LEE COUNTY LIBRARY SYSTEM

MW00467017

..., 1990-
...ssination in
Khartoum /

WITHDRAWN

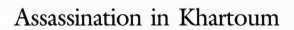

Assassination in Khartoum

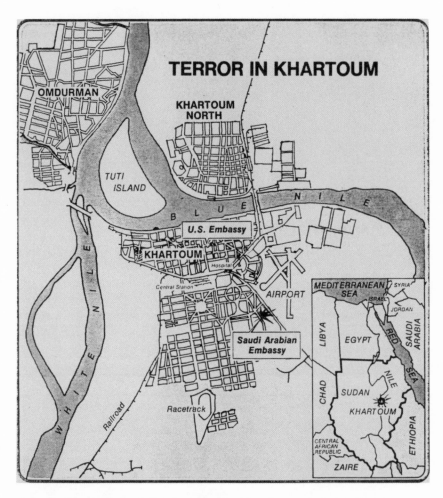

Map 1. Khartoum and Omdurman (Saudi embassy pinpointed); inset map showing Sudan, Egypt, the Red Sea, and the Mediterranean (*Newsweek*, 3/12/73, Ib Ohlsson/map "Terror in Khartoum").

AN INSTITUTE FOR

THE STUDY

OF

DIPLOMACY

BOOK

Assassination in Khartoum

DAVID A. KORN

INDIANA

UNIVERSITY

PRESS

BLOOMINGTON

AND INDIANAPOLIS

CAPE CORAL - LEE COUNTY LIBRARY

© 1993 by David A. Korn

All rights reserved

No part of this book may be reproduced or utilized in
any form or by any means, electronic or mechanical,
including photocopying and recording, or by any
information storage and retrieval system, without
permission in writing from the publisher. The
Association of American University Presses' Resolution
on Permissions constitutes the only exception to this
prohibition.

The paper used in this publication meets the
minimum requirements of American National Standard
for Information Sciences—Permanence of Paper for
Printed Library Materials, ANSI Z39.48-1984.

Manufactured in the United States of America

Library of Congress Cataloging-in-Publication Data
Korn, David A., date
        Assassination in Khartoum / David A. Korn.
            p. cm.
        "An Institute for the Study of Diplomacy book."
        Includes bibliographical references and index.
        ISBN 0–253–33202–8 (alk. paper)
        1. United States—Foreign relations—Israel.
        2. Israel—Foreign relations—United States.
        3. Terrorism—Sudan—Khartoum—History—20th
        century. 4. Israel-Arab conflicts—Sudan—
        Khartoum.   5. United States—Foreign relations—
        1969-1974.   6. Munazzamat Aylul al-Aswad—
        History.   7. Moore, George Curtis, d. 1973
        —Kidnapping, 1973.   8. Noel, Cleo A., 1973
        —Kidnapping, 1973.
        I. Title.
        E183.8.I7K67   1993
        962.6'204—dc20   92-46071
        1 2 3 4 5 97 96 95 94 93

CAPE CORAL - LEE COUNTY LIBRARY

TO

THE

MEMORY

OF

George Curtis Moore and Cleo A. Noel, Jr.

"Cleo and I will die bravely and without tears as men should."

*—George Curtis Moore, last letter
to his wife, March 2, 1973*

*"The sacrifice of the innocents in the name of an abstract
principle . . . is inadmissible."*

*—Aldo Moro, letter written from
captivity, March 1978*

CONTENTS

Illustrations follow pages 95 and 183.

Maps

PREFACE & ACKNOWLEDGMENTS

In the pages that follow, the reader will find the story of two American diplomats, George Curtis Moore and Cleo Allen Noel, Jr.—how they lived and how they died, how their government tried to save them, how and why it failed, how it tried to bring their killers to justice and once again failed, and then how it gave up trying.

The tragedy that befell these two men and their Belgian colleague Guy Eid on a day in March 1973 that was supposed to have been like any other in Khartoum, capital of what was then called the Democratic Republic of Sudan, erupted into headlines and onto television screens in the United States and Europe. It stirred outrage among the public and in the Congress of the United States. It shook the Department of State as few events before or since have. For years afterwards it was the subject of bitter controversy within the ranks of the Foreign Service of the United States of America. It is vividly remembered by those whose lives have involved them in the workings of American diplomacy, and by many others as well.

And yet the story is one that has never before been told. The press reported what was known of the circumstances of Moore's and Noel's abduction and killing at the time these events occurred, but then it turned to other news. Inside the State Department itself, no systematic study was made of what had occurred, no effort was undertaken to assess what had gone wrong and what might have been done differently. More than a year after the event, the department did commission the RAND Corporation to do an in-depth study, but RAND's report remained locked in a government vault. On the public record there were only a few press articles and occasional brief references in books on terrorism.

My interest in telling this story has personal origins. I worked for Curt Moore in the Department of State for a year and a half, from mid-1965 to the end of 1966, when he was officer in charge of Arabian peninsula affairs in the Bureau of Near Eastern and South Asian Affairs. After that, each of us went on to other assignments, but a little more than six years later, when Moore and Cleo Noel were seized, I was again in Washington working in State's Middle East bureau. Of the twenty-six hours that Moore and Noel were held hostage, I spent several in the task force room in the department's Operations Center, monitoring incoming cables and doing what I could to contribute to the effort to save him and Cleo Noel. Many of the scenes from that time that I have recorded in the pages that follow I myself witnessed, though everything I have written I corroborated through others who were there at the same time.

I knew Cleo Noel only through the superlative reputation that he made for himself within the Foreign Service. Curt Moore I admired as I did few others I came to know in thirty-one years in America's diplomatic service. Big, hearty, extraordinarily talented and keenly intelligent, impatient, restless for achievement, and demanding of himself and of his subordinates yet warmly human, he was, as others have said, a man who inspired devotion among those who knew him well.

It would not have been possible to write this book without the cooperation extended to me by Sarah (Sally) Moore, Curt's widow, and his two daughters, Lucy Wyatt and Katherine Bergeson. Mrs. Moore gave me many hours of her time; our discussions ranged over Curt's early years, through his Foreign Service assignments up to Khartoum, to his time there and his abduction and murder. Lucy and Katherine provided other valuable insights. Lucille Noel, Cleo's widow, agreed to speak with me about her husband's early years.

The help of others in filling in the details of a very broad canvas was equally indispensable. With the exception of three who asked to remain unnamed, they are James Akins, James J. Blake, Harry Blaney, Thomas Boyatt, Edwin L. Brawn, William D. Brewer, John R. Burke, Francis Deng, Herman F. Eilts, Robert E. Fritts, Samuel Gammon, John Gatch, Joseph N. Greene, Hassan (Cleo Noel's chauffeur), Jim Hoagland, Lewis Hoffacker, Hume Horan, Michael P. E. Hoyt, David Ignatius, Curtis Jones, Lucien Kinsolving, William B. Macomber, Henry E. Mattox, Armin H. Meyer, Hafeez A. M. Mohammed, George Naifeh, David D. Newsom, Shigeru Nomoto, Harry Odell, Joseph P. O'Neill,

Joan Peale, Barry Rubin, Ilsa Sanderson, George Thompson, Theodore Tremblay, and Timothy E. Wells. My interview with James Akins took place in March 1992; all other interviews and exchanges of correspondence were conducted in the late months of 1990 and the early months of 1991.

Several of the above generously opened their personal files to me and shared notes, documents, press clippings, and photographs relevant to the events recounted herein. Mrs. Moore and Mrs. Noel allowed me to peruse documents on the family history of their late husbands, and Mrs. Moore shared with me Curt's personal papers. Joan Peale, widow of Sam Peale, made available a copy of a letter written by her late husband in 1975 in which he analyzed at length the events of March 1 through 5, 1973. Joseph P. O'Neill, the deputy chief of mission at the American embassy in Khartoum during the time I was researching and writing this study, helped me locate and correspond with Sudanese who were employed at the embassy at the time of Moore's and Noel's service there.

Shigeru Nomoto, the former chargé d'affaires at the Japanese embassy in Khartoum, shared with me by correspondence what he witnessed during the two and a half hours he spent in captivity along with Moore, Noel, and Eid on the evening of March 1, 1973; it was the first time Mr. Nomoto had gone on record for publication about this harrowing experience. Material was also made available to me from the files of the American Foreign Service Association and the *Near East Report*, Washington, D.C.

The other indispensable element was access to official documents. Through the provisions of the Freedom of Information Act, I was able to obtain several hundred pages of U.S. government cables and memoranda relating to the Khartoum murders and their aftermath. Some of these documents had previously been declassified; others were declassified and released for the first time. Among them were several chronologies of the events that took place in Khartoum from March 1 to 5, 1973, that were very helpful in constructing the narrative that follows.

In addition, I was, after some delay, able to win declassification and release of the RAND study begun in 1974 and completed in 1976. It was enormously valuable. Including a chronology, it runs to more than eighty pages and draws on a wide range of classified documents and on interviews with those who participated in or closely observed the events in question, at a time when memories were still fresh. I also had the good fortune, in the course of my research, to be given a copy of a thirty-page report prepared by Theo L. R. Lansloot, the Belgian diplomat who was sent to Khartoum by his foreign ministry with instructions to attempt to rescue Guy Eid, and an English-language summary of the Sudanese court inquiry conducted during the fall of 1973 and early 1974. Taken together, these various documents helped fill in large gaps throughout the story, enabling me to reconstruct the scenes recounted in the two opening chapters and make sense of several episodes that otherwise would have remained scattered pieces in a chaotic puzzle. More detailed references to these and other documents used in the writing of this account will be found in the bibliography offered at the end of the book, along with a note on sources for each of the chapters.

To each of the persons named above, and to Mr. Eugene D. Price, Jr., of the American embassy in Tokyo for his good and diligent help in locating Mr. Nomoto and putting me in touch with him, I am deeply grateful, as I am to my wife Roberta for the encouragement and many helpful suggestions she offered during the course of my work on the manuscript.

Finally, I owe much thanks to Dr. Hans Binnendijk, director of the Georgetown University Institute for the Study of Diplomacy, and to Margery B. Thompson, the Institute's publications director, for the interest they have taken in this book and the help they have given in its publication. The findings and conclusions expressed in the book are mine alone, however, and do not necessarily reflect the views of the Institute for the Study of Diplomacy.

Assassination in Khartoum

1

Prelude

Later, during their interrogation, the one thing the young gunmen all remembered about the man called Abu Jamal—or would acknowledge remembering—was that he had a hand missing. As for the rest of him, the testimony was vague. He had dark hair and a mustache, which could have made him any one of a million or so adult male Palestinian Arabs. And he was a little older than the gunmen, which would have put him perhaps in his thirties and narrowed the search for him—if anybody were really searching for him—down to one among one or two hundred thousand. One of them recalled that he was "tall and bulky." But the missing hand was really his only distinguishing trait, and even its location was uncertain. Some thought it had once been attached to his right arm, others were sure it belonged to the left. And of course none of them knew how he had come to lose it. That was a question you did not ask a man like Abu Jamal.

It was understood that Abu Jamal was not his real name, only a code name, a nom de guerre, of the kind that all the militants took, from Yasser Arafat on down into the ranks. The code name served two important purposes: it gave you an identity within the organization, even a kind of persona; and unless you were someone famous like Arafat, or like Salah Khalaf, it hid your true identity, not only from those outside the organization but from most of those inside it as well. For a man in Abu Jamal's end of the business, that was particularly important.

Abu Jamal's job was not the most dangerous there was in the organization, but it was the kind of job that would make you want to keep your anonymity. He didn't kidnap or kill anybody, at least not in this operation; he only made the arrangements for the kidnapping and the killing. He was the man charged with setting up the operation, recruiting the gunmen, and drawing up the detailed plans. He went about it methodically and skillfully, in a way that showed that he was experienced in these matters. First he convoked the head of the organization's liaison office in the target city, which in this instance was Khartoum, the capital of the Democratic Republic of the Sudan. This person, whose name (his real name) was Fawaz Yassin Abdul Rahman, brought along his wireless operator, one Hassan Ahmad Hussein, for the operation would require special codes.

The three men met in Beirut on February 12, 1973. The Lebanese civil war was some three years in the future, so the city was still intact and bustling. The record, such as it is, does not reveal where they met, but an apartment in one of the buildings near Hamra Street, not far from where the intended victim once lived, would be a good guess. It also does not tell us what they discussed, but their talks must have been extensive, for the two men from Khartoum did not leave Beirut until February 16. When they did, they headed straight back to the Sudan.

Abu Jamal's next move was to pick his gunmen. The first chosen was a young man known as Tariq, who was, it must be assumed, experienced in commando operations, for Abu Jamal selected him to be the squad's leader. Tariq enlisted another. But it was Abu Jamal who chose the rest, five more. Like Tariq and his friend, all were young men in their early or mid-twenties. All had worked for Fatah for two or three years or more and had done commando operations for it; and all had switched over to the organization—they called it Ayloul, meaning September—not long after its big coup in September 1972. Presumably Abu Jamal selected them carefully, not just for their skills but for their toughness and reliability, because this time the operation had to be neither bungled nor abandoned, as the two immediately preceding ones had been. This time there was to be no giving up. This time the operation had to be carried out to the letter.

Abu Jamal told them all that the target was a notorious American intelligence agent, the CIA's top man in the Middle East, a man who worked for the Israelis, who had directed the killing of Palestinians in

Jordan in September 1970, and whose next assignment was to head a secret American missile base in Jordan. He did not tell them the country where the operation was to take place or the name of this American agent.

On February 22 Abu Jamal and Tariq flew to Khartoum. Again the record does not tell us everything they did there, but they must have had a busy time. It is safe to assume that they first did some reconnoitering, that they took a careful look at the embassy of Saudi Arabia, and at the American embassy and the American ambassador's residence. But they spent most of their time in the Fatah office, in the Blue Nile Insurance Building on Qasr Street, in the heart of downtown Khartoum not far from the presidential palace, conferring with Fawaz Yassin and with his deputy, a volatile, intense, angry man named Rizk al-Qas who went by the code name Abu Ghassan, and drawing up plans for the operation.

On February 25 Tariq flew back to Beirut. Two days later Fawaz Yassin sent a cable to Beirut. It was addressed to someone called Hisham and it read: "Completed well. It is high time. The merchants are gathered. Advise us promptly."

The reply came that same day: "The exhibits arrive on the Egyptian plane Wednesday morning."

The exhibits were Tariq and the six other gunmen. They came off an Egypt Air flight from Cairo early on the morning of February 28, a cloudless, brilliantly clear day. They were met at the airport, an unpretentious structure in every sense worthy of a poor third world country, by the driver of Fatah's Khartoum office, one Karam Ahmad Aram. Karam was well known to the airport personnel; on the Moslem holidays he habitually passed out gifts: packets of cigarettes, boxes of sweets, and small amounts of money. So when he presented the seven young men's Jordanian passports—artfully forged at the organization's head office in Beirut—and their immigration declarations listing them as students, the Sudanese immigration and customs officers waved them nonchalantly by. Had they troubled to examine the young men's luggage, they would have found no books, notebooks, or slide rules—only layers of well-worn clothing, under which were buried four disassembled Kalashnikov assault rifles, ammunition for the same, and eight small silver-colored hand grenades.

Abu Jamal waited outside the airport for the seven. He took them to the al-Arz hotel. They found no room available there, so they ended up staying at the Roxy, another small, shabby establishment.

Later that same morning they set out by twos, as Abu Jamal had instructed them, for the office in the Blue Nile Insurance Building on Qasr Street. There, at eleven o'clock, all assembled—Tariq and the six others from Beirut and Rizk al-Qas—to hear Abu Jamal and Fawaz Yassin give the final briefing. The time had come for Abu Jamal to instruct his team.

The code name of the operation would be "Abu Daoud." It was set for the next day, March 1, in the early evening. The mission would be to seize the embassy of Saudi Arabia, the CIA agent, and several foreign ambassadors. And Rizk al-Qas, who was fluent in English and had lived in Sudan for five years and knew everyone there, would be the team's "political leader."

Abu Jamal passed out a sheet of instructions to each member of the team that set out in detail his specific duties at every stage of the operation. All carefully studied a rough sketch done by Fawaz Yassin of the interior of the Saudi embassy. Pictures of the persons they were to take hostage were passed around and scrutinized.

To the eight of them Abu Jamal handed out the four Kalashnikov assault rifles brought in from Beirut in luggage the day before, and five pistols, together with a quantity of ammunition. Each was also awarded a dagger, to carry on his hip in a long sheath. Abu Jamal and Fawaz Yassin had assembled other supplies for them too: a bullhorn for talking with the authorities; a transistor radio, so they could know what the world would say about them, and so they could receive instructions from the organization's broadcasting stations; mimeographed sheets of paper proclaiming their demands; wiring of the type used for hooking up explosives; nylon rope cut in varying lengths, for binding the hostages; biscuits, cigarettes, and medical bandages. All were handily packed in tote bags for easy carrying.

Evidently it did not trouble the gunmen that they were going so lightly armed on their mission. The Sudanese were their brothers, they were told; they should not expect to have to fight them. The weapons were for the hostages only.

Early the next morning, March 1, 1973, Karam drove Abu Jamal and Fawaz Yassin and his wife and children to the airport, where they boarded a flight for Tripoli, the capital of Muammar al-Qaddafi's Libya.

Abu Jamal, the man with one hand missing, was a mid-level operative of the Black September Organization. After boarding the flight to Tripoli, he vanished without a trace.

Fawaz Yassin was the official representative in Khartoum of Yasser Arafat's Fatah, the main component of the Palestine Liberation Organization, also headed by Arafat. Like Abu Jamal, Fawaz Yassin would disappear into a void of silence. He would leave behind him only rumors—that he was hiding in Yemen, or had been sent to Baghdad.

At the moment the two men boarded the plane for Tripoli, no one saw anything suspicious in their departure. The trap they had set was about to be sprung in total surprise.

A Diplomatic Farewell

The residence of the ambassador of Saudi Arabia in Khartoum was a large, square four-story edifice of recent construction, with a pink and cream exterior that made it look like an ungainly multi-tiered cake. It was flanked on each side by a lower building, one the embassy's chancery, the other a warehouse, and was located on the Sharia al-Nus, which translated literally meant Half Avenue but more prosaically was called Middle Road, in the New Extension, a recently built suburb not far from the airport. An expanse of lawn cut by a semi-circular driveway separated the residence from the street gate. To enter it, the visitor climbed a half-dozen steps and passed through large plate-glass double doors which opened onto a spacious, high-ceilinged reception room.

Stairs at the rear led to the ambassador's family quarters, which occupied the second and third floors of the building. The fourth floor had a large patio, to which guests often repaired to enjoy the cool of the evening and get a view of the city lights. From the roof a forest of poles sprouted skyward, connected at their summit by a tangle of wires and antennas, for the top floor housed the embassy's powerful radio communications equipment. At the back there was a small garden. The entire Saudi embassy complex was surrounded by a high wall, as was customary in Khartoum.

In the early evening of Thursday, March 1, 1973, the street in front of the Saudi embassy was crowded with cars—not the usual collection of dusty ancient battered vehicles one ordinarily saw on Khartoum's streets but large, immaculately polished sedans mostly of recent manufacture. All bore diplomatic license plates, and they were decked with the flags of more than twenty nations.

The ambassador of Saudi Arabia, His Excellency Abdullah al-Malhouk, a man of medium height, thickening with middle age, was the dean of the diplomatic corps. He was giving a farewell reception for the counselor of the American embassy, George Curtis Moore, who was due to leave the Sudanese capital the following Monday after more than three and a half years there. Ambassador al-Malhouk's office had sent out invitations to the reception to the heads of all the foreign diplomatic missions in the Sudanese capital.

Ambassador al-Malhouk was married to a very attractive woman much younger than he who was, as it happened, of Palestinian extraction. But in the custom of his country, he did not hold functions at which the sexes mixed. This reception, like all others he gave, was strictly stag. It was to last only an hour, and it started early and was to end early, for the emperor of Ethiopia was in Khartoum on a state visit, and the ambassadors and chargés d'affaires were convoked to a dinner in his honor at eight.

Moments before 6:00 P.M. Moore, a big man, just over six feet tall and solidly built, with thick brown hair, glasses, and a neatly trimmed reddish mustache, joined his Saudi host near the large plate-glass doors. There the two greeted the guests as they arrived and sent them into the reception room, where trays of food and drink—all nonalcoholic, for this was the embassy of Saudi Arabia—awaited them. Some thirty minutes later the Saudi ambassador called his guests together to present Moore an engraved silver tray, a memento from the assembled diplomatic corps of their service together, and to deliver a short speech praising Moore for his achievements in the Sudan. Ambassador al-Malhouk predicted a brilliant future for Moore and wished him much success and happiness in the years ahead. These were sentiments that almost all there genuinely shared, for Moore had been easily the best-known, most active, and most popular diplomat in Khartoum, not just among his diplomatic colleagues but among Sudanese as well.

Moore's reply to the Saudi ambassador was full of jovial good humor and was punctuated by much laughter, for Moore was a warm, outgoing, and engaging man. And on this day and at this moment when he was being honored, he had every reason to be in high spirits.

At a little after 6:30, perhaps while Ambassador al-Malhouk and Moore were delivering their remarks, Rizk al-Qas and possibly one or two others stepped out of a Land Rover station wagon that had just pulled up half a block or so down the street, walked to the gate of the Saudi embassy, presented a diplomatic invitation card issued in the name of Fawaz Yassin Abdul Rahman, and were admitted to the building. A few minutes later, after verifying that the targets were in fact there, one of the men emerged from the Saudi embassy and returned to the Land Rover.

Moore's remarks were greeted by rounds of applause and followed by an exchange of orange juice toasts. After a few more minutes of conversation, the party began to break up. The British ambassador, R. G. Etherington-Smith, had departed earlier after excusing himself to the host and the guest of honor. He had to be at the airport before seven o'clock to meet a visiting Foreign Office official arriving from London. Two others with whom Moore had been on close terms, the ambassador of the Federal Republic of Germany and the ambassador of Ethiopia, had not come to the reception. The German was busy that day with a parliamentary delegation from Bonn. The Ethiopian had received two rather unusual telephone calls insistently inviting him to the reception, but he was in attendance upon his emperor and could not break away.

Just before 7:00 P.M., with night fallen outside, Ambassador al-Malhouk and Moore again placed themselves side by side in front of the plate-glass doors. The diplomats were still in small groups chatting among themselves, but they began to line up to say goodbye, to bid Moore a warm and affectionate farewell and wish him the very best of everything for the future.

The recently arrived American ambassador, Cleo Allen Noel, Jr., counted on other opportunities to express these thoughts. Noel and the Dutch chargé d'affaires, Jan Bertens, were among the first out the door. As Noel and Bertens chatted and walked toward the gate that opened onto the street, the Belgian chargé d'affaires, Guy Eid, a slender, dark-haired man in his mid-thirties, joined them and good-naturedly elbowed Bertens aside, explaining that he needed to speak with the American alone. The Dutchman broke away while the Belgian engaged Noel in conversation a few steps inside the gate.

Hassan, Ambassador Noel's Sudanese driver, sat behind the wheel of the long, white Chevrolet parked some yards away, a small American flag draped from a mast over the right fender and the ambassadorial pennant dangling at the left. Upon seeing his boss approach the gate, Hassan turned the key in the ignition and began to pull out to pick up the ambassador just as he stepped into the street. Hassan had driven American ambassadors in Khartoum for more than a decade. He took an almost chauvinistic pride in working for the Americans. When he spoke of the United States, he did so in the first-person plural. Two years earlier, while driving Moore down the U.S.-built highway from Khartoum south to Wad Madani to a ceremony marking the opening of a Soviet factory, Hassan had complained bitterly of the Russians' gall in putting their project on "our road."

Hassan prided himself also on his skill in cutting in ahead of other drivers to meet the American ambassador or chargé the moment he emerged from a reception or dinner, or from an official appointment, quickly and neatly with not a second lost in waiting.

But this time Hassan was not to make it. He had seen the Land Rover standing on the other side of the street some distance away, a vehicle that, like his, bore diplomatic license plates. Now, before he could move the Chevrolet more than a few feet, the Land Rover pulled swiftly ahead of him and came to an abrupt halt in front of the embassy's gate. This in itself was startling, but it was not all. To Hassan's amazement, armed men erupted from the van, their faces masked with checkered scarves. They brandished Kalashnikov assault rifles and pistols and carried tote bags, and as they charged into the Saudi embassy, they shot one of the Sudanese policemen at the gate and fired bursts into the ground and the air, forcing Noel and Eid and their colleagues who followed them back into the building. A bullet tore through the Belgian's lower leg. The American ambassador was struck in the ankle by a ricocheting fragment of metal or stone.

Bertens, the Dutch chargé, dashed into the street seconds before the gunmen slammed the gates shut. Though it was already too late, he turned to shout back to his diplomatic colleagues, "Run, run for your lives!" Then he followed his own injunction.

Two other Sudanese policemen posted as guards for the reception ran into the street alongside Bertens. Once safely there they stopped, stunned and shame-faced at having fled.

Hassan scrambled frantically out the door of his car and sprinted, as fast as his forty-some-year-old legs would carry him, to a nearby building. There, breathless, he telephoned the Marine guard on duty at the American embassy to report what he had witnessed.

The scene etched itself in Hassan's memory. Almost two decades later it was still vivid, but one thing stood out above all others: had the American ambassador not been stopped by the Belgian, he would have been clear of the Saudi embassy before the gunmen arrived.

3

Ambassador to Sudan

March 1, 1973, was a day to which both Cleo Allen Noel, Jr., and George Curtis Moore had looked forward with keen anticipation.

The day dawned clear and sunny, as it always did at that season in Khartoum. For Noel, a strikingly tall man, handsome, distinguished, and a bit younger-looking than his fifty-four years, it was the day on which he was to be sworn in, for the second time, as Ambassador Extraordinary and Plenipotentiary of the United States of America. Few envoys went through this ceremony twice for the same ambassadorship. Noel had done it the first time in Washington early in December of the previous year after he was given a recess appointment as ambassador to the Sudan by President Richard M. Nixon. Ordinarily, American ambassadors had to be approved by the Senate before they could leave Washington for their posts. But when it was deemed urgent for the ambassador to proceed, and the Senate was in recess and therefore unable to accord him or her a speedy hearing, the president could authorize an interim appointment, valid until the upper house could act.

Cleo Noel had been in Khartoum for a little more than two months when, late in February, the United States Senate gave its advice and consent to his appointment. He had been planning to join a group of Americans and others for a trip to the south of Sudan, but now he decided to stay in Khartoum. He set his swearing in for Thursday, March 1, the last day of the work week before the Sudanese government shut down for the Friday Moslem holiday.

Interim appointments were an exercise of presidential authority that the Senate liked less and less as it bridled against the broad uses—and, many felt, abuses—that Lyndon Johnson and Richard Nixon made of executive writ during the Vietnam war years. At a later time, the urgency that the Department of State saw at the end of 1972 in having Cleo Noel depart for Khartoum forthwith probably would not have been deemed sufficient to warrant his being sent to his post ahead of senatorial confirmation. It stemmed solely from the fact that the Sudan was the first of the Arab states to resume formal diplomatic relations with the United States after having broken them following the 1967 Arab-Israeli war. Getting Noel to Khartoum in a hurry was Washington's way of showing the Sudanese that it appreciated and wished to reward their gesture. Were it not for that, Noel very likely would still have been in the United States on March 1, 1973.

In Egypt, the colossus to the north that had played such a mighty role in the Sudan's history, in Syria and Iraq, even in Algeria and Mauritania at the opposite shore of the African continent, and in South Yemen at the tip of the Arabian peninsula, governments still adamantly refused to restore diplomatic ties with Washington. So long as the Arabs had not redeemed themselves from the crushing defeat they had suffered at Israel's hands in June 1967, so long as Israel remained in unmitigated and unrepentant control of the territories it had overrun in its astonishing burst of martial energy in six fateful days, and so long as the Americans continued to supply Israel with military equipment and economic assistance and did nothing to force it to disgorge its conquests, the American flag was not to be allowed to fly anywhere within their borders. The United States was to be made to know that it would remain a pariah.

Not that contact was to be broken off altogether. Only the firebrands in Damascus, Baghdad, and Aden went to that extreme. For the others, Washington was too important a player on the Middle Eastern and world scenes to be shunned absolutely. After the break in relations, American embassies in Cairo, Khartoum, and Algiers did not close their doors. Ambassadors went home, but their offices did not shut down. They simply changed names. Now they were called not embassies but interests sections. They operated with reduced staff under the flag of a protecting power chosen from among the United States' European friends. In Cairo, the Spanish embassy took the Americans under its wing; in Algiers, it was the Swiss. In Khartoum the Dutch assumed that role. After June 8, 1967, the flag of the Netherlands flew from the mast that protruded at a forty-five-degree angle from the drab five-story office building in downtown Khartoum that until then had been the U.S. embassy. And it was the robed and crowned portrait of Juliana, queen of the Netherlands, that hung on the wall behind the desk of the fourth-floor office of the chief of the United States interests section.

Cleo Noel was the first to sit at that desk. He had been assigned to Khartoum as deputy chief of mission, the embassy's second-ranking officer, at the beginning of 1967. It was, oddly, the Vietnam war that had brought him there. In the fall of 1965, after four years at the Department of State's block-long rectangular Washington headquarters, he had gladly accepted assignment as political counselor at the American embassy in The Hague. Earl Sohm, Noel's boss in the department, was going out to The Hague as deputy chief of mission. Sohm considered Cleo Noel one of the Foreign Service's best up-and-coming officers, and so he offered him the political counselor job. At the time, Noel was an FSO-3, a rank located on the threshold between the Foreign Service's mid and senior levels, roughly the equivalent of colonel in the armed forces. European postings were much sought after and the senior positions were all highly ranked, so the job of political counselor in The Hague was a plum for an officer of Noel's grade.

But he was to spend only fifteen months in The Hague. Early in 1966 Noel was promoted to FSO-2, and in the fall of that year, while in Washington for a brief time to serve on a promotion panel, he was asked if he would accept reassignment to Khartoum. The deputy chief of mission job at the U.S. embassy in the Sudan was unexpectedly coming open, well before the scheduled time. The incumbent was one of dozens of State Department officers who were being rushed to Saigon to back up the huge expansion in American military and economic assistance programs ordered by Lyndon Johnson.

For Cleo Noel and his wife, Lucille, a short, slender, angular woman who struck people as both intelligent and quite intense, the offer looked like another lucky break in their Foreign Service career. They had already spent three years in the Sudan. From 1958 to 1961 Noel had been the junior political officer at the U.S. embassy in Khartoum. The British had given up their colonial rule just two years earlier, and the place still had the air of a minor colonial outpost. It was quiet, unhurried, and unabashedly backward, with not a single paved road in all the immense expanse of the country outside the capital. There were constant electrical outages, and telephone service was so unreliable that most communication was by hand-written note, delivered by driver. There was no television; the Noels' children, John and Janet, were not to discover the animated screen until they returned to Washington in the second half of 1961.

In the mid-summer and early fall months, fierce sand and dust storms, called haboobs, darkened day into night and covered everything with a thick layer of dust. These alternated with infrequent but violent rainstorms that turned Khartoum's mostly unpaved streets first into lakes and then into quagmires and sent the humidity soaring. Gardens of the diplomatic residences would flood, and great African vultures, supremely ugly creatures, would assemble from out of nowhere and stand in eerie quiet in the water until it drained.

For nine months of the year the heat was ferocious. At midday temperatures would rise well above the 100 degree mark. If you could find a piece of pavement in Khartoum—not easy in the late 1950s— you could fry an egg on it; with patience you could bake a potato. But air conditioning was a rarity, even for the diplomatic community. Bedrooms were cooled by a contraption that blew air through wetted straw. Most Sudanese and many Westerners slept on their rooftops during the hottest months.

The sights, the sounds, and the smells were those of the poverty-stricken third world. Donkeys, camels, cattle, and crowds of unwashed, underfed humanity surged through the streets, competing for space with immense ancient smoke-belching, roaring, clanging trucks. The streets themselves reeked of urine and manure, and the colorful markets exuded overpowering odors of spices and decomposing foodstuffs. Dirty, ragged little boys with blotched skin vied with blind or mutilated beggars for the foreigner's charity.

But all this gave the place an aura of romance for Westerners jaded with the antiseptic and drably uniform life in the developed world. Most Europeans and Americans who lived in Khartoum came to love it; they became almost addicted to the place. The Sudanese were welcoming and hospitable and less morbidly obsessed with the Arab-Israeli conflict than other Arabs. It was easy to make friends with them, and making friends was a diplomat's business. The diplomatic community lived in comfortable houses surrounded by high walls, with well-kept gardens and servants to attend to almost everything. There were outings in the desert, sailing on the Nile, and endless rounds of receptions and dinners. There were visits to the lovely oasis at Al Fasher and infrequent but memorable trips by steamer down the Nile, to the south where one could ride in twenty-foot-long dugout canoes, be an honored guest at exotic tribal dances, glimpse the paradise flycatcher or a shimmering blue-green iridescent starling, gawk at crocodiles and hippopotamuses, bring back an elephant tail or a leopard skin, and even, perhaps, be received by the Reth, the king of the Shillouk, whose main occupation consisted in visiting his 120 or so wives at regular intervals, until his powers failed and he was (by tradition, but no longer) smothered to death.

For anyone with a tingle of adventure, there was nothing to match it; all the rest of the world, all the life of what was called civilization, was drab and dreary by comparison. For nine months of the year you could count on clear blue skies. After a while you adjusted even to the heat. Visitors who came off the plane at Khartoum's small airport right on the city's edge felt it strike like a huge, invisible sledgehammer. It was like stepping into an oven. But the Americans and Europeans who lived there would assure newcomers that the heat really wasn't bad at all. It was dry heat, they would explain, and therefore not unpleasant. The new arrival who failed to appreciate this, who continued to find the 115 degree temperatures of midday nonetheless too hot for words, would be looked upon as unforgivably obtuse.

The Hague was at opposite poles from Khartoum in every respect. Its chill, its incessant rainfall and gloom, and its Dutch order and cleanliness made the Noels look back with special fondness on their earlier years in the sprawling, chaotic Arab city in the middle of the desert at the confluence of the Blue and White Niles.

And now there was the prospect of going back, after less than six years, to represent the United States in the Sudan, this time in a senior position, one in which Cleo Noel could really hope to make an impact.

The Sudan was Africa's largest country, just shy of a million square miles, the size of the United States east of the Mississippi River. It spanned the two worlds of Arab North Africa and black Africa, but it was mainly Arab or Arabized. Of the 16.2 million inhabitants that it was officially estimated to have in 1972, 12 million counted one dialect or another of Arabic as their mother tongue. Most of them were dark-skinned people with mixed Semitic and Negroid features, reflecting the mingling of blood natural to borderland peoples. They lived along the banks of the Nile or in the desert and savannah lands that made up the northern two-thirds of the country.

The remaining 4.2 million—this figure, like the other, was just a guess—were coal-black Africans whose homes were the tropical swamps and rain forests of the south. Northern Sudan had been more or less opened to the influences of world civilization as early as the sixteenth century B.C., when the pharaohs of Egypt first extended their rule there. But the southern Sudan remained isolated for another three millennia, until the mid-nineteenth century A.D., its rivers—its only avenues of intercourse with the outside world—made impassable by the Sudd, a vast and until then impenetrable barrier of floating vegetation. The northern Sudanese were Moslems, but the southerners were animists.

The opening of the south brought Christian missionaries, but also Arab slave traders who made it a great plundering ground. Tens of thousands of black men and women were carted off to be sold in the slave markets of Khartoum and Arabia, across the Red Sea divide. Black Sudanese came to regard Arabs as cruel and hateful oppressors. The British put an end to the slave trade and in their half-century of direct rule over the Sudan protected the blacks from Arab exploitation. But they did nothing to heal the rift between the two peoples. Instead, it grew, and after independence exploded into an endless, debilitating civil war as the Arab north tried to reimpose its domination over the black south.

The Sudan was not a major player in the Arab or African arenas, even less so on the world scene, but its size and its problems (the latter wholly commensurate with the former) made it impossible to ignore. It was, moreover, looked upon as the soft underbelly of Egypt. For thousands of years Egypt had dominated the history of the Sudan. The pharaohs had extended their rule deep up the Nile; the remnants of their great stone monuments littered the halls of modern Khartoum's national museum. From time to time, native peoples drove the northerners out, or when Egyptian kingdoms collapsed from within, their governance in the southern provinces simply disappeared, like so much vapor in the desert. But inevitably the Egyptians returned to rule with a more or less heavy hand. In 1821 an Egyptian army under the nominal suzerainty of the Ottoman sultan made its way up the Nile as far as Khartoum. For the next sixty years Egypt governed there, and in as much of the rest of the country as it could subdue.

As might be imagined, Egyptian rule was less than kind or generous. It won the northern masters no love or gratitude. In 1884 a Moslem messiah, the Mahdi, a fundamentalist zealot much given to falling into religious trances and said to perform miracles, rallied the Arabs of the Sudan to throw out the hated Turks, as the Egyptians were called locally. The siege and fall of Khartoum to the Mahdi's army very likely would have attracted little outside attention had the Egyptian force there not been led by an extraordinary Englishman, General Sir Charles George Gordon. Perhaps the most famous and flamboyant of the European adventurers of the late nineteenth century, Gordon tried desperately to fend off the Mahdi's dervishes while an Egyptian army under British command made its way to his rescue. The city fell just a few days before it arrived. Gordon perished, pierced by a dervish spear (if one is to credit what is implied in the famous painting by G. W. Loy that hangs in the Leeds City Art Galleries), following which he was decapitated and his head paraded through town and presented to the victorious Mahdi (according to a contemporaneous account and drawing).

The Mahdi died shortly afterwards, but his successor ruled for the next fourteen years, until the British, having imposed their domination over Egypt, came back with an army of their own to subjugate the Sudan. For the British, as for the pharaohs and pashas of Egypt before them, it was axiomatic that he who ruled in Cairo had also to rule in Khartoum.

Sudan's accession to independence in the mid-twentieth century— on January 1, 1956, to be exact—did not bring a reversal of roles between the two countries. What happened in Egypt could and did still heavily influence developments in the Sudan. But by the same token, events in the Sudan could affect Egypt, and Egypt (though technically an African state) was the linchpin of the Arab world and of the Near East, an area in which Washington considered it had vital interests. And if this were not enough to persuade American policy makers of the Sudan's importance, one had only to look to the east and the south.

The government in Khartoum controlled four hundred miles of shoreline along the Red Sea, the artery through which much of the oil of the Arabian peninsula passed on its way to the West. And the Sudan's long, staircase-like border with Ethiopia gave it considerable weight in the affairs of that fragmented country, at the time still ruled by Emperor Haile Selassie. The Lion of Judah, as he styled himself, was a dear friend and ally of the United States of America. Since the early 1960s the emperor had been fighting off a growing insurgency in the northern province of Eritrea. The insurgency enjoyed the backing of a number of Arab countries, among them Muammar al-Qaddafi's Libya. The United States found itself, inevitably if unwillingly, smack in the middle of this contest, for it had a military communications station in Asmara, the capital of Eritrea, and was supplying and training the Ethiopian army in its effort to put down the Eritrean insurgency. What happened in the Sudan inescapably affected Ethiopia, and by extension American interests there, for by extending or denying assistance to the Eritrean guerrillas fighting Haile Selassie, a Sudanese government could undermine or strengthen the emperor's regime.

Farther south still lay the Sudan's borders with Zaire, ruled by another American friend, President Mobutu Sese Seku. Mobutu was a more controversial and considerably less savory figure than the Ethiopian emperor, but in Washington's scheme of things he was almost equally important.

So Khartoum, though not frequently in the headlines, was no backwater. Foreign Service officers assigned to the American embassy there could be sure that their colleagues in Washington would read the cables they sent back and would pay attention to their recommendations. And that was more than one could say for most U.S. embassies in Africa.

Beyond all this there was an important career consideration. The job of deputy chief of mission was a rung—really the most important rung—on the ladder that led to the coveted position of ambassador. It was not a mandatory one. There was no fixed requirement that one serve as deputy chief of mission in order to qualify for appointment as ambassador. But getting your ticket punched there marked you for serious consideration for advancement to the top of the American diplomatic service.

Cleo Noel did not like to think of it that way. The whole idea of getting one's ticket punched, of taking a job only or even mainly because it offered an avenue for promotion, he regarded as abhorrent. To be sure he was an ambitious man, but his ambition, as he saw it, was to serve his country. The idea of service to country, and of discipline in the service, was genuinely important to him, and he looked upon his forthcoming assignment as America's second-ranking representative in Khartoum as an opportunity to serve and at the same time to learn and to prove himself, and while doing so to cement relations between the United States and the Sudan.

Noel was a quiet, thoughtful man, friendly and affable, yet reserved. Some thought him austere, others a bit shy, perhaps something of an introvert, a man with a streak of sadness in him. But he was also a man of principle, of exceptionally strong character, disciplined and dedicated, yet fair and above all balanced. A man courteous by nature, with a kind of old world courtesy and dignity that at times could seem almost quaint in the turbulence of the second half of the twentieth century. Those who worked with him—peers, subordinates, and superiors—thought of him not just as a gentleman but as a truly gentle man, a man considerate of others, not only as a matter of form but quite genuinely so. He was also a man of intellectual interests. It impressed his Foreign Service colleagues—the Service did not, as a rule, attract true intellectuals—that he subscribed to and actually read *Daedalus* and other highbrow journals.

He had joined the Foreign Service in 1949 when he was just a few months under thirty-one, the age limit in force at the time. But after that, with the exception of the early Dulles years when almost all promotions were frozen, he advanced rapidly. Not too rapidly—he was, one might say, a five-minute miler. He ran a good steady pace near the head of the pack, but not so fast as to be in danger of burning out early; he had staying power. In the lower and middle ranks he won a promotion every other year, in the upper ranks once every four years. His steadiness and his dedication were important assets in his advancement. He did not try to shine or look smart. He did not need to, for he had an unusual talent for expressing his views cogently and deliberately, without exaggeration or bombast, a talent that gained him the ear of his superiors and the respect of his peers.

His second tour of duty in Khartoum was to prove a disappointment to Cleo Noel, though not by any means in every respect. The friends that he had made among the Sudanese during his earlier sojourn were still there. They too had advanced in rank and responsibility, in parallel to Noel. So he had ready access to the senior levels of the government offices with which he, as the number two American representative in the country, had to deal. And he was spared the difficulty that another would have experienced in building the personal relationships and the mutual trust so important for doing business in an Arab country.

He found that the number of personnel assigned to the American embassy in Khartoum had expanded enormously since he left in mid-1961. Most of the growth in staff came from the Agency for International Development. The U.S. aid program for Sudan had mushroomed during the first half of the 1960s, but the numbers of personnel assigned to that program had exploded; for when AID doubled a program, it habitually tripled or quadrupled the staff assigned to carry it out. There was one really good AID project, a highway south from Khartoum to the important provincial city of Wad Madani. It would be the first paved roadway in all of Sudan outside the capital. But Noel doubted that some of the other American aid projects would be as useful or produce the kind of benefits the Sudanese hoped for, or that the American taxpayer had a right to expect.

Noel did not have to worry long about the success or failure of the aid program and its ever-multiplying personnel. In June 1967, after Israel smashed Egypt's air force and army and President Gamal Abdul Nasser accused the United States of having taken part in Israel's opening air attack, the government of the Sudan broke relations with Washington. The Sudanese took this step with an obvious reluctance, and only out of a sense of duty to their Egyptian brothers; there were no anti-American demonstrations or riots and few evident hard feelings. Noel and the American ambassador, William Weathersby, warned their Sudanese friends that a break in relations would bring about the immediate closure of the American assistance program, that this was a matter of law and not of policy and was therefore automatic. The Sudanese simply refused to believe it, and when U.S. aid was cut off following the break in relations, they were surprised and resentful, as though the Americans had done something quite unwarranted and unexpected.

Washington chose Cleo Noel to stay on in Khartoum to head the new U.S. interests section in the Dutch embassy. The entire U.S. mission was reduced to nine diplomatic officers, a skeleton of what it had been until that time. A few of the Americans who were expelled departed leaving their dirty dishes in the sinks of their homes. This offended Noel's sense of propriety, for he was a man with strong views on what was right and proper. For him, neither haste nor resentment at being thrown out justified failing to clean up after oneself. He did not reprove his administrative officer when that official had the dirty dishes packed in with the clean ones and shipped malodorously to their owners' new address.

Noel and his newly assigned deputy, Lucien Kinsolving, spent the next two years working and hoping against hope for restoration of diplomatic relations. Some of Noel's friendships with individual Sudanese survived the break in relations, but many did not, and while he understood the pressures that the Sudanese were under, it nonetheless became a source of bitterness to him to see people he had regarded as friends turn away from him.

The time simply was not ripe for a renewal of diplomatic relations; probably no individual effort, no matter how skillful or superhuman, could have brought it about. And in June of 1969, after a military coup that brought in a left-wing regime headed by a big, ambitious, round-faced young officer named Jaafar al-Nimeiry (his name meant "the tiger"), there was another setback. The new government ordered the expulsion of six of the U.S. interests section's nine diplomatic officers.

The next month Cleo Noel turned over his responsibilities to his succesor and left Khartoum on reassignment to Washington. His successor was George Curtis Moore.

4

"Find Moore"

Just before 7:00 P.M. on March 1, 1973, Shigeru Nomoto, the chargé d'affaires of Japan, was standing somewhere toward the back of the reception hall of the residence of the ambassador of Saudi Arabia. Nomoto was chatting with the ambassador of Pakistan about nothing of real importance while both prepared to take their leave of the Saudi ambassador and his American guest of honor, George Curtis Moore, and be off to President Nimeiry's dinner for Emperor Haile Selassie. This prospect was abruptly and startlingly interrupted by a very loud noise that Nomoto, a veteran of World War II, first thought was a volley of machine-gun fire, and that he was sure came from outside but quite near the Saudi residence. Seconds later he heard another loud noise, this time the shattering of the glass entrance doors.

Then, as though on signal, the lights went out.

The decorum of the diplomatic reception gave way to pandemonium. The French ambassador, Henri Costilhes, and the papal nuncio fled to the garden in back, where before the startled eyes of two of the Saudi ambassador's children, who were at play there, they scrambled over its high wall. The Soviet ambassador, Felix Fedotov, was saying goodbye to Moore and to Ambassador al-Malhouk when he heard the shots. He too hurried to the garden. But he was a short, rotund man and could not make it over the wall, so he lay down flat behind a shrub.

Adli Nasser, the Jordanian chargé d'affaires, sprinted to the rear and up the stairs, to the Saudi ambassador's family quarters, where Mrs. al-Malhouk hid him in a bedroom closet.

Nomoto and a half-dozen others made their way in the darkness to the washroom, shut themselves in, and sat anxiously on the floor. Others hid in closets or behind drapes or furniture.

As unexpectedly as they had gone off, the lights came back on. Masked gunmen searched the residence, routing diplomats from their hiding places. They came to the washroom and pounded on the door, and one of those inside opened it. They led Shigeru Nomoto and the others back to the reception room and ordered them to sit on the carpet, in a horseshoe formation together with a number of others who had hidden elsewhere. One of the gunmen set about identifying the diplomats; he was evidently the leader of the group and someone who had been in Khartoum long enough to become familiar with the faces of the members of the diplomatic corps. Those he did not know, the Lebanese chargé identified for him. The gunmen were looking for the American, British, West German, Iranian, and Ethiopian ambassadors, but at the top of their list was George Curtis Moore, the reception's guest of honor. In fact, some witnesses were later to say that as they charged into the Saudi embassy, the gunmen shouted to one another in Arabic, "Which one is Moore? Find Moore!"

* * *

Curt Moore—he had since childhood been Curt, except to those who did not know him and addressed him, only once before he corrected them, as George—spent most of the morning of Thursday, March 1, 1973, in the office cleaning up last-minute odds and ends. He and his wife, Sally, a couple that seemed as well matched in personality as they were in physical likeness, both tall, comely, and outgoing, were due to leave Khartoum the following Monday morning.

Ordinarily they would have left the Sudan two and a half months earlier, after Cleo Noel had arrived there on December 18, 1972. The rule of thumb in the Department of State was that an officer who had headed a diplomatic mission for more than six months should be transferred when another arrived to take over from him, even if the newcomer bore the title of ambassador. Otherwise there were too many potential conflicts. Going from number one to number two was more than most people could handle; and a new ambassador was rarely comfortable having someone around to tell him, "We do things this way here."

By December of 1972, when Cleo Noel returned to Khartoum for the third time, Moore had headed the U.S. mission there for almost three and a half years. He had relieved Noel, and now Noel was coming to relieve him. In the interim he had nursed relations between the United States and the Sudan from a state of near terminal illness back to robust good health. July 25, 1972, the day that full diplomatic relations between the United States and the Sudan were restored, the day that he presided over the raising of the American flag at the embassy residence, had been one of the proudest of his life.

Now, in December, with the new ambassador on the job, he could have packed up and left, could have been back home in time for Christmas, had he chosen to do so. But he knew Cleo Noel not just as a colleague but as a friend, and he had enormous respect for Noel. The two had studied Arabic together for eighteen months a decade and a half earlier, first at the Foreign Service Institute in Washington and then at the State Department's Arabic language school in Beirut. Curt Moore was in no way a self-effacing man; no one who knew him ever described him that way. But for someone he liked and respected as he did Cleo Noel, he was capable of putting ego aside.

Noel wanted Moore to stay on; indeed, he needed Moore's help, since his new deputy chief of mission was not due to arrive until March, and relations between the United States and the Sudan were now busier than ever. And since Curt as yet had no onward assignment—there were rumors of assignment to New Delhi as deputy chief of mission, but the State Department had not yet found him a new job—staying on seemed the perfectly natural thing to do. Winter in the Sudan was the best time of year. The days were sparkling, temperatures rarely reached the 100 degree mark, and the nights were deliciously cool. Far better, since there was no urgency to their departure, Curt and Sally thought, to spend the next few months there than in the cold and gloom of winter Washington.

So, with the department's approval, they stayed in Khartoum. At their own insistence, they moved out of the spacious, comfortable ambassadorial residence that they had lived in since they arrived in the Sudan.

Cleo told them there was no need to do so, but they would not hear of it. They set their departure date for March 5, 1973.

On the morning of March 1, the next-to-last workday before their departure, Curt Moore penned a quick letter of welcome to Robert E. Fritts, the new deputy chief of mission who was to arrive a few hours after his departure. The staff, he wrote Fritts, was quite good, but there was one person he wanted especially to recommend: "You will learn particularly to bless whoever assigned Sam Peale to Khartoum." Peale was a slender, quiet, serious man in his mid-thirties who did the embassy's political and economic reporting. When Peale had first arrived in Khartoum, in December 1971, Moore had had doubts about him. Peale did not look all that impressive, and Moore set high standards for his subordinates, as he did for himself. But he soon discovered that Peale was smart, determined, and knowledgeable, and a very hard worker. In the fifteen months that followed, Curt Moore and Sam Peale became close friends, in a friendship that in some ways was like that of father and son or mentor and pupil.

"So at the close of three and one-half of the finest years of my life," he concluded his letter to Fritts, "I welcome you to Khartoum and hope you will be able to make the same statement when you leave." He signed the letter in a large, confident hand and gave it to his secretary, Margaret Thorsen, to deliver the following week.

Just before noon, Curt and Sally, Cleo and his wife, Lucille, and the embassy's small American staff—Sam and Joan Peale; Melville A. Sanderson, the lively, prematurely gray-haired administrative officer who went by the nickname of Sandy, and his German-born wife, Ilsa; his assistant Ed Brawn; the USIS chief George Thompson and his wife, Dorothy; the consular officer Carol Roehl; the CIA station chief and his wife; Marine Sergeant Timothy Wells and his wife, Carla, and the men of the embassy's Marine Guard unit; the embassy's two secretaries; and the two communications clerks—gathered in the wood-paneled ambassadorial office for Cleo's swearing in.

Lucille held the Bible, and Cleo carefully placed his left hand on it and raised his right. Standing beside the American flag, Curt read out the oath of office. Cleo repeated its solemn words in a firm, steady voice:

I, Cleo Allen Noel, Jr., do solemnly swear that I will support and defend the Constitution of the United States of America against all enemies, foreign and domestic, that I will bear true faith and allegiance to the same, that I take this obligation freely and without any mental reservation or purpose of evasion, that I will well and faithfully discharge the duties of the office on which I am about to enter . . .

And then, the oath:

So help me God.

Lucille Noel had stayed behind in Washington after her husband's departure for Khartoum in December. She arrived in the Sudanese capital in mid-February, and some thought she had been less than enthusiastic about returning there. After the ceremony, the Noels and the Moores lined up for a picture together, the two women in the center and the men on each side of them. As the photographer prepared to shoot the picture, someone made a funny remark. Curt mugged playfully, eyebrows raised and mouth wide open, and he, Sally, and Cleo laughed heartily. The camera caught Lucille in a faint, forced smile.

In the small talk of the reception that followed, someone mentioned terrorism. It was a subject much in the news. A few months earlier a group that called itself the Black September Organization had kidnapped and killed Israeli athletes at the Olympic Games in Munich. Before he had left Washington for Khartoum, Cleo Noel had been in a staff meeting where a new U.S. policy toward terrorism had been discussed. It was not a policy that had yet been formally announced, but it said in effect that if American diplomats were taken hostage, their government would pay no ransom—neither money nor the release of prisoners nor anything else—to secure their freedom or save their lives. The rationale was that paying ransom simply encouraged more terrorism and more kidnappings; by giving in to terrorists' demands, you saved a few but endangered many. Those present at the meeting had been asked what they would want if they were kidnapped and held hostage. Would they want their government to ransom their lives? Or would they hold to the principle of no ransom? All had declared that they would not want to be ransomed.

Cleo had brought word of the new policy out with him to Khartoum in December, and sitting around the table at the Moores' after Christmas dinner, he and Curt had talked about it. Both were very strongly for it, and neither had any reservations. They felt it was more than a matter of not rewarding terrorists; it was also one of service to country and being consequent with one's own actions. You signed up to represent your country abroad. You knew it involved risks, and so you had to be willing to accept those risks. It was a simple matter of duty.

Throughout 1972 and into the early months of 1973, a war of terrorism and counterterrorism raged in the Middle East, Palestinians hijacking aircraft and killing Jordanians and Israelis and being killed by them. Less than a week after the Christmas dinner discussion at the Moores, a team of Black September gunmen had seized the Israeli embassy in Bangkok and threatened to kill all there, but things had turned out all right. The Thais had put tanks in position around the embassy and called up a force of heavily armed infantry. Cowed by this show of firepower, the gunmen had allowed themselves to be talked into releasing their hostages in return for safe passage out of Thailand.

But the main threat to Americans seemed to be not in Asia or even the Middle East but in Latin America. In 1968 the U.S. ambassador to Guatemala, John Gordon Mein, had been shot to death while trying to escape being kidnapped there. In 1969 the U.S. ambassador to Brazil, Burke Elbrick, had been kidnapped and held under threat of death for ransom. And then at the end of January, the U.S. ambassador to Haiti, Clinton Knox, had been held at gunpoint.

Palestinian terrorists had never targeted American diplomatic personnel, and neither Cleo Noel nor Curt Moore felt himself in particular danger. They were, after all, in the Sudan, which for Noel was a place almost as much home as his native Missouri. He was sure no harm could befall him there.

"So long as I am in the Sudan," Noel remarked to someone after his swearing-in ceremony, "I will never be in danger."

No one there would have been inclined to dispute the American ambassador's assertion. The Sudan seemed to them all like the last place in the world where terrorism might strike.

Curt Moore had spent the past three and a half years of his life in the Sudan, and another seventeen before that in Arab countries or in Washington working to promote America's relations with the Arabs. He knew the Arabs well, had many, many friends among them, and felt at ease and at home in their world. Many American diplomats served in Arab nations without ever making a serious effort to learn the language, but Moore spoke Arabic fluently. He sympathized with the plight of the

Palestinians, and though he rejected extreme Arab views about the conflict with Israel, he felt that the Arabs had legitimate grievances and were, in general, more wronged by Israel than wrong-doing against it. Like Noel, he could not imagine that anyone in the Sudan, a country he loved and that he had worked so hard to bring back into good relations with the United States, could wish him harm.

*   *   *

The big event of March 1 for Curt Moore was the farewell reception that the dean of the diplomatic corps, the ambassador of Saudi Arabia, was to hold in his honor. Just how much of an honor it was, only those who were part of the diplomatic world could fully appreciate. When he had agreed to stay on in Khartoum after Cleo Noel's arrival, Moore had retreated from the position of de facto head of the American embassy to that of deputy chief of mission. It was still a position of considerable responsibility, but in the rigidly hierarchized protocol of diplomacy, ambassadors stood alone at the top of the heap. They were like little potentates, sovereign in their own realms. All were, at least theoretically, equal. The dean of the corps was *primus inter pares,* first among equals, but others were differentiated not by the size or might or wealth of their countries but by their date of accreditation to their host government, which determined order of precedence, which in turn determined such weighty matters as where one stood in official receiving lines or sat at the dinner table—in the inconsequential middle or at the honored end, at the right or left elbow of the hostess.

The diplomatic corps in Khartoum was a less snobbish ambassadorial club than in many other places, but it was virtually unheard of for the dean of the corps to give a send-off to a deputy chief of mission. The reception was to be the corps' way of recognizing the friendship and respect that Curt Moore had won from his colleagues during the years that he had led the U.S. mission in the Sudan. It was also acknowledgment that his achievement in bringing the Sudan and the United States to the resumption of diplomatic relations was something extraordinary, something that they all had to admire even if some of them, like the Soviet ambassador and his Eastern European colleagues, admired it grudgingly. It was also a personal gesture of friendship on the part of the Saudi ambassador, for Moore and al-Malhouk had become good friends during their time together in Khartoum.

After swearing in Cleo Noel, and after lunch at home, Curt Moore played a brief round of golf with Sam Peale at Khartoum's twelve-hole dirt and gravel golf course, which he himself had rescued from dereliction following his arrival in 1969. That day, as always, he wore a hat and a long-sleeved shirt to protect himself from the sun, for his light skin burned easily.

Then Moore dropped Peale off at Peale's house, drove home, showered, put on a neatly pressed suit and white shirt, and headed off for the Saudi ambassador's reception.

Was he in some way conscious that he had been followed in previous days, or had it escaped his notice entirely? Some later said that Moore had remarked something unusual, and that he had mentioned it to one or two of his colleagues. If so, no one at the American embassy thought the matter serious enough to warrant particular attention.

5

Hostage in the Saudi Embassy

Cleo Noel's wound, though minor, evidently made it difficult for him to flee and ensured his early capture. He was probably seized inside the residence, or perhaps even before he could get back there.

Curt Moore, it was said, was taken in the garden at the rear of the building as he was attempting to reach the wall to vault to safety. The gunmen beat Moore savagely, cursed him and called him "CIA pig."[1]

Guy Eid, the Belgian, was felled by the bullet that tore through his lower leg. His wound bled profusely.

As the gunmen identified the other diplomats, they began releasing most of them. They sent away the Soviet ambassador, and also the Pakistani, Romanian, Somali, and Spanish ambassadors. The Yugoslav ambassador, who was discovered hiding on the roof with his Hungarian colleague, had a moment of real fright. The gunmen took him for the West German envoy and were going to hold him, until he produced his diplomatic papers and persuaded them that it was a case of mistaken identity. Some of the Arab envoys were released, but those representing conservative, pro-Western governments—Morocco, Tunisia, the United Arab Emirates, Kuwait, and Qatar—were kept. Shigeru Nomoto, the Japanese, was held too.

While the others were being let go, Nomoto was still seated on the

[1]See Note on Sources.

carpet of the ground-floor reception room. After the identification, only he and a half-dozen Arab envoys remained in the room. They were ordered to rise and to proceed single file up the stairs to the family living quarters on the second floor. There the gunmen bound the hands of the Arab diplomats behind their backs and ordered them again to sit on the carpet. Nomoto was told to sit next to them, but his hands were left free.

The gunmen's masks were now off, and Nomoto could see that they were young men, in their early or mid-twenties. The leader looked a bit older—he might have been in his late twenties or perhaps thirty. To himself, Nomoto called the leader "the boss," for he was clearly in charge, and an aide was always close by to take his orders. The boss carried a Kalashnikov assault rifle; strapped to his belt on one side was a long knife that hung in a scabbard, and on the other side was a bag. Nomoto saw that it held grenades, for the boss extracted one—it was a small, round, silver-colored object—and displayed it. There were two other gunmen there, both armed with the Russian assault rifles.

While other gunmen looked on nervously, fingering their weapons, the boss launched into a loud discourse in Arabic directed at the Arab envoys seated on the carpet. Nomoto did not know Arabic, so he could not tell what was being said, but repeatedly he heard the word "Palestine," and he supposed that the boss was lecturing them on the Palestinian cause, for the gunmen had already identified themselves as members of the Palestinian Black September Organization.

Just as the boss finished speaking, Nomoto heard a strange sound rising from the stairwell, a thump thump thump. He turned and looked, and what he saw horrified him more than anything he had experienced that evening. A gunman was pulling a rope up the stairs, and attached to the rope was a body. Then there was a second thump thump thump, and another body emerged at the top of the staircase. The gunmen dragged the two bodies to the center of the second-floor living room.

The first was the man who not half an hour earlier had been the guest of honor at the Saudi ambassador's reception, the counselor of the American embassy, George Curtis Moore. The second was the American ambassador, Cleo Noel. Nomoto had not seen them since the lights went out at the moment the reception was stormed. They were both fully clothed. Moore's hands and legs were tied behind his body with a single length of rope wound and knotted around his waist. His face was red and swollen, marked with several dark bruises. He opened his eyes for a while and then closed them, but he did not look around or even seem to see; he rocked a bit from side to side but uttered no sound.

Noel's binding was less constricting. His hands and legs were tied, but tied separately. His face was unmarked, Nomoto saw, but was absolutely white. He was breathing, but his eyes were closed, and he did not attempt to move or speak.

The two Americans had been brutally assaulted after their capture, beaten insensate. They were left to lie there, on the carpet in the center of the Saudi ambassador's ample family living room. The young gunmen stood over them, and Shigeru Nomoto and the Arab envoys looked on in shock and terror.

*　*　*

Just before 7:15 P.M. the telephone rang in the apartment of Sergeant Timothy E. Wells, the noncommissioned officer in charge of the United States Marine Guard detachment assigned to protect the American embassy. Wells was a short, slender man, quick, intelligent, and lively. He and his wife Carla—they had been married only a few months earlier—were dressing to go out to dinner.

On the line was the U.S. Marine who was standing watch at the embassy that evening. His message was terse: The Saudi embassy had been stormed by Palestinian gunmen, there had been shooting, and Ambassador Noel and Mr. Moore were inside. Wells ordered his watch-stander to get in touch immediately with Sandy Sanderson, who was both the administrative officer and the post security officer, and who was next in the State Department chain of command after the ambassador and the deputy chief of mission. The guard replied that he had already called Sanderson's home but had gotten no answer.

Wells dashed down the stairs and out of the building to his car and drove wildly to Sanderson's house. There was no one at home, so he headed for the Saudi embassy. It was about 7:30 when he got there. He found he was the only American at the scene. Sudanese police were just beginning to arrive, and a few of the diplomats whom the gunmen had released were nervously making their way out the embassy gate. Wells questioned those he could stop. From them he learned that the gunmen had identified themselves as belonging to the Black September Organization. They were holding Moore and Noel and some others. They had passed out leaflets demanding the release of Palestinians in prison in

Jordan and Israel, of Sirhan Sirhan, the killer of Senator Robert Kennedy, and of imprisoned members of the West German Bader-Meinhoff gang. They had threatened to kill their hostages if these persons were not immediately released.

Wells garnered one further bit of information from Hassan, Ambassador Noel's driver, whom he found nearby: the Land Rover that had delivered the gunmen to the Saudi ambassador's residence bore diplomatic license tags assigned to the Fatah office in Khartoum.

*　*　*

Sally Moore was at home waiting for her husband to return from the Saudi reception. They were to go that evening to the home of Beshir Mohammed Said, a Sudanese journalist and one of their earliest and dearest friends in Khartoum, for a farewell dinner. Just after 7:20 she received a phone call from the French ambassador, quite breathless, who recounted that the Saudi embassy had been seized by Palestinian gunmen. The French diplomat explained that he had managed to escape over the garden wall. Curt and others were inside, he said, but there was no cause for worry. He was sure they would be released in a few hours at most.

*　*　*

Sanderson arrived at the American embassy at about a quarter to eight, in the company of William Cole, the State Department's regional security officer, who was stationed in Addis Ababa and happened to be in Khartoum on one of his routine visits to his area of responsibility. The two men hurriedly sent off to Washington a flash cable, a message bearing the highest category of urgency, with a terse first report: "Ambassador Noel and DCM Moore being held in Saudi Embassy by armed group possibly Palestinians. Entire diplomatic corps also being held. Details will be flashed as they become available."[2]

[2]Khartoum telegram 0371, DTG 010814Z Mar 73, unclassified.

Map 2. Drawing of a street map of the New Extension showing the Saudi embassy, the Triplex Apartments, and Khartoum airport. Source: Hafeez A. M. Mohammed.

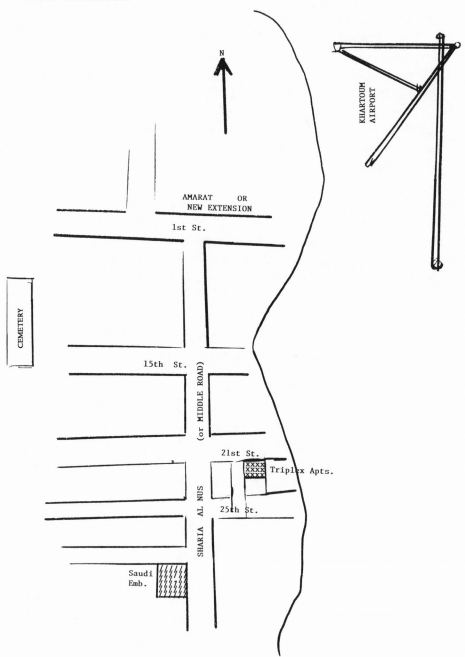

6

Fury of the Black September

After getting Hassan's story, Sergeant Timothy Wells went to the Triplex Apartments, a six-story building a short block away in which the American embassy had rented units for its subordinate staff. The building offered an unobstructed view of the embassy of Saudi Arabia. There, in one of the top-floor dwellings, Wells and others set up a watch that was to last for almost sixty hours. With field glasses sent from the embassy, Wells repeatedly scanned the facade of the pink and cream building, trying to divine what was going on inside. He was not to sleep a moment of the time; in fact, all told he was not to sleep for five days.

Wells wondered if he had been tagged by fate to be a witness to violence and tragedy. He had been in the Marines in Vietnam. A booby-trapped 105 mm shell had killed a buddy standing in front of him, and he himself had been hit by shrapnel and suffered a concussion and a damaged eardrum. After his tour of duty in Vietnam he had decided to stay in the Marines and had applied for the elite U.S. embassy guard unit. He had been sent to the American embassy in Amman, Jordan. He had been there in September 1970 when King Hussein's bedouin Arab army moved to crush the Palestine Liberation Organization, the event that gave rise to the creation of the Black September Organization. He had by chance been in Cairo in November 1971 when Black September gunmen shot down the prime minister of Jordan—the same Black September that now, hardly more than fifty yards down the street, held Curt Moore and Cleo Noel and threatened to kill them if their demands were not met.

So Sergeant Timothy Wells of the United States Marines knew something about the Black September. He knew that they were a ferocious gang, and that their threat to kill was no bluff. He had no illusions that it would all end happily in just a few hours.

* * *

The origins of the Black September Organization were not entirely what the name implied. The name implied vengeance for the thousands of Palestinians killed in Amman in September 1970 when King Hussein ordered his army into action against Palestinian guerrilla organizations that, through the numbers of their armed militants and the power they had accumulated over the previous three years, threatened his rule. Hussein's order sent tanks and artillery into action against Palestinian guerrilla fighters holed up together with their families in residential areas of Amman. The result was a blood bath. Estimates of the number of killed ranged between two and seven thousand, and many of them were women and children.

The events of September 1970 did in fact spawn a rage among Palestinians, a thirst for revenge against everybody who was, or was imagined to have been, responsible for the bloodletting—against Hussein and those Jordanians who served him, and against the Americans and the Israelis because they were believed to have backed and encouraged him in his decision to crush the Palestinians. But the Black September Organization's roots went back further than September 1970. And its genesis had as much to do with the rivalry between two of the Palestinian organizations, Fatah and the Popular Front for the Liberation of Palestine, as with the events of the month from which it took its name.

Fatah was the creation of Yasser Arafat and Salah Khalaf and a handful of other Palestinians of their generation. Arafat and Khalaf met as students in Cairo in the early 1950s. Arafat was a distant relative of the mufti of Jerusalem, Haj Amin al-Husseini, but his parents had moved from Jerusalem to Cairo in the 1920s, and Arafat is said by some to have been born in Cairo (though he claims Jerusalem as his birthplace). Arafat's family was well off and comfortably established in Egypt. Not so Khalaf's. The son of a Jaffa merchant, Khalaf was in his teens when his family fled to Gaza in May 1948 under the threat of Israeli guns, and under the illusion of a quick return in the wake of victorious Arab armies. The family had relatives in Gaza, but they lost almost everything in their flight, and in exile they led a precarious, poverty-ridden existence. Through distant family connections, young Salah managed to eke out the means to get to Cairo for university studies. There, in the best of revolutionary traditions, he and Arafat encountered one another in prison, each arrested by the Egyptian police in the fall of 1951 for political agitation.

Arafat was the leader. He was short and plump, but he was a fiery and inspiring orator and an effective organizer. And he was totally dedicated to the Palestinian cause. There was nothing else in his life—no women, no drink, no known vices or distractions. Khalaf was more the intellectual, the quiet, meticulous planner, a little taller than Arafat, solidly built, with dark eyes and a piercing gaze. Together, Arafat and Khalaf took over the Palestinian Student Union, Arafat becoming president and Khalaf vice-president and then president when Arafat finished his time at Cairo University. Their idea was armed struggle by the Palestinians themselves to regain control of their homeland. Although they were all of middle-class background, they drew their inspiration from the writings of the revolutionaries, of Franz Fanon, Lenin, and Mao Tse-tung. But they were inspired above all by the Algerian uprising, for they reasoned that if the Algerians could fight the French—who were, after all, a European nation of more than forty million—the Palestinian Arabs could surely do as much against a mere two million Jews. Other young Palestinians who were later to play leading roles in Fatah, or in Black September, gathered around them: Khalil al-Wazir, Mohammed Yussef al-Najjar, Kamal Adwan, and Mahmud Abbas.

Arafat went to Kuwait in the late 1950s, set up an engineering business, and became moderately wealthy. Khalaf joined him there after a stint as a teacher in Gaza. In October 1959 they and others began meeting to lay the basis for an armed Palestinian resistance movement independent of the various Arab governments that were host to the Palestinians. Their idea was unique, for at that time, and for some time afterwards, it was generally believed that the liberation of Palestine could come only at the hands of the Arab states. Arafat and his associates wanted Palestinians to do the job themselves. They first thought of calling their organization "Harakat al-Takrir al-Filistini," the Palestinian Liberation Movement, but that was just a little too prosaic. They had a flair for the dramatic. So they reversed the name and made of the first letters of the three words an acronym, Fatah, meaning in Arabic "conquest" or "victory."

They worked quietly through the early 1960s to gather membership and support for their organization. When the Palestine Liberation Organization was set up in 1964, at a congress held in Jordanian Jerusalem, Fatah had no chance of asserting leadership. For at its inception the PLO was the creation of Gamal Abdul Nasser, the president of Egypt and a charismatic figure. Not only Palestinians but Arabs everywhere looked to Nasser for the liberation of Palestine. Nasser chose Ahmad Shukeiry, a rabble-rousing orator, to head the new organization. The Palestine Liberation Army that Shukeiry proceeded to bring into being was, like the PLO itself at the outset, meant to be simply an adjunct of Egyptian policy.

Arafat's day came after the Arab debacle of June 1967, when in seventy-two hours Israel crushed Egypt's army and swept all the way to the Suez Canal, and in another seventy-two took the West Bank from Jordan and the Golan Heights from Syria. Nasser remained as president of Egypt, but he was now more a symbol of Arab defiance than a leader. The defeat of the Arab armies, and the pitiful showing made by Shukeiry's force, opened the way for the era of the Palestinian guerrilla. Arafat and his associates found an abundance of recruits for Fatah among the large Palestinian refugee population in Jordan and Lebanon, some from the 1948 war, but many of them new refugees from the recent Israeli conquest of the West Bank. Arafat himself slipped into the West Bank to organize resistance there, cleverly eluding the Israelis. Fatah began infiltrating teams of guerrillas into Israeli-held territory to carry out acts of sabotage. It set up its main operational base in a town called Karameh, in the Jordan Valley a few dozen miles south and east of the Allenby bridge.

It was at Karameh that Fatah and Arafat were to win themselves fame and adulation among Palestinians and Arabs everywhere. In March 1968 the Israelis moved to eliminate the Fatah base there. But the Israeli army, puffed up by its 1967 victories and under the command of newly appointed chief of staff Haim Bar Lev, had become careless and overconfident. Its plans became known to Jordanian intelligence, and in any event it telegraphed its punch by dropping leaflets to warn away the civilian population the day before its assault. Arafat decided that Fatah should stand and fight. At the time it must have seemed a mad, long-shot gamble, almost suicidally risky. But it paid off. At the end of a day of hard battle, the Fatah fighters were pushed out by the Israelis, but with the help of Jordanian artillery they gave almost as good as they took and exacted an unexpectedly heavy price from their opponent: the Israelis lost thirty killed and left at least one disabled tank and several other vehicles behind when they withdrew. Militarily the battle of Kara-meh was a defeat for Fatah, but psychologically it became a victory.

Arafat had redeemed the pride of the Palestinians; he had shown that they could do battle with the vaunted Israeli army. Now his organization's ranks swelled with volunteers. And not long afterwards, Karameh catapulted Arafat into the chairmanship of the Palestine Liberation Organization in the place of the discredited Shukeiry.

Fatah's tactics were to fight Israel on its borders and in the occupied territories and—to the extent that it could—inside Israel proper. But the Israelis were no easy target. They cut Fatah's Jordan Valley infiltration routes with mine fields, barbed wire, and electronic warning devices. Those Fatah teams they did not stop at the Jordan River line they relentlessly hunted down and killed in the hills to the west of it. Fatah's guerrilla war stalled, and while it was stalling, a rival organization, the Popular Front for the Liberation of Palestine, came along with a different tactic and a determination to steal the show.

On July 22, 1968, PFLP gunmen hijacked an El Al plane and flew it to Algiers. The Algerian government was deeply embarrassed. It ended up freeing the passengers and the plane, but only after Israel agreed to release sixteen Arab prisoners.

The PFLP's hijacking grabbed headlines around the world. Arafat's dead infiltrators, if they were noticed at all, garnered at most a few lines on the back pages.

The PFLP was the creation of Dr. George Habash, a Christian Palestinian and a native of the town of Lydda, known since 1948 as Lod and famous today mainly as the site of Ben Gurion International Airport. A Haganah force under the command of Moshe Dayan took Lydda in May 1948 and gave the Arab population a few hours' notice to leave. Habash and his parents walked all the way to Jerusalem, a distance of less than thirty miles but a traumatic thing for the middle-class people that they were. From Jerusalem George Habash went to Lebanon, to study medicine at the American University of Beirut.

He became a doctor, but he was not to follow a career of healing.

Habash and Arafat were rivals from the very beginning, and their tactics were to differ at every stage of their lives. While Arafat sought Palestinian regeneration through Palestinian efforts, Habash at first looked to Gamal Abdul Nasser for salvation. He joined the Arab Nationalist Movement, a group that operated under the sponsorship and guidance of Nasser, and he became one of the ANM's leading Palestinian figures. The ANM was predicated on the belief, conventional and accepted before 1967, that it was Egypt and the other Arab states that were going to liberate Palestine, and that the Palestinian role would be secondary. The June 1967 defeat shattered both the ANM and the expectation that Egypt and the other Arab states would liberate Palestine for the Palestinians.

Habash proceeded to set up his own organization, and here again he took a different path from Arafat. As a Christian, he could not rally the kind of mass following that Arafat, a Moslem, could command; one Beirut newspaper later wrote that if his first name had been not George but Ahmad, the entire history of the Palestinian movement would have been different. But Habash and the men he grouped around him—among others Ahmad Jibril, Wadi Haddad, Naif Hawatmeh, and Bilal al-Hassan (several were to defect and set up their own organizations)—had a tactic that made them an attractive alternative to Arafat for some Palestinians. They saw no point in confronting Israel head on, at its borders or inside them. To go up against the enemy's hard defenses was wasted effort. Instead, they would strike at Israel's soft spots, its aviation and its interests abroad. They called their tactic "revolutionary violence."

After the Algiers hijacking, the PFLP struck again and again, always seeking the soft, unprotected civilian target. On December 26, 1968, PFLP gunmen attacked an El Al Boeing 707 as it was about to leave Athens airport for New York. They killed one passenger and wounded two others. On February 18, 1969, PFLP gunmen shot up another El Al plane, this time at Zurich's airport, fatally wounding the pilot. Two days later a PFLP operative, a young woman from Ramallah, planted a bomb in a Jerusalem supermarket. The explosion killed two Israeli shoppers and wounded more than twenty. On August 29, 1969, PFLP gunmen hijacked a TWA jetliner and flew it to Damascus. On September 8, 1969, Palestinians identified with the PFLP threw grenades at the Israeli embassies in Bonn and The Hague and at the El Al office in

Brussels. On February 10, 1970, PFLP gunmen attacked a bus carrying El Al passengers at the terminal of the Munich airport, killing one Israeli and wounding eleven. All these operations kept Habash and the PFLP in the headlines while Arafat and his associates smarted in the shadows, their guerrilla war against Israel in a state of collapse.

The PFLP spawned imitators. A group called the Popular Struggle Front (rumored to be under Egyptian sponsorship) threw a grenade into the El Al office in Athens in November 1969, planted a bomb at the El Al office in Istanbul the following April, and in July 1970 hijacked an Olympic Airlines plane in order to free from Greek jails the Palestinian perpetrators of other bombings. Another to dabble in terrorism was the PFLP General Command, set up by Ahmad Jibril, a breakaway from Habash's own PFLP. It claimed credit for blowing up a Swissair plane in flight, killing all forty-seven of its passengers and crew, on February 22, 1970, though its spokesman soon retracted the claim.

But the imitators and the defectors did not put George Habash and the PFLP out of business. Habash's big coup came on September 9, 1970. In an operation without precedent to that time—and that has remained without comparison since—the PFLP simultaneously hijacked four airliners. One, a Pan American Boeing 747, it flew to Cairo and there blew up after the passengers were freed. The other three— Swissair, TWA, and British Airways jetliners—were flown to Dawson Field, a landing strip built by the British in the Jordanian desert during World War II and long since abandoned. There the passengers were held in the planes in sweltering heat while demands were made for the release of prisoners in jail in Israel. Three days later, after removing the passengers, the PFLP blew up the planes.

This spectacular operation stunned the world and precipitated a confrontation long in the making between King Hussein's government and the Palestinian organizations in Jordan. Arafat was furious with the PFLP, and he suspended it from the PLO's Central Committee. He and his supporters knew that Fatah was not ready for a showdown with Hussein's army, but the Dawson Field operation triggered one anyway.

For a brief while the outcome appeared in doubt. As Jordanian tanks and artillery began to blast Palestinian strongholds in Amman, Syria sent a large tank force across the border into Jordan. Hussein panicked. Through the American embassy in Amman, he asked Israel to intervene to stop the Syrians. But the Syrians themselves were divided. The tank force was dispatched at the order of Salah al-Jadid, Syria's military strongman, but Defense Minister Hafez al-Assad refused to give it air support. Israel moved troops toward the Golan Heights, and the United States sent a carrier task force to the eastern Mediterranean. This, together with a vigorous Jordanian resistance, shattered the Syrians' less than robust determination to come to the aid of their Palestinian brethren. The Syrian tank force turned tail and headed back home.

With the Syrians out of the picture, the Palestinians in Amman came close to being annihilated. What saved them from that fate was the intervention of Nasser. At the Egyptian president's insistence, and through the good offices of a committee whose members included President Jaafar al-Nimeiry of Sudan, a series of truces were arranged, and finally an agreement was signed that put an end to the fighting. Arafat escaped from Amman to Cairo, disguised as a woman, on one of the planes carrying the Arab mediators.

Well before the September 1970 showdown with Hussein, Arafat, Khalaf, and others in Fatah had begun to toy with the idea of terrorism. It posed a dilemma. Arafat was both the head of Fatah and chairman of the Palestine Liberation Organization. In the latter capacity he was the embodiment of the Palestinian movement as a whole; in fact, he saw himself—and aspired to be recognized—as the legitimate leader of all Palestinians. He and others realized that an open resort to terror would be enormously damaging to him and to the Palestinian cause, for it was one thing to fight Israel along its borders and inside them but quite another to hijack airliners and kill defenseless civilians in European airports. Identification with terror would give both Arafat and the Palestinian cause a bad name. A facade of moderation had to be maintained.

And yet the fury among the Palestinians, and among other Arabs, was such that a great many felt the resort to terror fully justified. And the September 1970 massacre in Amman heightened the fury. Fatah could not afford to leave it to the PFLP and splinter groups that began to vie with the PFLP in aircraft hijackings and killings to occupy center stage, to be the only outlet for this Palestinian rage. If it did, it risked losing the support of an important segment of Palestinian opinion.

The solution that was hit upon was a simple one: an organization with no avowed links to Fatah or Arafat but that would draw its personnel and its financial and logistic support from Fatah. It would be a clandestine organization, with no known offices and no address; an organization to which Arafat, Fatah, and the PLO could deny any connection. The PFLP would have a Fatah competitor, even if that competitor could not be openly associated with Fatah.

* * *

The code names taken by the Palestinian guerrilla chiefs all began with the word "Abu," which in Arabic means "father of." When a man had a son, it was a thing of pride, of honor, so others would call him, for example, Abu Hassan if his son's name was Hassan. The names that the Palestinian guerrilla chiefs chose were not those of their sons—Arafat was not married and had never had a son—but names that had a family or historical connotation, or that simply gave the bearer a certain panache. Arafat was Abu Ammar. Salah Khalaf, co-founder with Arafat of Fatah and by the late 1960s head of its intelligence branch, the Jihaz al-Rasd, was Abu Iyad.

Abu Iyad became the secret chief of Black September. A man who called himself Abu Yussef, and whose real name was Mohammed Yussef al-Najjar, became the organization's chief strategist. One who called himself Abu Hassan, and whose real name was Ali Hassan Salameh, became its head of operations. Still another senior Fatah figure who was to play a prominent role in Black September was Khalil al-Wazir, who went by the code name Abu Jihad. All four were members of Fatah's ten-man governing council, the General Command.

Ali Hassan Salameh was, without question, the most colorful of all of Black September's leading figures. The Israelis nicknamed him "the Red Prince," not because of his political inclinations—he was not, in particular, a leftist—but because of the blood on his hands. He did not kill people himself; he may never in his life have pulled the trigger on a victim. But he was the brain, the organizational genius, behind the killing of many Israelis and Arabs.

Ali Hassan was the son of Hassan Salameh, one of the leaders of the Palestinian Arab guerrilla war against the Jews during the late 1930s and the 1940s. Hassan Salameh's hatred of the Jews, and of the British, led him to join his patron, Haj Amin al-Husseini, the mufti of Jerusalem, in Germany during World War II. When toward the close of the war the mufti proposed a plan he hoped would wipe out a large part of the Jewish community in Palestine, Salameh was chosen to carry it out. Early on the morning of November 5, 1944, the Luftwaffe parachuted Salameh, another Palestinian, three German officers, and several large crates into the rocky, cave-pocked wastes of the Jordan Valley not far from Jericho. The crates held bags of poison intended for Tel Aviv's water supply. The team's mission was to kill the population of Tel Aviv.

The British mandate police learned of the air drop within a day after it took place. They quickly tracked down and arrested two of the Germans and the other Arab and seized the poison. Salameh, however, got away.

He made his way slowly across British Mandate Palestine, staying at the homes of friends, and then crossed over into Lebanon, where he had family. But in November 1947 he returned, to play a leading role in the Palestinian Arab uprising aimed at crushing the Jewish state before it could see the light of day. Salameh was second in command to Abdel Kader al-Husseini, and when Husseini was killed in the battle for the Kastel (the hilltop that the Arabs sought to seize so as to block Jewish access to Jerusalem), Hassan Salameh took over as supreme commander of the Palestinian Arab forces. But only briefly. On May 31, 1948, in a battle with forces of Menachem Begin's Irgun for control of the village of Ras el-Ain, the source of Jerusalem's water supply, Salameh was mortally wounded.

Ali Hassan Salameh was seven years old when his father was killed. His mother vowed to raise him to follow in his father's footsteps, but the child was recalcitrant. The burden of living up to his father's legend was too onerous. Besides, he had little other personal reason for bitterness. Most Palestinians who fled their homes in 1948 ended up leading miserable existences in refugee camps in Gaza, on the West Bank, or in Lebanon. But Salameh's family had money, and after his father's death, his mother took him to a comfortable life in Beirut. He went to school with the sons of well-to-do Lebanese, and he acquired their taste for luxury and high living. He grew to be an extraordinarily handsome young man, with fair skin and dark hair that he let grow modishly long. Fun-loving and pleasure-seeking, he had a pronounced fondness for flashy Western clothes and for women both Western and Eastern. And he was very attractive to women. Despite his mother's urgings, he showed little interest in joining the ranks of the Palestinian fighters.

It was the Arab debacle of June 1967 that changed everything for Ali Hassan Salameh. He went to Jordan and signed up with Yasser Arafat's Fatah, and because of the prestige of his family name and his own keen and quick intelligence, he was soon brought to work directly with Arafat and Abu Iyad. His first job was in counterintelligence in the Jihaz al-Rasd, ferreting out Jordanian and Israeli agents from Fatah's ranks. In 1969 Salameh was sent to Cairo together with several other promising young men selected by Arafat for training by the Egyptians in intelligence and in the arts of sabotage. There were ten in the group altogether. One was a tall, lean young man, Mohammed Daoud Mahmud Awda, who went by the code name of Abu Daoud.

Joining Fatah and rising to a senior position within it did not make Ali Hassan Salameh change his personal style of living. In Beirut he continued to live the life of a European playboy, frequenting nightclubs, bedding women all around town, and spending large sums of money. He liked to dress all in black, and he wore a gold chain around his neck. This flamboyance brought Salameh to the attention of the U.S. Central Intelligence Agency station in Beirut, and a young CIA officer there, Robert Ames, was assigned to make contact with him. At the time, the agency's main interest in Ali Hassan Salameh, it appears, was to have someone in the Palestinian movement who could alert them if the terrorism that was beginning to sweep the area were to turn against Americans. But the CIA knew the Palestinians wanted more, so Ames represented the contact he offered Salameh as one aimed at establishing a political dialogue.

It may never be possible to know precisely what happened between Ames and Salameh. But, as the story goes, after a series of indirect contacts in Beirut, they met in Kuwait in 1970 in a CIA safehouse. Salameh made clear that he had no intention of working for the CIA— of becoming, in the terms of the trade, a CIA "asset"—but he indicated that he would be ready to act as liaison with the agency, and that he would do this with Arafat's knowledge and agreement. To his bosses, Ames sensibly advocated accepting Salameh on his own terms. But at CIA headquarters in the Washington, D.C., suburb of Langley, Virginia, the view prevailed that an effort should be made to sign Salameh up, make him a controlled agent. Under instructions, Ames set up a meeting for Salameh in Rome with a senior CIA officer from Washington. The senior officer came with a written contract and a briefcase loaded with a million dollars in greenbacks. Salameh exploded in rage; he was not going to be a spy for the CIA, he roared. He hurled the briefcase across the room and stalked out.

The disastrous meeting in Rome ended the CIA's first attempt at contact with Fatah. It also ended the agency's first hopes for gaining early warning of Palestinian terrorist attempts against American officials, and thereby of foiling them. Contact between the CIA and the PLO was not to be resumed until more than three years later, after the October 1973 Arab-Israeli war.

*　*　*

Black September turned its fury first against King Hussein's men, and it chose as its target Jordanian prime minister Wasfi Tal. A tough, wily man with a thick brush mustache, Tal was a member of Hussein's inner circle. Palestinians held him responsible for the September 1970 slaughter in Amman; and he was indisputably the architect of the Jordanian army's move in July 1971 to crush Palestinian guerrilla units in northern Jordan.

Black September gunmen stalked Tal and finally caught him in Cairo at 1:25 P.M. on November 28, 1971, as he walked into the lobby of the Sheraton Hotel after an early lunch with Arab League Secretary General Abdul Khalek Hassouna. Five bullets, fired at close range, struck Tal in the chest and head. He collapsed and died on the spot. It is said that one of the gunmen knelt and licked Tal's blood as it flowed from his wounds and then shouted, "I am proud, finally I have done it, we have taken our revenge on a traitor."[3] The Egyptian police arrested the four members of the Black September team. Soon thereafter, however, the Egyptians released the killers and allowed them to go their way. It was a practice that others were soon to emulate.

*　*　*

Black September's next target, less than three weeks later, was Zaid Rifai, Jordan's ambassador in London and a boyhood friend and confidant of King Hussein. A Black September gunman, in this instance an Algerian, stood on a traffic island in the Belgravia quarter of London waiting for Rifai's limousine to pass. As it approached, the assailant pulled a submachine gun from under his coat and fired off a magazine of ammunition. Rifai ducked to the floor of the car and, miraculously, suffered only one hit, in his hand. The gunman fled to a nearby house and then slipped out of Britain to France. There was some speculation that the British were glad not to have caught him. The French certainly did not want him; they hurriedly put him on a plane for Algiers. In the

---

[3]Christopher Dobson, *Black September* (New York: Macmillan, 1974), p. 1; and Michael Bar Zohar and Eitan Haber, *The Quest for the Red Prince* (New York: Morrow), 1983, pp. 111–12.

early years of the terrorist era, even European governments did not want to have on their hands a prisoner whose sponsors would hijack and kill to win his release.

After the unsuccessful attempt on Rifai came an avalanche of attacks on Jordanian targets in Europe—attacks against Jordanian embassies in Paris and in Berne and the Jordanian Airlines office in Rome, an attempt to bomb one Jordanian Airlines plane and to hijack another, and the mass slaying in the cellar of a house in Bonn of five persons suspected of being Jordanian intelligence agents.

Black September took credit for all these actions, while Arafat and Fatah stoutly denied any connection to them or to Black September. The Egyptians, who surely interrogated Wasfi Tal's killers before releasing them, suspected that Tal's assassination was the work of Abu Yussef (Mohammed Najjar). But the actions in Europe were most likely directed by Ali Hassan Salameh. Europe was Salameh's special area of operation. He spoke good French, passable English, and some German, and he traveled frequently to Europe.

Europe was to be the starting point for Black September's next major operation. It was another aircraft hijacking, but a particularly unusual one. On the afternoon of May 8, 1972, a team of four Black September operatives, two men and two women, seized control of a Sabena Boeing 707 airliner as it flew over the Greek island of Rhodes en route from Brussels to Tel Aviv. Brazenly, they directed the pilot to continue his flight to Tel Aviv. When the plane landed at Lod, the head of the Black September team—he went by the alias of Captain Kamal Rifaat, but his real name was Ali Abu Sanina—demanded the release of 317 Palestinians imprisoned in Israel and threatened to blow up the plane with all passengers aboard if this demand was not met. In a stall for time, Defense Minister Moshe Dayan promised to do what the Black September required.

The day, however, was not to end with jubilant Palestinians flying off to safe haven in an Arab capital. A team of Israeli commandos posing as maintenance crew stormed the plane, killing Sanina and the other male hijacker, and capturing the two women. In the brief exhange of fire between the hijackers and the Israelis, one passenger was killed and two or three others were wounded, but the rest were freed unharmed. Interrogation of the two women hijackers led the Israelis to the conclusion that the mastermind behind the Sabena hijacking was Ali Hassan Salameh.

According to Israeli sources, the Black September's next operation was carried out in collaboration with its rival, the PFLP, with the Japanese Red Army furnishing the gunmen. It was to be the bloodiest action to that time. On the night of May 30, 1972, three young Japanese arriving at Lod airport on an Air France flight out of Paris pulled submachine guns from their luggage as it came off the conveyor belt and sprayed the hall with bullets. Twenty-seven people were killed, sixteen of them Puerto Rican tourists who had come to the Holy Land on a religious pilgrimage, and seventy-two were wounded.

But Black September's most spectacular coup, more spectacular even than the PFLP's September 1970 hijacking of four airliners, was yet to come. Salah Khalaf was to be its mastermind, but both Salameh and Mohammed Awda (Abu Daoud) were to go to Germany to participate in or oversee the preparations for it.

At about 4:00 on the morning of September 5, 1972, six young men wearing track suits and carrying tote bags scaled the wall of the Olympic Village in Munich, where the first Olympic Games to be held in Germany since Hitler's 1936 Berlin spectacular were under way. German guards saw them but did nothing to stop them; the guards assumed they were athletes returning from an unauthorized late-night outing. Inside the village the six were met by two others. Pulling Kalashnikov assault rifles from their bags, the eight proceeded to the Israeli pavilion, burst through the door, shot and killed two Israelis who resisted, and seized nine others and bound them. The leader of the Black September group went to the window and threw out a list of demands. It called for the release of some two hundred Palestinians jailed in Israel.

Prime Minister Golda Meir's first reaction was a trenchant no. But as hours passed and the Israelis despaired of saving the lives of their athletes in any other way, they secretly offered a compromise. The Israeli hostages would be exchanged for German volunteers who would be flown together with the terrorists to an Arab country. Two or three months later, Israel would release fifty jailed Palestinians, disclaiming any connection with the Munich kidnappings. The Germans passed the Israeli offer to the leader of the Black September team. He in turn telephoned the number in Tunis that he had been instructed to call to get approval for terms other than those stated in his initial set of demands. But his contact was not there, so the momentary prospect for a deal vanished.[4]

[4]Bar Zohar and Haber, *The Quest for the Red Prince*, pp. 127–28.

The Black September team leader then demanded a plane to take his men and the hostages to Cairo. The Germans promised to comply, but they set a trap: German sharpshooters would pick off the gunmen as they transferred to an empty Lufthansa Boeing 707 on the Munich airport tarmac. But, incredibly, the Germans sent only four sharpshooters, equipped with bolt action rifles, to gun down eight terrorists armed with automatic weapons. The result was a disaster: all nine Israeli hostages were killed. Five of the Black September team died along with the Israelis, but three survived.

The three Black September survivors did not have to stay long in their German jail. A few weeks later, Black September hijacked a Lufthansa airliner. This time they offered the Germans a deal: the release of the passengers and crew in exhange for the imprisoned terrorists. The Germans acceded without hesitation. The Munich three flew to a hero's welcome in Libya.

Arafat, Khalaf, and their associates in the PLO and Fatah denied any connection to the Munich operation, but they nonetheless refused to condemn it. Libya's leader, Colonel Muammar al-Qaddafi, praised it, and his offer of safe haven to the surviving three terrorists highlighted the growing connection between Qaddafi and the Black September. The Black September team had gone to Munich from Libya via Rome. It seemed likely that Qaddafi was privy to the secret of the operation, and he was said to be the largest single contributor to the Black September's coffers, giving $30 million a year.[5] Khalaf, moreover, was believed by American intelligence to receive an independent direct subsidy from Qaddafi.[6]

Munich was to be the apogee of the Black September. After Munich, it dispatched a flurry of letter bombs to Israelis and to prominent Jews in the diaspora. One of the first of the letter bombs killed the agricultural attaché at the Israeli embassy in London, Dr. Ami Shechori. But after that police and postal authorities were alerted, and most of the missives were discovered before they could reach their mark.

The locus of the next major Black September operation was to be almost as much of a surprise as Munich. On the evening of December 28, 1972, the policeman on guard at the Israeli embassy in Bangkok,

[5] US Embassy Khartoum telegram 0686, DTG 291130Z Mar 73.
[6] State Department Confidential/Exdis telegram, 15 March 1973.

Thailand, saw two men in white tie and tails open the gate and walk into the embassy compound. The policeman thought they were diplomats returning from the big event of the day, the investiture that evening of the crown prince of Thailand, until he saw two other men with submachine guns scale the wall. The four bolted the embassy's door and took hostage six Israeli diplomats, including the Israeli ambassador to Cambodia, Shimon Avidor, who was on a visit to Bangkok. The gunmen raised the Palestinian flag over the Israeli embassy and threw out a leaflet demanding the release from prison in Israel of thirty-six terrorists, including the lone Japanese survivor of the Lod airport massacre and the two Arab women who had taken part in the Sabena airliner hijacking.

The Thai authorities brought up tanks and armored cars and threw an imposing cordon of storm troopers around the hostage embassy. They then began an extended series of negotiations with the four Black September gunmen, leading them on and on, getting them to break deadline after deadline. Finally, overawed by the Thai government's show of force and exhausted and confused, the four Palestinians accepted an offer of safe passage to Cairo in return for release of their hostages unharmed. The Egyptian ambassador, under instructions from President Sadat, who in December 1972 still hoped to gain American support for a political settlement of his dispute with Israel, played a key role in persuading the terrorists to accept the Thai offer.

The Bangkok operation was a humiliating failure for the Black September. The organization lost both face and credibility; who would again believe them when they threatened to kill their hostages unless their demands were met? The operation itself had obviously been well planned, and it had been executed with considerable precision and skill; the gunmen and their arms had been brought into Bangkok without being discovered, and the seizure of the Israeli embassy had come off with surprising ease. The gunmen's orders had been precise: if the Israelis did not meet their demands, they were to blow up the embassy with the hostages inside it and turn themselves over to the Thai authorities. The critical weakness was their resolve: when the test came, they were not ready to kill and be killed.

The lesson for Black September planners was clear: the next team to be dispatched to seize an objective would have to be a team of "tried militants," and everything possible would have to be done to ensure that its resolve was ironclad and beyond question. Perhaps with that in mind, an emissary was dispatched from Beirut to Cairo to question the Bangkok gunmen, and *Al Muharrer,* the Beirut newspaper that spoke for the Palestinian guerrillas, reported that they were to be put on trial.

But before another operation could be mounted, the Black September suffered yet another humiliating setback. On February 9, 1972, Abu Daoud, one of the organization's top agents, was arrested in Amman, where he had gone in disguise to lay the groundwork for an operation whose target was to be either the American embassy or the office of the Jordanian prime minister. Under interrogation, which almost certainly included torture, Abu Daoud sang. He admitted that Black September was the secret arm of Fatah, said that Abu Iyad (Salah Khalaf) was the brains behind the Munich operation, and gave a detailed—if very likely not wholly truthful—account of the planning for Munich. The Jordanians broadcast Abu Daoud's confession over Amman radio. In Beirut, Palestinian leaders countered that the voice in which Abu Daoud spoke was not his, and that the confession was phony.

A Jordanian court put Abu Daoud under death sentence. Either the Black September did not consider his confession genuine or, if they did think it so, it was one they themselves wanted to punish. So while Abu Daoud sat in jail in Amman awaiting execution, his associates in Beirut began planning an operation to get him out.

They decided to call it "Operation Abu Daoud."

* * *

After Munich, Prime Minister Golda Meir called in retired generals Aharon Yariv and Zvi Zamir, the latter the head of the Mossad, and charged them with setting up an organization to hunt down and kill Israel's Arab terrorist tormentors. One by one, Black September and other Arab terrorist agents in Europe began dying by bomb or by bullet. In mid-February, Israel mounted a combined air, sea, and land operation against two Palestinian refugee camps in northern Lebanon where the Black September trained its terrorists and from which the Munich team had come. Over a hundred Palestinians were reported to have been killed in the Israeli raids. One of the camps bore the name Nahr al-Bard, or Cold River.

Both Israelis and Arabs were keyed up and on edge, and on February 21 this tension brought on a tragedy. A Libyan civilian airliner carrying 113 persons on a flight from Tripoli to Cairo got lost in a sandstorm over the Egyptian capital and strayed into Israeli-occupied Sinai. Israeli fighter planes immediately rose to intercept it. The Israelis claimed that the pilot of the Libyan plane ignored their order to land, but the tapes from the plane's black box showed that if an order to land had been given, the pilot, a Frenchman, had not understood it. The French pilot did, however, realize that he was in the wrong place, for when he was shot down by air-to-air missiles fired by the Israeli interceptors, he was heading back east toward the Suez Canal. The Israelis had shot first and left questions for later.

One hundred and six people died in the crash of the Libyan craft. Throughout the Arab world there were calls for vengeance, and these were not confined to fringe groups. Even a figure so respected as Mohammed Heikal, editor of the prestigious Cairo daily paper *Al Ahram,* was to write: "Are we now forced to say [to the Palestinians] . . . no one would blame you if you carried out your vengeance in any place: strike where you want and against any target you choose!"[7]

Arab leaders called on the United States to condemn the Israeli action, but Washington remained silent. Defense Minister Moshe Dayan belatedly acknowledged that the shooting down of the airliner was a mistake, and that the blame lay at Israel's doorstep. The Israeli government offered to pay compensation to the families of the victims. But these gestures did little to calm Arab outrage, which was now directed almost as much at the United States as at Israel.

* * *

By the end of 1972 the militants, those who saw terror as a legitimate weapon in the struggle of the Palestinians, were gaining the upper hand within the PLO. The influence of Salah Khalaf was on the rise, while the stock of Khaled al-Hassan and his brother Hani and others who wanted to keep the Palestinian cause's name clean of terrorism dropped sharply. Arafat sided with Khalaf, and when the Palestine National Council, the 450-member Palestinian parliament in exile, met in Cairo in January 1973, it formally committed the PLO to a policy of overthrowing King Hussein. Getting rid of Hussein had always been on the PLO's agenda, but never before had the organization so brazenly proclaimed the fact.

Arab governments were moving in just the opposite direction. That same month, at the Arab League Defense Council meeting in Cairo, they granted Hussein partial rehabilitation. The two Arab governments

[7] *The Arab World,* January 16–31, 1973.

that took the lead role in bringing Jordan out of its isolation were those of Saudi Arabia and Sudan. Behind all this, PLO leaders saw the hand of the United States, for Hussein himself would be going to the United States late in February, and that same month President Sadat would be sending one of his top advisors, Hafez Ismail, to Washington. They suspected that the Arab governments and Washington were about to make a deal at their expense.

The PLO's new militancy, and its anger at the United States, were reflected in speeches delivered by Salah Khalaf in Cairo late in January and by Arafat at a public rally in Baghdad early in February. "We will not limit our arena to the Palestinian field, the land surrounding Palestine, or the Arab arena," Khalaf proclaimed. "We will set forth to pursue our enemy in all directions."[8] Arafat was even more threatening. "Welcome to the American efforts and the American conspiracies," the PLO chief roared defiantly in his speech in Baghdad. "We are going to turn this region, like Vietnam, into a center of revolutionary radiation for the entire world."[9]

*   *   *

It was Salah Khalaf, the head of Jihaz al-Rasd, who planned Operation Abu Daoud, after first getting Yasser Arafat's approval.[10]

Evidently Khalaf had learned the lessons of Bangkok and was determined that that failed operation's mistakes should not be repeated. The team charged with carrying out Operation Abu Daoud was to number not four, as in Bangkok, but eight gunmen: the larger their number, the less likely the group would be to agree among themselves to capitulate. And to fire them with enthusiasm for their mission, they were to be told that they were going to seize the top agent of the American Central Intelligence Agency in the Middle East, an individual who had been at the U.S. embassy in Amman in 1970, who had directed King Hussein's killing of their Palestinian brethren that September, and who would soon be going back to Jordan to head a secret American missile base there—a certain George Moore, the number two man at the U.S. embassy in Khartoum.

[8]In a speech to Palestinian students in Cairo, January 21, 1973 (*Arab Report and Record*, January 16–31, 1973).

[9]"Arab Leaders Fear They May Be Target of Palestinians," *Washington Post*, March 14, 1973.

[10]See "Note on Sources" for chapter 6.

7

To Be a Foreign Service Officer

George Curtis Moore's forebears came to America in pre-revolutionary times. He could trace his ancestry back practically to the beginning of eighteenth-century Scotland. And, in fact, he did, for he was the kind of person who was curious about everything. He compiled a genealogy, and it told that his ancestor was one Samuel Moore, who was born in Scotland and emigrated to northern Ireland in the second or third decade of that century. Samuel married a woman named Sarah Morrison. They had a son, John, who was born on June 21 or 22, 1732, near Newry, Ireland.

John Moore was the first of the family to come to America. He emigrated to the New World in 1757, not long after marrying. He and his wife, Ann, settled in western Pennsylvania; they had eight children, seven boys and a girl. At the time, western Pennsylvania was the frontier, the Wild West. John Moore suffered the fate that frontiersmen were liable to suffer in those days: he was killed by Indians. After his death, his wife kept a tavern on the Old Cumberland Trail at Union, or Uniontown, Pennsylvania.

It was from John Moore's second son, Robert, born three years after his parents reached America, that Curt Moore was directly descended. Robert Moore struck out across the Appalachians to stake his claim to land in Ohio. By the last years of the nineteenth century, his descendant Abraham Moore, a man who looks out at the world from old photographs with the stern and direct gaze customary of the times, was comfortably established in farming, though by no means well-to-do. Abraham Moore's son, Paul, put himself through medical school, working in the hours when he was not studying or in class at Western Reserve University Medical School to earn the money he needed to sustain his education. Paul Moore married Lucille Munn, an attractive young woman from Portage, Ohio, and on September 7, 1925, George Curtis Moore came into the world.

Paul Moore had a romantic, inquisitive streak. He was curious about the world, and he did not want to settle down and practice medicine in his native Ohio. An uncle of his wife's who had recently retired in Los Angeles wrote of the delights of the climate and the beauties of the Pacific coast—freeways and smog lying still some years in southern California's future. After finishing his studies at Western Reserve and doing a year of specialization at the University of Pennsylvania medical school, Dr. Paul Moore packed his wife and young son into the family car and headed westward.

They arrived in Los Angeles in the late summer of 1930, just as the Great Depression struck the West Coast with full force. The Depression was not to affect their lives for long, however, for Paul soon established a thriving practice that included celebrities of the movie industry, among them Walt Disney. Paul and Lucille eventually bought a large house in a well-to-do residential section of Hollywood. Curt's friends of college days were to think the house a bit grand and pretentious, but they found Dr. and Mrs. Moore quite the opposite—unassuming, warm, and always welcoming.

Curt was to be Paul and Lucille Moore's only child. They had the money to pamper him but declined to do so. They enrolled him in public schools, and in his high-school summers they sent him off to earn his pocket money by picking fruit and carrying mail, for they believed in the early American virtue of self-reliance. The postal service was so well satisfied with young George Curtis Moore's work that it declared him eligible for re-employment upon graduation.

For Curt was a serious and diligent boy. Though he grew to be over six feet tall and well proportioned, he was not much inclined to sports in his early years. Poor eyesight was no doubt one reason. His vision tested at 20/200. Throughout his youth and his adult life he wore thick-lensed glasses, and in those years before the invention of contact lenses, the wearing of glasses ruled a young man out of the sports that dominated high-school and college life. But there was more to it than that. He loved books. As a child, and throughout his life, he spent long hours reading. And he loved school. From kindergarten—where he got top marks for diligence, comportment, and judgment—through high school and college, he was an outstanding student. He had a prodigious memory and a delight in and talent for music. His parents arranged lessons for him in the flute. For a child it was a challenging instrument, but he worked at it and mastered it, with the same determination and thoroughness that were later to enable him to excel in difficult academic subjects and to become fluent in German and Arabic. The flute became a part of his life. He played it in his junior high school orchestra, and he continued to play it throughout his later years, finding pleasure and relaxation in it.

All this came at a price, however, and the price was that George Curtis Moore was different from most other youngsters. Adults delighted in him—he was so well behaved, such a friendly, polite boy and so hard-working. A neighbor later told investigators who came to do Moore's security check for the Foreign Service that he was "the kind of boy I would have liked to have had as a son." These, however, were not the traits that won popularity with one's peers, and they were compounded by Lucille Moore's sense of propriety. She sent her son off to southern California's public schools dressed as though he were attending an exclusive New England academy. His home-room picture from the yearbook of his first year at John Marshall High School in Los Angeles shows Curtis Moore as a round-faced youth dressed in a dark double-breasted suit, white shirt, and dark tie, all buttoned up, with hair neatly barbered and in place. No other boy wore a suit, and only two others wore ties, one of them knotted with deliberate carelessness an inch or so below the collar. The others sported open-necked shirts or jerseys.

Had he been a natural loner, he might have been happy to be different, even have gloried in it. But he was not. For inside the shell cast of his parents' affluence, his only-child upbringing, and his own intellectual vitality and curiosity was a gregarious, fun-loving youth who liked people, very much wanted to be liked by them, and was pained to find himself not particularly accepted or popular among his peers. By the time his home-room picture was taken in his second year of high school, he had shed both suit and tie, though with a sportscoat and a white shirt with collar neatly folded over the lapel, he was still the best-dressed boy in the group.

Sacrificing his academic standing might have been another way to join the crowd, but he was too bright and intellectually curious to take it. In one of southern California's best public high schools, and at a time when making good grades required both intelligence and real effort, he kept a record of As mixed with an occasional B, never lower. Over and over the notations made by classmates in his John Marshall High yearbooks spoke of him, in the jargon of the day, as a brain. "To a swell kid, and a Brain," read one entry. "To Curt, the Brain of all Brains," read another. "To a swell guy and 'A' student. . . . To a smart boy in biology. . . . To one swell guy and trig brain," read still another.

There was, however, a way to make good grades and be popular at the same time. It was simple. Curt used his mastery of difficult subjects to help classmates. And they appreciated it, as other yearbook inscriptions testify:

"To Curt, who got me through Latin last year and (I hope) will do the same next year."

"To the source of all my English answers."

"To the smartest kid in chemistry, and my savior."

His junior and senior years at John Marshall were a time of blossoming for Curt Moore. They were also a time of discovery of the attractions of the opposite sex. As in his other enterprises, here too he evidently had considerable success, as these entries in his 1942 school yearbook attest:

"To my first love, Darling. I hope there's a spot in your heart for me. Your ity bity Darling." And elsewhere, in a different hand:

"You know, there's no one else, Darling."

There was also an inscription, this one in his 1941 yearbook (that summer he was still three months shy of sixteen), that foreshadowed what was to come. "To a future foreign counselor," it read, "when I'm in Spain will you help me out? ha, ha." His junior high school yearbook, the year before, bore the notation "wants to be a foreign counsel" beside his name. From very early on, from at least his fifteenth year, a time when most boys had little if any serious notion of what they wanted to do with their lives, Curt Moore knew: he wanted to be a Foreign Service officer. He dreamed of it, and he spoke about it to his friends.

But in the summer of 1943, when he finished high school (ranked

24th academically in a class of 418), it was to the military, not to diplomacy, that young men were going. He signed up for a naval officer candidate program at the University of Southern California. He was evidently still not sure enough of his own intentions to allow them to override parental influence, for he enrolled in a pre-med course. But his heart was not there, and when he found that his eyesight would disqualify him from becoming a naval officer, he quit the program and enlisted in the army.

At the beginning of 1944, with World War II at its height, poor eyesight was no bar to becoming a foot soldier. He was assigned to the infantry. His unit was on the point of being shipped off to Europe, to replace one that had been chewed up in battle, when he came down with measles. Instead of going to the fighting front, he went into the base hospital, and from there he joined the medics and was assigned in the early fall of 1944 to a U.S. military hospital in England, at a small town called Arrington, near Cambridge. There he met an attractive young nurse, Lieutenant Sarah Stewart.

The name Sarah never quite stuck. Her family and her friends called her Sally, and it was as Sally that she came to be known. She was born in southern New Jersey not far from Philadelphia, grew up and went to high school there, and then took a three-year course in nursing at Samuel Hahnemann Hospital in Philadelphia. In a sense she was following in her mother's footsteps, for Gertrude Stewart had, while studying education at Columbia University under John Dewey during World War I, answered a call for young women to become what in those days were known as "reconstruction aides," later occupational therapists. She worked at Walter Reed Army Hospital in Washington, D.C., helping to rehabilitate wounded veterans of the war in Europe, and it was there that she met her future husband.

Sally Stewart finished her training as a nurse in the summer of 1943, and the day she turned twenty-one she enlisted in the army. She was sent to Arrington as a psychiatric nurse—it was the specialty in which she had trained—but there were hardly any psychiatric cases, only a few soldiers who had been kept waiting too long in England to get to the front and had developed hysterias or neuroses. The surgery wards, however, were overflowing with wounded from combat on the continent. Sally answered a call for volunteers for surgery, and there she met Private G. C. Moore, a corpsman in the surgery ward. She called him

George—that was the name on the tag on his uniform—and he replied: "You'd better get used to calling me Curt. That's what my friends call me."

In June 1945 Curt was transferred to an army clinic in Frankfurt. Sally was assigned to a hospital in Karlsruhe, but did not stay long. She went back to the United States at the end of the year and was discharged in March 1946. Curt could have gone back then too, but his curiosity about Europe made him stay a while longer. Enlisted men who agreed to extend got leave time to travel to Switzerland and Italy, so he extended for six months to take advantage of the opportunity.

Curt and Sally thought they would get married when Curt returned home in the summer of 1946, but they found that marriage at that stage of their lives was "not very practical." So Sally enrolled at the University of California at Los Angeles, which at the time was one of the few schools in the United States that offered a B.S. in nursing education— and which, not coincidentally, was a short drive from the University of Southern California, where Curt was enrolled in the School of International Relations. His service in the army in Europe and his travels there had confirmed him in his earlier aspiration. He was going to make the diplomatic service his life's work.

When Sally graduated, in the summer of 1949, she was offered a fellowship for a master's program in education at Syracuse University, in New York State. In November, at Thanksgiving, when she was home in New Jersey, Curt called to propose. He did it in a way that was wholly characteristic of him: "I'm going to go into the Foreign Service; are you coming with me or not?" Sally's fellowship was for two years, and she really loved the work, so it was a hard decision. But she called Curt back and said she would.

He was a brash, self-confident young man, but his self-confidence was not misplaced. By November 1949 he already had his B.A. behind him and was enrolled in an M.A. program in international relations that he would complete the following June. In his undergraduate years he had been Phi Beta Kappa and had been inducted into Blue Key, the National Honor Fraternity. Long gone were the days when he had felt himself an outsider among his peers. He had been president of the student body of the School of International Relations and had joined Chi Phi, a social fraternity, and Delta Phi Epsilon, a foreign service fraternity. He had passed the written examination for the Foreign Service but had failed the French language test. When he called Sally, he had just learned that he had passed in French on his third try. But the big hurdle, the oral examination, was still in front of him. He was not to take it until June of the following year. There was no way that he could know he would pass and be accepted into the Foreign Service, but he was sure he would.

Getting past the French examination proved to be an undertaking in and of itself. On the first try, Curt and Theodore Tremblay, a fellow student at USC and like Curt a veteran of World War II, both got 65, a failing score. The second time around they did hardly better. Frustrated but determined to find out how this could be overcome, Ted Tremblay went to the Los Angeles Public Library, cornered the librarian, and told her his problem.

"What you want," the woman said, "is Vanderveet's word list." It was the five thousand most commonly used words in the French language, arranged in lists of one hundred. Ted saw that the first ten words on earlier State Department examinations were drawn from Vanderveet's first one hundred, the next ten were from the next one hundred, and so on down to the last ten, which were nowhere to be found. So Curt and Ted studied Vanderveet's lists. They made up cards and flashed them at one another. When they took the exam again, they passed handily, each with the score of 82.

They went together to Washington for the oral examination. Crossing the country by air in June 1950 was no simple matter; nonstop transcontinental flights were rare. Curt and Ted got on a plane that landed, it seemed, at every airfield between the West and East coasts. At each stop they would hop off, grab something to eat, and get back on. In this manner they arrived in the nation's capital after three days and two nights of continuous travel.

They were called together for the oral exam on a morning in June of 1950. Ted went in first. Facing an imposing panel of three senior Foreign Service officers, he answered questions for nearly an hour. Then, as the interview drew to a close, one of the examiners remarked: "I see that you and Mr. Moore took the written exams together and that you both got 65 on the first French test and 82 on the make-up. How do you explain that?"

Ted hesitated for a moment. Obviously they were going to ask Curt the same question, but Ted would have no opportunity to warn him.

What to do? Better to tell the truth, he concluded, for Curt surely would. So he explained that he and Curt had studied together using Vanderveet's word lists and flash cards. When Curt's turn came, they asked him the same question, and he gave the same answer.

At noon, the examiners informed both that they had passed. Curt went to a small park near the White House to find Sally—she had waited there while he took the exam—and tell her the good news. They were married the next day, at the home of Curt's Aunt Frances in Washington. Dr. Edward R. L. Elson, pastor of the Presbyterian Church on Sixteenth Street, conducted the ceremony.

* * *

Cleo Allen Noel, Jr., was also a descendant of men and women who emigrated to America in colonial times. His forebears came from England in the second half of the eighteenth century. The Noel ancestor, his given name now lost to history, settled in Virginia, but he was a pioneer and was not content to stay there. He moved to Kentucky and there sired a son that he named Joel, who continued in the pioneering tradition of his father. Opportunity beckoned westward. Joel Noel moved on to Missouri, to Monroe County, just north and west of Saint Louis and not far from the Mississippi River, where he staked a claim to a large tract of land. There, on April 15, 1832, Charity Davis, Joel's wife, bore a son, James D. Noel, who, in the quaint turn of phrase of a local chronicler, became "a substantial and representative exponent of productive farm industry." In addition to farming, James Noel also set up a general store. His business prospered, and he became a man of means and a figure of local note. He was known as a dedicated member of three organizations: the Christian Church, the Democratic Party, and the Masons.

His son William P. Noel, born April 26, 1861, followed in his father's footsteps. He too was to be a Democrat, "unswerving in his allegiance to the Democratic Party," and a Mason. He was also to become, in the words of the same local scribe, "one of the influential and popular citizens and public officials of Randolph County." In his later years, William P. Noel would be the inspiration and the guiding influence in the early life of his grandson, Cleo Allen Noel, Jr.

William P. Noel began his working life as an elementary school teacher in rural north-central Missouri. But he was a man of determination, and he aspired to more. In 1892, when he was already thirty-one years of age, married, and the father of a child, he enrolled in Southwest Missouri State Teachers College. Four years later he graduated with a degree that bore the interesting title of "Bachelor of Scientific Didactics." Degree in hand, he became first a high-school teacher and then superintendent of schools of Salisbury, Missouri. But education did not offer sufficient outlet for his energies. He turned to business, and from there to politics. He was a vigorous man, and in 1926, when he was sixty-five, an age at which most men of his generation were dead or retired, he ran for the office of county executive—it bore the humble title of county clerk—of Randolph County, and he won. He held the office for eight years, until 1934, when he was elected judge on the Randolph County Court. In the small-town society of Moberly, Missouri, the seat of Randolph County, William P. Noel was a man of vast importance. When he died, in July 1938, all county offices closed for the funeral. County employees came as a group to pay their last respects.

For his family, William P. Noel was a patriarch. Cleo, his only child, was to live much of his life in his father's shadow and was never to attain his father's prominence. Cleo married and settled first in Oklahoma City, where he opened a general store and where a son whom he and his wife named Cleo A. Noel, Jr., was born on August 6, 1918. Soon thereafter they moved back to Missouri, to Centralia, a small town some twenty miles southwest of Moberly. Cleo transferred his business to Centralia, and during the boom years of the 1920s he thrived. But the stock market crash of 1929 and the bank closures that followed swept it all away. Cleo and his wife and son returned to Moberly to live in the parental home.

For Cleo Junior, the family misfortune had a silver lining. The young Cleo Noel worshiped his grandfather and yearned to be like him, and William Noel returned his grandson's affection many times over. Now, living in the same household, they were together frequently. His grandfather's tales of the family past aroused in Cleo a passion for American history. He had discovered another passion as well, for nature, for flowers and trees. Botany and American history became his two best subjects in school. He grew to almost six feet three inches, a tall, gangling boy, serious and dedicated as a student, not much interested in athletics, and perhaps a bit of a loner. He graduated from high school with high marks. His academic standing would have won him entry into any university in the country, but his family's means dictated that he settle for Moberly Junior College, and then for the University of Missouri at Columbia, only some forty miles south of Moberly. Even then he had to work to help pay his way at Columbia. Thanks evidently to his grandfather's Democratic Party political connections, he found employment in the state tax office.

He had planned to major in botany at the University of Missouri. But when he arrived there, he found that the science credits he would need for a botany major would require him to spend an extra year as an undergraduate. The added expense was too much, so he turned to his other love, American history, and chose it as his major.

He got his B.A. in 1939, then went on for an M.A. in 1940, and for the year after that he taught American history at Missouri. But war was clearly coming. Cleo Noel's upbringing and his study of his country's history had imbued him with a strong sense of duty and patriotism. In June 1941, six months before the Japanese attack on Pearl Harbor, he joined the navy and was sent to an officer training program, and then to gunnery school. He spent the war years on the high seas as a gunnery officer on merchant marine vessels, hauling supplies and men all around the globe, never experiencing combat but seeing parts of the world that to a young man from Moberly, Missouri, were more exotic than distant planets—the east coast of Africa, the Persian Gulf, Australia, and the Pacific islands. He logged a total of forty long and lonely months of sea duty and, just as he was to do later in the State Department, rose steadily in rank. He was a lieutenant commander at the time of his discharge.

Having seen the world, he was ready to go back to Missouri. In the box marked "job preference" on his navy separation papers he entered "teaching in Missouri," and under "preference for additional training" he put "history." So when he got out of the navy in the fall of 1945, he went back to the University of Missouri intending to enroll in a Ph.D. program in American history and settle down to a career in teaching and a quiet life. At the university, they were ready and eager to have him, but they told him it would be to his advantage to have a degree from another institution before returning to teach there. With his financial problems solved by the GI Bill, and with his excellent academic record, he could pick any university in the United States that he wanted.

So he went to Harvard. And there, while working on his doctorate, he came across a notice one day on the university bulletin board. It announced the dates for a written examination for the Foreign Service of the United States of America and invited candidates to apply. He still intended to become a history teacher, but taking the exam would cost him nothing. He took it, and he passed easily on the first try, with a perfect score of 100 in the section on American history. His GI Bill was running out, and the world beckoned. He left the study of history behind him so as to take a part in the making of it.

His first assignment with the Department of State was in Washington, in the personnel office. There he went to work under the supervision of a young woman named Lucille McHenry, like him a naval officer in World War II, but with service behind a desk in the United States. Those were times when few women applied for the Foreign Service and even fewer got in, for the standards that were set for them were higher than for men. Lucille McHenry had taken and passed the written examination, but was turned down at the oral. She could not become a Foreign Service officer, but she was offered a staff job. Until the Foreign Service underwent democratization two decades later, staff was a separate—and lower—category. Staff performed many of the routine administrative and consular tasks, while officers filled the more exalted political, economic, and executive functions.

Lucille McHenry and Cleo Noel worked together for eight months in Washington in the personnel office and then went their separate ways, Cleo to the U.S. consulate general in Genoa, Italy, and Lucille to the American embassy in London. Not for long, however. In September 1951 they were married in London. Lucille resigned from the Foreign Service—she had no choice, for in those times once a woman married, she was not allowed to continue her Foreign Service career—and went off with Cleo to Genoa and to a new life.

8

To Be an Arabist

The ways in which George Curtis Moore and Cleo Allen Noel, Jr., came to the Arab world were as different as those that brought them into the American diplomatic service.

In September 1950, barely three months after he and Sally were married, Curt was assigned to Germany. They sailed for France, to Le Havre, on the USS *Independence* together with some two dozen other young Foreign Service couples. It was an extraordinary time, an exhilarating time, to be twenty-five and going off to represent the world's most powerful nation on the morrow of its victory in history's greatest and most devastating war, in a Europe that was just beginning to take its first steps along the road to recovery. America was running the world, at least that part of it west of the newly descended Iron Curtain, and Curt Moore was to run, or at least to guide, a small part of it for America. He was to be a *Kreis* officer, an American official working at the German equivalent of the county (*Kreis*) level, seeing to it that neither Nazis nor Communists made their way into positions of local authority and, in general, "teaching the Germans democracy." When he first arrived in Germany there was no kreis officer position open. So he was assigned to run the Amerika Haus—the U.S. information and cultural program—in Würzburg, a pleasant city of some 100,000 halfway between Frankfurt and Nuremberg. It was a temporary position, filling in for an official of the United States Information Agency who was on extended absence. But he did the job so well that when the American occupation ended and the kreis officer jobs were abolished, USIA brought him back to Würzburg to head the Amerika Haus in his own right.

He had arrived in Germany not knowing more than the few words of the language that he had picked up during his brief military service there five years earlier. In Frankfurt he and other new officers were given six weeks of training in German language and German history and culture, then left to fend for themselves. Six weeks was not enough time in which to learn so difficult a language as German. But Curt Moore had an extraordinary memory, a fine ear for tone and pitch, and a talent for putting himself inside the skin of the people with whom he was dealing—as well as an enormous fund of enthusiasm. He worked and worked on the language, and well before he left the Federal Republic in the summer of 1953, Moore spoke German fluently and with an almost flawless accent.

With German to his credit, he could have chosen specialization in European affairs, as many of his contemporaries in the Foreign Service did. Europe was a far safer and more comfortable place to be assigned than almost any other part of the world. But he did not want to stay in Europe. The State Department's personnel office, in its wisdom, assigned him to the American consulate general in Madras, India, a spot exotic enough to meet almost any taste. But he did not want that either. In Washington on home leave, he went to his personnel officer and asked for a change.

"I want to be an Arabist," he announced.

He wanted to study Arabic and serve in the Arab world. The idea had come to him well before he entered the Foreign Service, from somewhere in his reading and his imagination of the world. He had never been to the Middle East or taken instruction in Arabic—in the 1940s it was not offered at USC—but for his master's thesis he chose the topic "Bases and Prospects for Arab Unity." The Middle East, he wrote in it, was "one of the strategically important areas of vacuum in the world today." The vacuum would be filled, he said, either by the Arabs themselves or by outside powers. There was, he declared, "no serious, objective bar to the establishment of a strong union among the Arabs." What was lacking was an enlightened and mature leadership and a strong popular will. The leaders of the Arab countries for the most part ignored the benefits to be obtained from unity. They were intent on maintaining their own local power. Few Arab nationalists would have disagreed with this analysis, then or later.

Like others at the time, he thought the recently founded Arab League might become a vehicle for Arab unity. Otherwise, he saw only one way: "Unification of the Middle East could occur at the hands of a modern Arab Bismarck," he concluded, "but such men are rare." And the influence of foreign powers in the area made it doubtful that such a man would be allowed to carry out his program. The words were written in the spring of 1951, two years before Gamal Abdul Nasser emerged as the leader of Egypt.

To qualify for the Department of State's Arabic language training program, a young Foreign Service officer had first to serve at least one tour of duty in an Arab country. The assignment to Madras was broken, and Curt went off to Cairo in November 1953. Sally followed three months later with their two infant daughters, Lucy and Catherine. Sally's plane arrived over the Egyptian capital in the middle of a sandstorm—one of the worst the crew had ever seen there—and had to fly on to Beirut and wait it out before returning to land in Cairo. It was their first encounter with Middle Eastern sandstorms.

His service at the American embassy in Cairo confirmed Curt Moore in his determination to make his diplomatic career in the Arab world. He studied Arabic after work. It was a hard language but a fascinating one. Challenges attracted him. As he learned bits and pieces of Arabic, he spoke what he knew without shyness or fear, and in January 1956 he got his coveted Arabic language training assignment. It was to start with six months of instruction in Washington and then another twelve to eighteen months at the State Department's Arabic language school in Beirut.

* * *

From Genoa, Cleo Noel was assigned to Dhahran, Saudi Arabia. It was not an assignment that he had asked for. Like almost all assignments of junior personnel—Curt Moore's to Cairo was a rare exception—it was the work of circumstance. The end of his tour of duty in Genoa happened to coincide with the opening of a slot in Dhahran for which he was deemed qualified. Some invisible hand in the department's personnel system decided that Noel, rather than another with more or less the same qualifications, should go there.

The hot, dusty town just a few miles from the Arabian peninsula's east coast was the headquarters of ARAMCO, the Arabian-American Oil Company, the mighty conglomerate of American oil companies that held a monopoly on Saudi Arabia's oil production. The Saudi kingdom was not then the colossus of the oil world that it would later become, but its production figures were not negligible, and its potential was enormous.

In 1952, when the Noels arrived there from Genoa, Dhahran was a desolate-looking place. ARAMCO dominated it in every sense. At night one might look out into the desert and think it had become an inferno. Great flames leapt skyward into the darkness from the flaring of gas from ARAMCO's refineries. There were frequent sandstorms, and wild donkeys from the desert would walk right into the yard of the Noels' house. But ARAMCO maintained an excellent hospital, and there was an American air base in Dhahran (a relic of World War II that lasted into the mid-1950s) and thus a PX. The Noels' two children, John and Janet, were born in the ARAMCO hospital.

In Saudi Arabia there was no mixing of the sexes at social functions; what social life there was with Saudis was all male. And neither Saudi nor foreign women were permitted to drive or to appear alone in public. Lucille accepted all this. It was simply the way things were. It was part of her husband's career, and she had his same sense of discipline and duty. It never would have occurred to her to rebel.

For Cleo it was a good assignment. The post was small; he did the economic reporting and some of the political reporting as well. He had a lot of responsibility and more freedom than he would have had in a large, stratified consulate or embassy in Europe. The Saudis and other Arabs he came in contact with were pure bedoins, proud men who lived in a world entirely different from the one he had known to that time. The Dhahran consulate was responsible for relations with the Trucial Sheikhdoms, the principalities of Bahrain, Qatar, Abu Dhabi, Sharjah, and Oman, all under British protectorate at the time. The consul general took Cleo along on his frequent visits there. Cleo was already making a reputation for himself as an exceptionally able young officer and a hard and serious worker.

In Dhahran Cleo Noel also made his fame as an amateur gardener. With water, which ARAMCO provided in abundance, the desert would bloom. He planted trees around Dhahran, and the trees and shrubs and flowers that he planted—unlike those planted by some others—grew and prospered. Years later, State Department colleagues visiting Dhahran would be told that "those were the trees that Cleo Noel planted." He had, a colleague was to say of him, "the greenest thumb of anyone I ever knew." Next to his work, gardening was his love and his passion. He could coax plants to life out of the most reluctant of soils. He devoted long hours to his gardening. It was like music—a thing that gave pleasure and beauty to his life, and a retreat in which he could find relaxation from the responsibilities of career and family.

In the summer of 1954, Cleo and Lucille Noel pulled up stakes again. Cleo was assigned to the consulate general in Marseilles. The personnel officer in Washington who made the assignment must have thought he was doing them a favor, rewarding them with France and the Mediterranean for their two years in the desert wastes of Arabia. But there was a terrific housing shortage in Marseilles in the early 1950s, and the consulate had neither a house nor an apartment to offer them. It was months before they found a place of their own. In the meantime, Lucille had to tend to the needs of two small children in a cramped hotel room. They didn't like Marseilles, and France itself held no particular charm for them. They were nostalgic for Saudi Arabia. The nostalgia brought Cleo to a decision: he would apply for Arabic language training. They left Marseilles at the close of 1955, after only fifteen months there.

They were happy to be gone, and to be launched on a path that would take them back to Arabia.

* * *

The paths of Curt Moore and Cleo Noel came together for the first time in Washington, in the Arabic language class that began in January 1956 at the Foreign Service Institute, in the basement of an office building in Arlington, Virginia. They were together with three other aspiring Arabists, John Gatch, Ned Schaefer, and Chester Beaman. When they finished their six months in Washington, they all signed up to sail to Beirut together, with their wives and children, on one of the American Export Line's Four Aces.

In Beirut, the Moores and the Noels rented apartments in the same building, just off Hamra Street, the city's main shopping and business district. Their children played together—they were almost the same ages—and they and the others in the Arabic program went together on picnics in the Lebanese mountains. They studied Arabic together, traveled together, and hosted one another at dinners and luncheons. Later when they looked back on it, they felt that the year in Beirut had been a halcyon time, even though all the while a turbulence was brewing in Lebanon.

Slowly, the country was moving toward its first civil war. Nasser's nationalization of the Suez Canal in July 1956 and the Sinai war in October of that year roused Lebanese Moslems to a frenzy and dealt a heavy if indirect blow to the country's fragile structure. But Lebanon continued to develop and to prosper. Despite the unrest—and unlike a later time—nothing happened that endangered Americans or even particularly restricted their activities. Beirut was still, with much justification, called "the Paris of the Middle East."

In May 1957 Curt and Cleo took their area orientation tour together, driving a 1956 Chevrolet sedan over the Lebanese mountains to Damascus and then northward to the ancient and infrequently visited cities of Homs, Hama, and Aleppo. They then headed eastward into Iraq, to Irbil in the heart of Iraqi Kurdistan, to Kirkuk, the oil capital, and on to Baghdad, which for all its fame in history was in the 1950s a very common and rather miserable-looking place, its architectural glories having been destroyed some six centuries earlier by the Mongol hordes. From the Iraqi capital they drove back westward across the desert into Syria and over the mountains again down to Beirut and the blue, sparkling Mediterranean. All along their way they noted road conditions, the price of gasoline, places to eat, the comfort or discomfort of hotels, the sights offered by each itinerary, and the helpfulness of the people encountered. The hotel at Dor el-Zor, they warned the future traveler, was awful; better to camp out. Syrians they found generally suspicious but civil, Iraqis open and friendly (the pro-Western Hashemite monarchy still ruled in Baghdad at the time). Take along an extra spare tire, spark plugs, headlamps, coils, and distributor points, they advised, just in case.

Soon after their return to Beirut, Cleo wound up his studies, and he and Lucille went off on assignment to Jidda. He had worked hard to learn Arabic, but it just didn't take the way he had hoped. He was older than the others and, he found, had little aptitude for languages. His time studying Arabic had not been wasted, but he realized that he would never gain true fluency in the language. Curt was the best in the class and got the highest score on his final exam. With Arabic, as with German, he had a talent for putting himself inside the people and the language, capturing the vocabulary, and getting the accent just right. He would leave the Beirut language school fluent in Arabic.

But before moving on, Moore joined a group of some forty State and Defense Department officials for a month-long trip through the Middle East, visiting capitals, where they had meetings with government officials and briefings by American ambassadors. They went to Istanbul, to Ankara, to Baghdad, and then on to Tehran, and from there back westward to Saudi Arabia, Cairo, and, as their last stop, Israel. He found Istanbul a fascinating place, a city, he later wrote, of "six or eight tremendous, multi-domed, bulbous grey mosques scattered in a sea of black and jumbled buildings, with ship traffic up and down the straits." It was, he felt, a true city, like New York, London, or Cairo; it had spirit, movement, and life. In Iran he was impressed by the poverty, and by the wealth. He spent a day at the country home of an Iranian family that owned the village in which their house was located and several hundred more like it, altogether some twenty thousand acres of land. During stops in Saudi Arabia at Ras Tanura and Dhahran, he took time off to go swimming in the Persian Gulf. The water was hot, and it "looked and felt, but did not taste, like thick pea soup."

It was of Israel, however, that he wrote most extensively, and it was plain that he did not like, and perhaps was not prepared to like, what he saw there. In Israel, Moore wrote later, the group talked with, "and were talked at by," Israeli leaders of all persuasions. They spent two hours with Prime Minister David Ben-Gurion, visited kibbutzim, met with Arabs from Nazareth, saw factories and neat Western-style housing developments. The program was so crammed with activity and the group was briefed by their Israeli hosts with such energy and determination that he thought it amounted to a shrewd attempt at brainwashing. As he wrote later,

And from all this, these are my thoughts: a group knowing all the methods of western technology has been set down in the area of the Middle East best endowed by nature; it receives an annual unearned income from various foreign sources (United Jewish Appeal, Israeli Bonds, international bank loans, U.S. Point Four, German reparations, etc.) of about one-quarter of a billion dollars, that is, a sum of slightly more than $125.00 per every man, woman and child in the country . . . ; the people have tremendous energy and are violently and narrow mindedly nationalistic; they have the great asset of having the 'cake of custom' broken for them so that they do not have to struggle against the tremendous weight of past habits in developing their country; in spite of their continued protestations to the contrary, they are not willing to make peace with their Arab neighbors on any but their own rigid terms, are not willing to accept repatriation of any Arab refugees or to make more than a very limited token compensation for [Arab] property and goods which the Israelis have usurped; they absolutely intend to continue a policy of unlimited immigration by which they expect to take in two million more Jews . . . whenever the USSR allows its Jews to emigrate, and thus their potential expansion presents a real danger to their Arab neighbors.

"And so it goes," Moore concluded. "I was impressed by what the Jews have accomplished in Palestine, but I was depressed by their cockiness, narrowness, and the threat which I feel they, in and of themselves, pose to peace in the Middle East." He was depressed also "by the way they treat the one hundred or so thousand Arabs which now live as a third class minority in their territorial boundaries."

He was happy to get back to Beirut. The Lebanese capital was, he wrote, "really a delightful spot—one of the nicest in the Middle East."

* * *

That was his second and last visit to the Jewish state. His first had been some three months earlier. He and Sally had driven over to Damascus, then south to Amman and westward to East Jerusalem, where they had crossed through the Mandelbaum Gate into Israel, as tourists, simply to see the sights. Their brief transit in the late spring of 1957 through Amman on their way to Israel, and back again homeward-bound to Beirut—no more than a few hours altogether—was the only time in his life that George Curtis Moore was ever to be in that city or in Jordan.

9

A Wrong Turn in Omdurman

On an evening in mid-May 1969, Lucien Kinsolving and his wife Mary drove across the Nile bridge linking Khartoum and neighboring Omdurman for dinner at the home of the director of the British Council. Omdurman was founded in 1884 by the Mahdi after he expelled the Egyptians, took Khartoum, and slew Gordon. During the fourteen years of his and his successor's rule, it became the capital of the Sudan. The Mahdi's descendants still lived there, in a large walled compound located, as it happened, not far from the residence of the director of the British Council.

In the dark, Kinsolving missed his turn and drove into a dead-end street. As he stopped to try to figure out what he had done wrong, Sudanese policemen emerged from the shadows and shined flashlights on Kinsolving and his wife, and on their car's license plates. By mistake they had driven to the rear gate of the al-Mahdi compound. The policemen were there not to guard the Mahdi residence but to check on who went in and out, for the Mahdi clan headed the opposition. What, they wanted to know, were the two Americans doing there? "I'm lost," Kinsolving answered. He asked directions to the British official's house and drove off. He thought no more about the incident until several months later, after he had left the Sudan.

Lucien Kinsolving was a short, articulate man with a wry sense of humor who wore his hair in a crew cut long after that style went out of fashion. He drove an ambulance in combat in World War II, first as a volunteer with the British in campaigns in Lebanon, Syria, and Libya, and later with U.S. forces in Italy. After the war he went to Harvard for his B.A., and from there to the University of Virginia for a law degree. He passed the Virginia bar exam but decided that a life practicing law would be altogether too dull. In 1951 he joined the Foreign Service, and the next year he was sent to Libya. That launched him on a long career in Arab affairs. He was in the Arabic language program in the class ahead of Curt Moore and Cleo Noel and finished his training in Beirut just a few weeks after they started there.

Kinsolving arrived in Khartoum in August 1967, two months after the break in relations. The U.S. embassy had been converted into an interests section under the Dutch flag. The conversion had been made easily, for the Dutch chargé was an affable, accommodating man. The main problem was on the U.S. side: Americans assigned to the interests section found it hard to adjust to the fact that the Stars and Stripes could not be raised in the Sudan, that America's business had to be conducted under a foreign flag, albeit a friendly one.

But at the end of the summer, when the Dutch ambassador returned to Khartoum, it began to look as though the United States might have made a mistake in putting its Khartoum office under the Dutch flag. The ambassador, it turned out, was a rather literal-minded man. On paper, the American mission in Khartoum was simply a section within the Dutch embassy. When the Americans wanted to send a diplomatic note to the government of Sudan, they gave it to the Dutch ambassador or chargé, and he transmitted it; replies came back through the same channel. The Americans had no objection to this arrangement, but the Dutch ambassador wanted to take things a step further. If the Americans were part of his embassy, he reasoned, he should know exactly what they were up to. He wanted to see the classified cables they sent and received. This, of course, was out of the question, and Cleo Noel told him so.

But the Dutch ambassador was stubborn. He persisted. Finally, one morning in his office, they came to a confrontation. Under Cleo's gentle, courtly manner, there was a firmness that surprised those who did not know him well. There was also a temper for those who provoked it. The meeting that morning was intended to iron out the matter of the cables, but the Dutchman was unyielding; he repeated his demand that they should be handed over. That, Cleo replied, was impossible. Exasperated, he crashed his fist down on the coffee table in front of him, so hard that the cups jumped in the air, and then stalked angrily out of the office. Still gritting his teeth, he returned to the interests section and gave Lucien a graphic, blow-by-blow description of what had happened.

The Kinsolvings lived across the street from the Dutch ambassador; their children played with his, and the two couples had become good friends. When Lucien went home after work that day, the Dutchman came over, still steaming, and recounted what had happened. The two versions, Lucien found, were exactly the same. "The cups jumped in the air!" the Dutchman exclaimed in his quaintly accented English. Lucien mediated a reconciliation. And in due course the ambassador was instructed by The Hague to drop the issue, after the American embassy in the Dutch capital spoke with the Foreign Ministry there.

Lucien soon discovered that Cleo Noel was an extraordinarily thorough person. He also learned that Cleo took gardening very, very seriously. Cleo, who had now moved into the ambassador's residence, was horrified at the way the gardening had been done there to that time. "How could these people have been so casual about it?" he exclaimed to Lucien, as though something truly shocking had been allowed to happen. He took charge of the garden, cleaning out debris and planting new shrubs, flowers, and trees, and installing lights to show it all off to evening guests. He was particularly proud of a palm tree he planted, just a seedling that hardly came to his knee but that grew to be taller than the house itself.

Kinsolving found Noel easy to work for. He had been assigned to Khartoum as chief of the political section. With the break in relations, his section disappeared out from under him, but political reporting continued to be his main job. Noel had served in Khartoum earlier and was far better informed about the Sudan than Kinsolving, but he was not the kind of person who pretended to know it all. He did not try to impose his opinions or tell Kinsolving what to put in his reports back to Washington. If Noel disagreed with what Kinsolving wrote, he would set out his views in the weekly confidential letter he wrote to Washington, to Matt Looram, the State Department's office director for Northern African affairs.

Since it had become independent in January 1956, the Sudan had alternated between civilian and military governments. The government that took over from the British was a parliamentary democracy, but it was also an Arab government; southern blacks had almost no role in it. The first thing it aspired to do was to impose Arab domination over the south. This caused civil war to flare there almost immediately. The burden of war drained the treasury, and economic conditions deteriorated throughout the country. No single party could achieve a majority in the parliament, and coalition politics left governmental stability at the mercy of the politicians' squabbles, their ambitions, their petty rivalries and conspiracies. So the Sudan's first experiment with parliamentary democracy lasted less than three years. On November 17, 1958, the army moved in, as the new military leader, General Ibrahim Abboud, announced, to "save the country from the chaotic regime of the politicians."

Abboud ruled for close to six years before being forced from office by a series of public demonstrations and riots. He had had no program other than that of ousting the politically bankrupt parliamentary regime. He had had no plan, other than more repression, for dealing with the civil war in the south; and he had had no notion of what to do to reverse or even arrest the country's continuing economic decline. So in October 1964 the politicians came back to replace the discredited military regime. From the time of independence, Sudan's relations with the United States had been ambivalent. The Sudanese wanted, but also did not want, good relations with the Americans. When the United States proposed economic aid in 1957, the Sudanese parliament debated for almost a year before deciding to accept the American offer, and the vote was close. Washington felt no such ambivalence. From 1955 on, with the exception of the first two years of the Kennedy administration, the United States was on the outs with Nasser's Egypt. Cultivating good relations with the government in Khartoum was a natural response, one designed to checkmate Nasser's influence there and elsewhere in Africa.

Elections, held in 1965, once more produced a splintered parliament. Mohammed Ahmed Mahgoub was the first prime minister to emerge from the new parliament. Mahgoub was a member of the Umma Party but not its leader. That position was held by Sadiq al-Mahdi, the great-grandson of the fabled Mahdi, Oxford-educated and imbued with modern ideas and a burning desire to lead the country that his illustrious forebear had given its earlier brief taste of independence. Sadiq had been too young to run for parliament in 1965—the law required candidates to be thirty—but in 1966 he came of age, and in July of that year he became prime minister. Paradoxically, the Mahdi's heir was the most pro-Western of all the leading Sudanese politicians. His brief tenure (it was to last only until May of 1967) was the high point of relations between Sudan and the United States. After Sadiq fell, Mahgoub returned to office, albeit with a very shaky parliamentary base.

Lucien Kinsolving was persuaded that the key to improving relations between the United States and the Sudan lay in Sadiq al-Mahdi's return to power. He pushed this idea in all of his reporting. Noel was far from sure Kinsolving was right. He held a much more nuanced—and more realistic, Kinsolving acknowledged in retrospect—view of the situation. But Kinsolving's views were known not only in Washington but around the Khartoum diplomatic community and, evidently, to some Sudanese as well.

On May 25, 1969, a bloodless coup by the army, backed by communists and leftists, put an end to hopes both for Sadiq al-Mahdi's return to power and for improvement in relations between the Sudan and the United States. The coup's leader, Colonel Jaafar al-Nimeiry, announced his takeover in much the same terms as those used by Abboud a little more than a decade earlier: the new regime, he said, would put an end to the "instability, corruption, and chaos" of the rule of the politicians. Spokesmen for the new regime said it would strengthen relations with Egypt and "other progressive Arab states." Since 1956 the country had been called the Republic of Sudan. To emphasize its leftist leanings, the new regime added the word "Democratic" as a prefix: the Democratic Republic of Sudan. Broadcasts over the government radio condemned "reaction and imperialism." The new regime promptly issued a virulently anti-Israeli statement and moved to establish diplomatic relations with East Germany.

All this, of course, was bad news for the United States. The Americans waited, expecting trouble. But nothing happened, and things seemed to quiet down, enough so that Lucien and Mary Kinsolving could fly off to Greece late in June for a short holiday. They were vacationing on the island of Skiatos when a policeman came to their seaside hotel looking for Lucien, to tell him that he should call the American embassy in Athens urgently. The message he found there was short and to the point: the Sudanese government had given him and five other members of the staff of the U.S. interests section ten days in which to leave the country. He should return immediately to Khartoum to pack.

Kinsolving flew back to Khartoum, only to find that he would have to build his own crates for packing, his five colleagues having in the meantime preempted the services of the city's only packer. The State Department sent him off to take charge of the American embassy in Lomé, Togo, in the extended absence of the U.S. ambassador there. After a brief stay in Togo, Kinsolving got a cable from Khartoum advising him that the Sudanese government had published a document allegedly written by someone in Sadiq al-Mahdi's entourage that said that Lucien and Mary Kinsolving were "trying to help us by stocking plastic explosives at kilometers 68 and 69." There were also incriminating documents that the government said were in Kinsolving's own handwriting.

It was a skillful forgery, probably the work of the East Germans. Lucien Kinsolving had no idea where kilometers 68 and 69 were. And he had never in his life even seen plastic explosives, much less delivered them to the Mahdi or anyone else.

The only thing he could think of was his bumbling into the rear door of the Mahdi compound back in May.

10

To Make a Difference

Curt Moore arrived in Khartoum on July 9, 1969, at the lowest point, the absolute bottom of the abyss. Six of the nine diplomatic officers of the U.S. interests section had just been expelled. To help him run the mission, he would have only an administrative officer and a junior officer who would be jack of all trades. The Sudanese government's radio and press were spewing out vicious anti-American propaganda. The day before Cleo Noel turned over charge of the mission to Moore and departed Khartoum, someone set off a bomb at the American library. "Cleo," Curt wrote Sally, only half-joking, "was glad to go."

Moore was shunned by everyone except his Western diplomatic colleagues. For his first six weeks in Khartoum he was trailed everywhere he went by an agent of the security police riding a small blue motor scooter. Then came the forged document purporting to implicate Lucien and Mary Kinsolving in a conspiracy against the regime.

He had not expected a red-carpet welcome to Khartoum. But he certainly had not thought it would be quite that bad.

The assignment to Khartoum was one that he had eagerly sought, in fact had lobbied hard to get. For years he had wanted a posting there, because he had heard that it was a very special and fascinating place. But now, in his nineteenth year in the Foreign Service and just two months short of forty-four, he had particular reason for wanting to be sent to the Sudan. As chief of the U.S. interests section, he would for the first time in his career be his own boss, have his own post. It was an opportunity to make his mark now, without having to wait several more years for the promotions that could give him a shot at being ambassador. And he very much wanted to make his mark.

After Arabic language school in Beirut, Moore had been posted to the American consulate in Asmara, in the job of political officer and deputy to the consul. Asmara was the capital of the former Italian province of Eritrea, now federated with Ethiopia. For someone in whom the State Department had just invested almost two years of training in Arabic, it was a nonsensical assignment. The personnel officer in Washington who made it had never been to Asmara, but he had heard that people spoke Arabic there. Indeed, over a quarter of the population did speak Arabic, but they were the quarter that did not count, politically or even much economically. By 1958, Emperor Haile Selassie was well along in his plan to scuttle Eritrea's federal statute, abolish its autonomy, and integrate it into Ethiopia's centralized administrative structure, making it a province like any other. The emperor considered the Arabs an alien, hostile influence, and he strictly banned their language from official or public use. The languages of government, and of the media, were Amharic and Tigrinya, Semitic languages as distantly related to Arabic as English is to German. Sally was to make more use of Arabic there—in Asmara's teeming markets—than Curt.

They stayed in Asmara only a little more than a year and a half. In September 1959, Moore got a transfer to Libya, to the American embassy office in Benghazi, on the eastern shore of the Gulf of Sirte. In one way, but in one way only, Ethiopia and Libya were alike. The U.S. military had a base in each—in Ethiopia the Kagnew communications station, in Libya Wheelus Air Force Base—and Washington's consuming, overriding, and myopically short-sighted interest in each country was the preservation of that base. But otherwise they were entirely different places. Libya was a sparsely populated bedouin Arab kingdom, ruled by a very traditional Arab monarch, King Idriss of the Senoussi tribe. Not only was Arabic the language of the country, but most Libyans spoke nothing else. Oil had been discovered in Libya some years earlier, and by the close of the 1950s, American companies were drilling wells and pumping crude at a rapidly expanding rate.

Moore was still relatively low in the hierarchy—his job title was economic officer—and Tripoli, not Benghazi, was the main seat of government. But King Idriss moved back and forth between the two cities, and so the American ambassador, John Wesley Jones, came frequently to Benghazi. Jones quickly took notice of this young officer who, unlike many who came out of the Beirut language school, actually spoke Arabic, spoke it well, with gusto and with flair, who was never shy, was self-confident without being cocky or boastful, who met people warmly and with great ease and made them feel at ease. The ambassador moved Moore to Tripoli and took him along on his travels, as aide, interpreter, and notetaker. When Idriss decided to move his capital to Baida, on a mountain ridge overlooking the Mediterranean a hundred miles or so east of Benghazi, Jones chose Moore to open and head the American embassy office there.

Idriss was a devout Moslem. Baida, in addition to its natural attractions—the coolness of its summer months and its striking views of the sea and the mountains—was a minor Islamic shrine. The prophet Mohammed's standard bearer had died in Baida while on his way back from a campaign in North Africa, and his tomb was there. It was just a village when the king decided to make it his capital. There was nothing there, no services, no school for foreigners, and no hospital, so Sally and the children stayed behind in Benghazi. Curt spent the work week in Baida and came down to Benghazi on weekends.

George Naifeh, a USIS officer assigned to Baida early in 1963, after Moore had already been there a year, was full of admiration for what Moore had accomplished. "He was very effective, he knew everybody there, and he was warmly received by the Libyans," Naifeh later recalled. Through his Lebanese parents, Naifeh was a native speaker of Arabic, and he admired the fluency of Moore's Arabic and the effort he put into his job. "He spoke a very good Arabic, and he worked very, very hard at his job. But he was not just a one-track kind of person. He was fun to be with, and he was interested in everything and could talk about everything. And he and Sally were always ready to help if you needed it."

Moore was always received by Idriss when the monarch came to Baida. He had better access to the king than any other American in the country except the ambassador. For the first time, he held a position of real responsibility, and he proved himself in it.

In September 1963 he was transferred to Washington. It was his first regular assignment there since he had entered the Foreign Service thirteen years earlier. The six years that he was to spend at the State

Department's headquarters in Foggy Bottom were not to be the best of his life or of his career. He found the department's stratified bureaucracy frustrating. He could work frantically through a ten- or twelve-hour day, and at the end of it find himself wondering if he had accomplished anything useful; it often seemed like so much spinning of wheels in a void. The place where you could get your hands into things, he felt, get them dirty and leave an imprint, was overseas.

He was assigned to the Office of Near Eastern Affairs, the office that handled America's relations with Egypt, Israel, and all the Arab states of the Near East. His job was desk officer for the Arabian peninsula—Saudi Arabia, the two Yemens, and the Persian Gulf principalities. In 1964, after he was promoted to FSO-3, a grade on the threshold between the middle and senior ranks, he stepped up to be officer-in-charge of that area. But in 1966 Secretary of State Dean Rusk, the archetypical organization man, decided that relations with the rest of the world would be better run if put in more senior, experienced hands. He directed that the offices handling large numbers of countries be broken up into smaller units, each to be headed by an officer of ambassadorial rank or equivalent. Rusk's move immediately created a gigantic bureaucratic inflation. All around the Department of State new offices sprouted. The Office of Near Eastern Affairs ceased to exist, and in its place appeared four new country directorates, as they were called. Curt Moore had quite handily run the United States' relations with the states of the Arabian peninsula with one assistant and a secretary. In place of this tidy arrangement there was now an office staffed by five officers and two secretaries. No longer did Moore have the rank required to do the job that he had performed more than satisfactorily, and with a much smaller staff, to that time.

So he went off on temporary assignment with Ambassador Julius Holmes, working on a long-range study of American policy in the Persian Gulf. When that was done, he took a job in the personnel office for a year, and after that went on to join the State Department contingent at the National War College at Fort McNair, just across the Potomac from Washington's National Airport, where beneath the incessant roar of ascending and descending jetliners, lieutenant colonels and colonels jogged puffing and sweating around the main concourse at dawn and before lunch, boning up earnestly on international affairs, in the hope of one day becoming generals.

But the years were passing, and he was not being promoted. By 1968 he had four years in grade, all the time needed to qualify for promotion to FSO-2, the next-higher rank. But his name did not appear on that year's list. Neither was it to be found there the following year. Bouncing around from one assignment to another was simply not the way to get promoted in the State Department, no matter how good one's record. The boy of fifteen who had aspired to be a "foreign counsel," and who in his whole life had not seriously wanted any other career for himself, was now approaching forty-four. If he was to be a success in his life's work—and he was determined that he should be a success—he had to have that next promotion, and soon. The assignment to Khartoum, if successful, would ensure that he got it.

* * *

No one in the Sudanese government wanted to receive Moore, even for a courtesy call. It took almost a month to arrange his first meeting with the chief of protocol at the Foreign Ministry, the most routine of calls that a newly arrived diplomat can make. And when he got to the ministry he was met by a junior aide who told him that the chief of protocol was otherwise occupied and would not be able to see him. Private Sudanese citizens were almost equally reluctant to associate with him, for in the summer of 1969, being seen with an American diplomat was a sure way of attracting the attention of the Sudanese security police; interrogation or even torture might follow. Even foreign businessmen felt they had to be careful. One, an Armenian, had lunch with him and later said he would not be able to see him again, not before diplomatic relations were restored. The only contacts he was able to establish outside the diplomatic corps were with a very few of Cleo's closest Sudanese friends who were not part of the government and were not scared of incurring its displeasure.

He could have resigned himself to this situation. He could have retreated into the cocoon of the diplomatic corps and the small international community and spent his time sending Washington reports on what he could pick up from the rumor mill there. That would have been the comfortable solution. But it was not his. He was determined to turn this situation around, to break out of the isolation imposed on him and, ultimately, to bring the United States and the Sudan together again.

He was by nature enormously inventive. When Washington sent out a film of the landing of American astronauts on the moon, he invited

Sudanese officials and educators to come see it. Only a few showed up, but that did not discourage him. When the State Department's regional medical officer stopped in Khartoum, Moore invited Sudanese physicians to meet him. This time his plan worked. Sudanese doctors were starved for contact with Western medical science; they all came. He joined the local Rotary Club, went to meetings regularly, and got to know the Sudanese and foreign business community. He brought Mal Whitfield, the black U.S. Olympic medalist, to Khartoum and arranged for him to coach local basketball and track teams. In these and other ways he set about building bridges.

On Moslem holidays, when ministers and other senior officials held open house, he went around to their homes to pay his respects. He knew they wouldn't see him, and they didn't, but he left his calling card anyway.

An early misjudgment set him back. The June 1969 expulsions had wiped out the CIA station in Khartoum. The agency badly wanted to get an officer back in. Moore allowed himself to be talked into agreeing to this, or perhaps he was ordered to agree to it. He should have known that the time was not ripe. There was still too much suspicion of the United States. The Soviet and East European intelligence services were working hand in hand with the Sudanese. No matter how good a cover the CIA officer had, and even if he were to do nothing but sit in his office all day long—an unlikely hypothesis—the Sudanese would be sure to spot him. And they did. The CIA officer arrived in Khartoum in August; the Sudanese expelled him in April the following year.

Events came to Moore's rescue. Early in August 1970 an American-mediated cease-fire brought an end to fighting between Israel and Egypt that had raged along the Suez Canal line for the previous seventeen months and had developed into a virtual war. The next month President Gamal Abdul Nasser of Egypt died; he was replaced by Anwar Sadat, a man of more moderate, pro-Western inclinations. Nimeiry began to move away from the leftists in his government and closer to Sadat. In November, after meeting leftist opposition to a proposed federation between the Sudan, Egypt, Libya, and Syria—an idea opposed also by the Soviet Union—Nimeiry dismissed from the government several far left army officers who had played prominent roles in the coup that brought him to power. Nimeiry had never been an ideologue. He had associated himself with the left because it offered him the opportunity to grab power. But he felt no commitment to it. His commitment was to whatever worked, and, in particular, to whatever would keep him in power.

At the end of November 1970, Moore decided to try his luck in a cast of the dice. He had been in the Sudan for well over a year and had never been able to meet with Nimeiry, even to shake his hand. But Moore sensed that events were now giving him an opening. It was the first day of the Eid al-Adha, the Moslem feast of the sacrifice. President Nimeiry was holding open house at the officers' club. With much relish, Moore told a young *Washington Post* reporter, Jim Hoagland, the story of what happened next. Hoagland later wrote of it: "Moore walked up to the President and stuck out his hand, identifying himself. Nimeiry did a double take, thought for a second, and then proved that Moore had read him correctly. He responded with a broad smile and a firm hand-shake."[11]

It was a small breakthrough, one that began to open doors for him. Khartoum had a population of several hundred thousand, but it was more like a small town. Those who counted numbered only in the hundreds. Word of the handshake got around quickly. In a country where everyone looked to the leader to set the tone, it gave a signal. If Nimeiry could exchange greetings with the head of the American diplomatic office in the Sudan, so could others. It was no longer quite so risky to be seen with this American.

But not all of his problems were solved. He still could not get meetings with cabinet officers and other senior officials, and the staff of the interests section still had a hard time obtaining permission to travel outside of Khartoum. But by the time Hoagland came to Khartoum, in May of 1971, Moore was able to arrange an interview for him with Nimeiry. Hoagland, who was based in Nairobi and covered Africa for the *Post*, was much impressed. It was not often that he met an American diplomat of this caliber. He later wrote of Moore:

> Open, imaginative, he had an enthusiasm for virtually everything and everybody that he came into contact with. . . . A visitor to his office in

[11]"The Diplomacy of G. Curtis Moore," *Washington Post*, March 10, 1973.

the drab American embassy quarters . . . was certain to be greeted with a great friendly smile, a pumping handshake and an invitation to call him Curt.[12]

Hoagland was also impressed by the ease and confidence with which Moore handled a potentially embarrassing situation. At a luncheon that he held to introduce Hoagland to a group of Sudanese business and professional men, several of the Sudanese unexpectedly began to speak of their opposition to Nimeiry's policies and to urge that the United States do something to get rid of the Sudanese leader.

Instead of retreating into self-righteous platitudes, Moore quickly began pouring more beer into their glasses and quietly explained that "the United States doesn't do that here—anymore." In the pause, a broad smile flashed across his face, and the Sudanese laughed uproariously.[13]

Hoagland's interview with Nimeiry was encouraging. The Sudanese president told him, in so many words, that he wanted to move toward better relations with the United States. It was not the usual line that Sudanese officials took in talking to Western journalists. It was so novel, in fact, that when Hoagland went to the Khartoum telex office to file his story back to Washington, the officials there refused to take it. He had to carry it out of the country with him and send it from Nairobi.

Under the influence of Nasser and of the leftist officers who had backed his May 1969 takeover, Nimeiry had aligned the Sudan with the Soviet Union. He had reoriented trade toward the East bloc and nationalized banks and other large business holdings. Militarily, this seemed to pay off. The Soviets sent plentiful supplies of military equipment and large numbers of personnel to advise and train the Sudanese army. But already by early 1971, Nimeiry had begun to be disappointed with the results of his economic partnership with the Soviets. The nationalizations caused a sharp drop in the Sudanese economy, and Soviet economic aid did not turn out to be nearly as generous or effective as the Western aid had been previously.

Disappointment over trade was even more pronounced. The Soviets bought a substantial part of Sudan's cotton crop—the country's main export earner—under a barter arrangement. Sudanese were outraged

[12]Ibid.
[13]Ibid.

when they learned that the Soviets were reselling much of it on the world market at a price that undercut their own. And they found the manufactured goods supplied by the Soviets under the barter arrangement to be overvalued and shoddy. The Soviets charged 30 percent more for their tires than the Japanese did for theirs, and 55 percent more for earth-moving equipment than the Italians did. Soviet tractors, the Sudanese discovered, were a complete failure. They broke down almost immediately in the Sudan's hot climate.

Nimeiry was soon to feel he had reason to be dissatisfied with Soviet military assistance. On July 19, 1971, in the blazing heat of midafternoon when most of Khartoum was on siesta, Major Hashem al-Atta, one of the officers Nimeiry had dismissed the previous November, moved tanks into position around government buildings and took Nimeiry and several dozen of his followers prisoner. Al-Atta declared himself and two other officers earlier ousted by Nimeiry, Colonel Babakr al-Nur Osman and Major Faruk Hamadallah, in charge of the government. All three were rumored to be communists. They denied it, but the new regime's first actions seemed to belie their denials, for it lifted the ban that Nimeiry had slapped on the Sudanese communist party and its affiliated organizations. In a policy statement read over the official radio, al-Atta said the new regime would link the Sudan more closely with communist and socialist countries and bring Sudanese communists into a coalition government.

The coup at first seemed a walkover. It met no resistance either from the Sudanese military or from the population. Sudanese communists turned out in Khartoum to demonstrate in favor of the new regime. Osman and Hamadallah were in London—Osman had gone there for medical treatment, and Hamadallah had gone with him—when al-Atta sent his tanks to seize power. They speedily wound up their sojourn in the British capital and prepared to fly home, Osman slated to become chief of state in the new regime.

In fact, however, despite the ease with which it was carried out, the coup had little popular support. The Sudanese communist party was the Arab world's largest, but it commanded the loyalty of only a relatively small element of the country's population. Most Sudanese were devout Moslems; they considered communism abhorrent and its acolytes dangerous atheists. Sudan's neighbors reacted to the coup with dismay. None wanted a communist or communist-sympathizing government on its border. Egypt's president, Anwar Sadat, first sent a "fact-finding" mission to Khartoum and then ordered Egyptian troops stationed south of Khartoum to resist the coup. Libya too rallied to Nimeiry's support. Colonel Muammar al-Qaddafi had seized power in Tripoli less than two years earlier and was at that stage virulently anti-communist. Qaddafi was from the beginning a practitioner of the spectacular. He sent fighter planes to force down the British Airways jetliner on which Osman and Hamadallah were returning to Khartoum, and he took the two off the aircraft and held them under arrest.

The Saudis too were worried about a leftist government on their western flank across the Red Sea, but if they took any action it was clandestine. An Iraqi airliner carrying a delegation from the Baath government in Baghdad to congratulate al-Atta and his colleagues (Iraq was the only Arab government to give public support to the coup) crashed in mysterious circumstances as it crossed Saudi Arabia on its way to Khartoum.

On the morning of July 22, al-Atta, not knowing of Qaddafi's action, went to the airport to greet Osman and Hamadallah. He sensed that he was on shaky ground and had already taken measures he hoped would prevent a countercoup. He had ordered the army to immobilize its tanks in the Khartoum area, had furloughed most of the armored brigades and paratroopers, and had locked up the arms and ammunition of those soldiers whose loyalty was in doubt. Rumor had it that Soviet military advisors had helped him carry out these precautions.

When al-Atta learned that the plane from London would not arrive, he went to the center of Khartoum to address a rally he had called to welcome Osman and Hamadallah back. He tried desperately to muster support for his coup, but the crowd was thin, he was heckled, and there were calls for Nimeiry's return to power. Within hours, Sudanese army units loyal to Nimeiry moved into Khartoum and freed him. After a brief battle, Nimeiry's forces prevailed. Al-Atta and half a dozen other coup leaders—including Osman and Hamadallah, who in the meantime had been forcibly returned to Khartoum by Qaddafi—were summarily executed.

It was a close call for Nimeiry. He had narrowly escaped death, and he was furious not only with the coup leaders and the Sudanese communists but with the Soviets and their East European allies, for he saw the Soviet hand behind the coup. Later investigation showed that this very likely was not so, but perception was more important than reality. Nimeiry moved to crush the Sudanese communist party, and in speech after speech he vilified the Soviet Union. "We found out that some countries, who pretended to be friendly towards us, were leading figures in the conspiracy against us," he proclaimed at a rally on September 9 outside Khartoum. "The European communist countries, with the exception of Yugoslavia, colluded in the conspiracy. Those countries, led by Moscow, conspired to bring their hirelings in the Sudan to power." Nimeiry's conclusion was simple and straightforward: "We have committed a mistake by seeking friendship with Moscow."[14]

The Soviets replied bitterly, denouncing "the ruthless persecution, wholesale arrests and execution of patriots." *Izvestia* charged that "an atmosphere of savage terror against all progressive forces, and above all the communists, has been created in the Sudan."[15]

Nimeiry's remarks were a clear signal to the United States. Curt Moore was in the United States on home leave when the coup occurred—in July 1971 he had been in the Sudan for two years. He broke off his leave to rush back to Khartoum, but before doing so he drafted and got approval for a letter to Nimeiry from Secretary of State William Rogers offering an improvement in relations with the United States.

On August 17, 1971, for the first time since he had come to the Sudan more than two years earlier, Moore got a meeting with the foreign minister, Mansour Khaled. He handed over Rogers's letter. After reading it, Khaled declared that the Sudanese government shared the United States' desire for better relations; in particular it hoped that the Americans would be able to help with the Sudan's economic problems. The foreign minister added that it had to be understood that full diplomatic relations would be out of the question so long as the United States continued its "one-sided support for Israel."

Moore said yes, of course, he understood that full diplomatic relations were not under discussion, but this did create a small problem. U.S. legislation prohibited the granting of economic assistance to a government that had broken relations with Washington. But maybe there were some things that could be done anyway. He would look into it.

He knew there was no point in arguing about the resumption of relations. For he knew that this time he really had his foot in the door,

[14]"Sudan Turns Sharply Away from Russia," *Los Angeles Times,* October 3, 1971.
[15]Ibid.

and he could foresee that with patience, with tact, and with the right amount of encouragement and pressure, it would be possible to swing that door wide open.

He sat down to map out what could be done on the economic side short of resumption of relations. The U.S. Foreign Assistance Act, which forbade aid to countries with which the United States had no formal diplomatic relations, had one large loophole. It was food, and food was one of the things the Sudan needed most, and one of the things that the Soviets had been unable to offer even in modest quantities. Humanitarian food aid, the Act said, could be given "to friendly people regardless of the attitude of their government." Under the provisions of the Act, food could be donated for distribution to starving people. And under the Commodity Credit Corporation Act, the United States could extend a line of credit to the government of Sudan to buy surplus American agricultural commodities. But that was not all. The World Bank could be encouraged to look more favorably on loans for projects in the Sudan, and so could the U.S. Export-Import Bank.

Moore had other ideas as well. He would try to get the Ford Foundation to resume a program in the Sudan. He would bring back Mal Whitfield to coach the Sudanese track team, he would get an American professor to teach at Khartoum University, and he would start sending Sudanese journalists, educators, and labor leaders to the United States on visitors' grants. The list of things he could think of to do went on and on.

When he discussed the possibility of food aid with the Sudanese, he did not earmark it for any particular region. He marked it simply as "area to be determined." But he could already see how it could be used to help bring an end to the destruction and bloodshed of civil war in the south, and to promote stability both in the Sudan and in neighboring Ethiopia.

Nimeiry had pledged, when he seized power in 1969, that he would bring the civil war to an end by granting the south a large measure of autonomy. But during his first two years in office, he did almost nothing to fulfill this pledge. Instead, like his predecessors, he resorted to more repression. So the civil war continued to fester, like a great gangrenous wound that would not heal and that increasingly sapped the Sudan of its economic and political vitality. Al-Atta and the other July coup leaders had taken up the call for autonomy for the south; along with strengthening of relations with communist and socialist governments, it was the main plank in their platform. Now Nimeiry decided to make it his own. He realized that without autonomy there would not be peace in the south, and that without peace neither there nor elsewhere would conditions improve. And if conditions did not improve, very soon his own rule would be imperiled.

But putting an end to the civil war in the south was not a simple matter. It involved more than just making a grant of autonomy to that region. Emperor Haile Selassie's government had to be brought to agree to end its assistance to the southern Sudanese guerrillas, the Anya Nya; and to obtain this, the Sudan would have to cut off the aid it was giving to separatist guerrillas in Eritrea. This latter move was bound to be unpopular with other Arab states, since some of the Eritrean separatists were Arabs and the Eritrean separatist movement enjoyed broad support in the Arab world. Qaddafi, who was an ardent backer of the Eritrean insurgents, would be particularly unhappy.

An agreement along these lines would nonetheless be a boon for both the Sudan and Ethiopia. It would also be to the advantage of the United States, for it would reduce pressures on Haile Selassie's government and strengthen Nimeiry's incipient moderate tendencies. Washington warmly encouraged both sides to move toward agreement. For the government of Sudan, the prospect of U.S. aid to help rehabilitate the war-torn south was a powerful incentive.

After Moore's August 17 meeting with Foreign Minister Khaled, his schedule—to that time sparse in official calls—began to fill up with appointments with cabinet-level officials: the minister of agriculture, the minister of planning, the minister of finance, the minister of interior, the minister of rural development, the minister of southern affairs, the director of the Agricultural Development Bank, all threw their doors wide open to him.

The time came now to settle the matter of the forged documents implicating Lucien and Mary Kinsolving, to prove to Nimeiry that in expelling Kinsolving and the five others, his government had acted on East bloc disinformation. At the end of November, a CIA technical expert (handwriting was one of his specialties) arrived in Khartoum. The expert stayed at the residence with Curt and Sally. Curt arranged several meetings for him with Sudanese officials, but the decisive one was with the deputy minister of interior. It was to be held at a secret location in Khartoum. Curt and the expert left the residence at six in the morning for the meeting. They felt they had all the proof needed to show that the documents were forgeries, but they were uncertain how the meeting would turn out, for they did not know what the intentions of the deputy minister were. Was he on their side, or was he in the pay of the other side? Did he genuinely want to clear up this matter, or would he use the meeting to try to befog it further? Sally sat anxiously by the telephone all day long until late afternoon when Curt and the expert returned, smiling and confident that the task had been accomplished.

After that the last barriers seemed to come down. In the second half of December, the U.S. assistant secretary of state for African affairs, David Newsom, visited Khartoum. From the schedule of meetings that Moore arranged for Newsom, one would have thought the two countries had always been the greatest of friends. The foreign minister was out of town, but the deputy foreign minister gave a dinner in Newsom's honor, and Newsom and Moore met with top figures all around the government, and at the end with Nimeiry himself. It was the first time since Nimeiry had taken power in July 1969 that he had received a visiting American delegation.

James Blake, the State Department's office director for northern African affairs, was with Newsom. Blake was struck by the obvious respect that the Sudanese accorded the chief of the U.S. interests section. Blake was not one to dispense praise lightly, but he was impressed by Curt Moore. "He had a warm and ready smile," Blake was to say later, "and he was the type of person you immediately knew was a genuine article. People didn't keep him at arm's length."

* * *

Moore was also a man of boundless energy—he needed only four or five hours of sleep a night—and of great enthusiasm and seemingly limitless interests.

In Benghazi he had played the flute in a small amateur chamber orchestra with Italian and other European expatriates. There was no similar talent in Khartoum, and in any case he would not have had time there to practice and to play regularly. But on evenings when he and Sally had no social commitments, he would take the instrument from its case and play Vivaldi, Handel, or Mozart, sometimes for hours on end, until late in the night.

He was also an amateur astronomer, fascinated by the universe and the stars. During his time in Libya, he had bought a large telescope and a stand to hold it, and he and Sally and the girls had hauled this rather substantial piece of equipment with them all around the desert. On clear winter nights in Khartoum, when the heavens blazed away as though on fire, he would take Lucy and Cate onto the rooftop of the residence. They would peer through the telescope into the vastness above, and he would point out the planets, the dippers, and the other constellations and talk about the origins of the universe and of life. He would make the heavens spring alive for his daughters, just as he had history, walking through Gettysburg with them years earlier and talking about the battle there, or in a Roman amphitheater in Libya, conjuring up the crowd, describing the gladiators and the games.

He was an amateur chef as well, in an unusual kind of way. There was no particular recipe that he specialized in. For him, cooking was more a challenge than a hobby. The dishes he undertook were never simple. His projects always required long planning and great marshaling of ingredients, and then a final heroic dash toward completion—a kind of culinary assault on the summit of Everest. He did not always succeed. Lucy and Cate remembered the beer soup, the recipe for which he found in his *Larousse Culinaire*. "It was awful," each exclaimed when recalling it later. "Nobody could eat it."

In Khartoum he became an amateur sailor too. He had never sailed before in his life, but sailing on the broad expanse of the Nile was a popular sport. Khartoum had a nautical club, the Blue Nile Sailing Club, headquartered on the *Melik*, a large antique boat anchored in the Nile, one of the gunboats used by the British in their conquest of the Sudan in 1898. The club sponsored sailing races on weekends and holidays. Moore bought a small wooden boat and taught himself to sail. One afternoon he came home and announced, to Sally's astonishment, "We're going to buy a racing boat." Racing boats in Khartoum were steel-hulled vessels. Sally did not understand how they could stay afloat, much less race. But buy one they did. And they raced, competing relentlessly, losing some races but also winning their share.

He was never bored. One summer at the beach, when he had nothing else to do (because of his very light and sensitive skin, he couldn't spend his time lazing on the sand), he took up bird-watching. As with everything else he did, he went at it enthusiastically. By the time the vacation was over, he announced triumphantly that he had identified twenty different varieties of seagull.

He was never aloof or distant. At the Fourth of July parties and other events organized by the American community in Khartoum, where he was the chief of mission and therefore everybody's boss, he was always to be found out with the others, running the three-legged race or competing in one of the other games. He knew how to be one of the boys and yet maintain his dignity and his authority. He could have a wonderful time at the parties the Marines organized at the American club. He could get a great kick out of letting the Marines, young men in their early twenties, throw him into the swimming pool. But because they knew he was genuinely enjoying himself, that it was not all just an act, he could retain their respect.

He loved life and everything about it. But he took it very seriously, and he was not always cheery and enthusiastic. He held himself to extraordinarily high standards, and when he felt that he had not met those standards, or that he had made a mistake or lost his temper, he could fall into a gloom, almost a depression, and be silent for hours. Although he hardly ever talked about it, he believed deeply in service to his country. And he believed just as deeply that people had a responsibility to be consequent in their actions. When Lucy told him that one of her professors at college in the States who was a reserve officer in the air force had balked at going to Vietnam, he had nothing but scorn for the man. If you were in the service, you did your duty—there was no other way. He felt the same way about himself. He was in the service, and he was there to do his duty.

It mattered to him that he should make his mark in life. He wanted the world to know that he had been there, and he wanted to leave the world behind him changed and, if only in a small way, a better place than he had found it. He had a code, and it told him that people came into the world not just to enjoy it but to accomplish something there, to make a difference. One evening he asked Lucy what she wanted out of life, and after a moment's hesitation she replied: "To be happy." He exploded. "What kind of a goal is that!" he exclaimed. "You have to want more from life than that. You have to want to make a difference in the world."

* * *

On July 25, 1972, the day that the United States and the Democratic Republic of Sudan restored diplomatic relations, Moore could truly say to himself that he had made a difference. No other Arab state that had broken relations with the United States in June 1967 had yet restored them. Sudan was the first to make the move. To be sure, it was the failed July 1971 coup that opened the way. But there was nothing inevitable about what happened after that in relations between the United States and the Sudan. For all Nimeiry's anger at the Soviets, he could well have held back from extending his hand to the Americans; he could have waited for others to go first. It was in very large part because George Curtis Moore had so diligently prepared the ground before the coup, and because he had known how to seize the opportunity it presented, to shape events and direct them afterwards, that the American flag was raised in Khartoum on an afternoon in July just a year later.

Washington recognized his contribution. Two days after the flag raising came a cable from Secretary of State William Rogers congratulating him and praising the work he had done in Khartoum.

Others who were not happy about the Sudan's resumption of relations with the United States, or about its agreement with Ethiopia, were ready to give him even more credit. The Cairo newspaper *Akhbar al-Yom*, leftist and hostile to both Nimeiry's and Anwar Sadat's pursuit of better relations with the United States, wrote:

> The most powerful foreign personality in the Sudan today is Mr. Curtis Moore, the American Chargé d'Affaires. The authority acquired by Mr. Moore has been a subject of rejoicing for Americans. . . . For the first time after years of hostility, hatred and boycott, Americans read of applause for their country in Khartoum.[16]

Nimeiry's resumption of relations with the United States amounted, in the eyes of some—in particular the Palestinians and Muammar al-Qaddafi—to a breaking of ranks, a betrayal of Arab solidarity. After all, Israel remained firmly in occupation of all the territories it had taken in the June 1967 war; and America continued to give Israel what all Arabs called its one-sided support, continued to provide it arms and economic aid, and to back it politically. Nimeiry's abandonment of the Eritrean rebels, and his conciliation of the black south, they considered another betrayal.

The American they tagged as having led the Sudanese president along the path of betrayal was thenceforth to be on their list.

---

[16] *Akhbar al-Yom*, October 28, 1972, article bylined to Ibrahim Saeda.

Curt Moore at a U.S. Marine Security Guard detachment party, at Khartoum's American club, being thrown in the swimming pool. Sam Peale and Sandy Sanderson are at rear. Photograph taken sometime between fall 1971 and February 1973. Courtesy of Joan Peale.

Curt Moore raising the American flag on July 25, 1972, at the American ambassador's residence, Khartoum, with Netherlands Chargé Jan Bertens. USIS photograph.

Cleo Noel being sworn in as U.S. ambassador to Sudan by Curt Moore on March 1, 1973, in the office of the ambassador, U.S. embassy, Khartoum. USIS photograph.

Curt and Sally Moore and Lucille and Cleo Noel after the swearing in, March 1, 1973. USIS photograph.

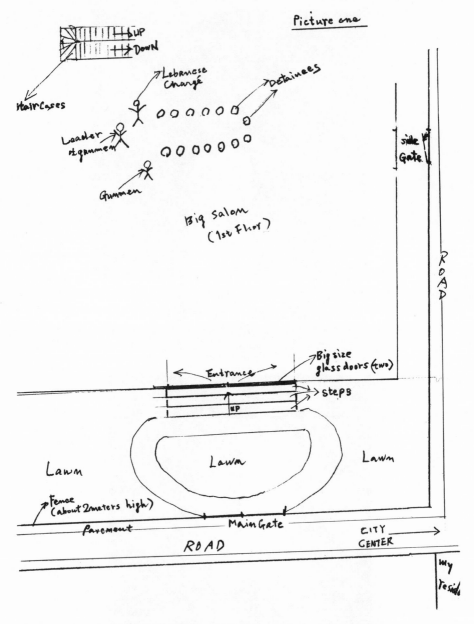

Picture One. Front entrance of the Saudi ambassador's residence and reception room after seizure by Black September terrorists. Shigeru Nomoto and other diplomats are seated on the carpet guarded by gunmen. Drawn by Shigeru Nomoto.

98

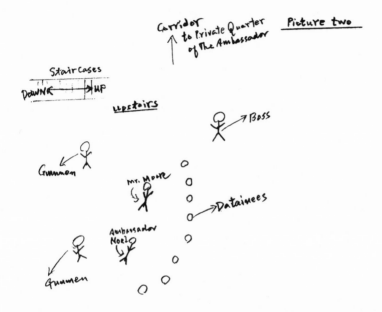

Picture Two. Shigeru Nomoto and the Arab diplomats are transferred to the Saudi ambassador's upstairs living room and seated on the carpet. Moore and Noel are bound and prostrate. Drawn by Shigeru Nomoto.

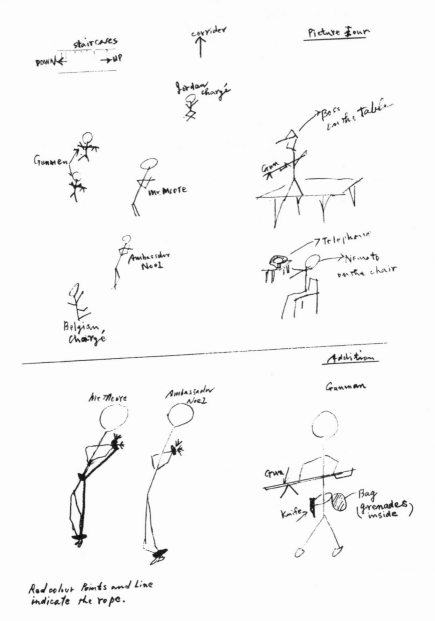

Red colour Points and Line indicate the rope.

Picture Four. After the Arab diplomats are released, Moore, Noel, Belgian Chargé Guy Eid, the Jordanian chargé, and Shigeru Nomoto are held by terrorists in the upstairs living room. Drawn by Shigeru Nomoto.

Addition. How the terrorists bound Moore and Noel. Drawn by Shigeru Nomoto.

100

Top left: Guy Eid (AP/Wide World Photos); *bottom left:* Adli Nasser (*Al Sahafa,* 3/5/73); *right:* Saudi Ambassador Abdullah al-Malhouk (*Al Sahafa,* 3/3/73).

11

In the Operations Center

Sanderson's flash cable, numbered Khartoum 0371, hit Washington like a bombshell. There had been no warning, not even a suspicion that a plot to seize American diplomats might be in the making.

The time difference between Khartoum and Washington was seven hours. The cable was clocked in at the State Department's sprawling communications center at 1:14 P.M. Washington time.

An aide hurriedly fetched William B. Macomber, the State Department's deputy under secretary for management, from the elegant executive dining suite on the eighth floor, above the offices of the secretary of state. Another was sent to summon Armin H. Meyer, State's coordinator for combatting terrorism, from lunch with the ambassador of newly independent Bangladesh at a restaurant across the street from the department.

Others were called with equal abruptness from the State Department's cafeteria on the ground floor or learned the news as they drifted back into their offices to finish what had promised to be a quiet, routine Thursday afternoon's work.

They all converged on the department's Operations Center, a sprawling complex of offices on the seventh floor in the east wing of the building, down the hall from the secretary of state's suite. The first to arrive was Harry Odell, a big, red-freckled bear of a man who had spent two years in a German prisoner-of-war camp in World War II and was now deputy director of the Office of Northern African Affairs.

The Operations Center was the place from which crises were handled, but for the personnel who staffed it, crises were routine, day-to-day occurrences.

"I guess you'll be setting up a task force," the official on duty in the center remarked to Odell rather laconically. He gave Odell a spacious room with rectangular meeting tables aligned in its center and, behind them, rows of folding chairs, as in a makeshift theater. From the wall facing the chairs hung a screen. Onto it were to be projected messages received from the embassy in Khartoum; it was a device designed to permit anybody entering the room to take in the latest news at a glance.

John Gatch came in moments after Odell. Gatch was Armin Meyer's deputy in the terrorism office. He had studied Arabic with Moore and Noel in Washington and in Beirut seventeen years earlier; he counted both men good friends, and so there was a personal urgency about the job he had to do there. Both Gatch and Odell were to stay in the Operations Center throughout the crisis.

Then came the top people, Macomber, Meyer, Joseph Sisco, the assistant secretary for Near Eastern and South Asian affairs, and a little later David Newsom, the assistant secretary for African affairs. A crowd of others came either because the abduction of the two American diplomats in Khartoum touched in one way or another on their official responsibilities, or because they were friends of Curt Moore and Cleo Noel, were anxious for the latest news, and wanted to be there, in a simple act of solidarity, to do anything they could to help; or for no reason other than that they were curious to find out what was going on.

Odell managed to get a telephone connection to the embassy in Khartoum, but it was full of static and was in any case impossible to keep open indefinitely. So he and Gatch proceeded to set up a secure teletype link with the embassy in Khartoum. Messages were typed out at each end—in the State Department Operations Center and at the embassy in Khartoum—on the keys of a telex machine. This procedure, called telecon, cut through the formal steps involved in processing cables and thus speeded up communication, but it had a major drawback that was to become evident later. The information conveyed over the telecon circuit between the Khartoum embassy and the task force in Washington was not directly available to anyone else. The telecon messages were not

sent laterally to other U.S. diplomatic posts and were not even dis-
tributed around the Department of State or to other U.S. government
agencies or entered into the Department of State's formal records. Only
those in the task force room had access to them. For the messages to
gain wider circulation, the task force team had to retype them onto the
thick green forms then used for regular State Department cables and
send them to the communications center for retransmission to other
overseas posts, a time-consuming job.

Even before the telecon link was set up, messages from Khartoum
began to flash onto the screen in rapid succession. The Spanish chargé
had emerged from the Saudi residence and told the Americans—errone-
ously, as it quickly turned out—that the Black September assailants
were demanding that the United States turn King Hussein over to them.
Then came the text of the leaflet passed out by the Black September
gang. It set out their terms: the freeing of Abu Daoud, the Black
September leader imprisoned in Jordan, of other Palestinians, and of
two Jordanian army officers; the release of Sirhan Sirhan from jail in the
United States and of members of the Bader-Meinhoff gang held in
Germany; and the freeing of "Palestinian women in prison in Israel."
The leaflet accused the American embassy in Khartoum of aiding Israel
and of being behind efforts to stop Black September's "revolution." It
warned that if its demands were not met within twenty-four hours, the
hostages would be executed.

These last words seemed to rivet themselves into the screen's white
canvas fabric.

The man in charge at the task force room in the State Department's
Operations Center was William B. Macomber. No one who stepped
into the room could mistake it.

He was not physically a big man. But he was like a welterweight
fighter, his whole being packed with energy and wound taut, as though
it might explode at any moment and in exploding injure someone
nearby. His nickname around the department—earned two decades
earlier but still merited, most felt—was Wild Bill. Macomber graduated
from Yale in 1943, joined the Marines, fought in the Pacific, and
finished World War II as a first lieutenant. After the war he went back
to school, first to Harvard, where he earned two graduate degrees, and
then on to the University of Chicago.

Macomber was a Republican, and he rode into the State Department on the tail of the mighty wave that swept Dwight D. Eisenhower to the presidency in January 1953 and made John Foster Dulles his secretary of state. A political appointee, Macomber came in at a senior grade that most career people had to slave a lifetime to reach. After working as Dulles's chief special assistant, Macomber was appointed assistant secretary for congressional relations in November 1955, at the relatively tender age of thirty-four.

But there was nothing tender about Bill Macomber. In an organization that cultivated an air of refined gentility, whose members addressed one another in their correspondence as "Esquire," where orders were most frequently couched as suggestions, Macomber came on like a Marine Corps boot-camp drill sergeant. As aide to Dulles he ordered assistant secretaries around as though they were freshman plebes. As assistant secretary for congressional relations he could be ferocious. One evening toward the end of the Eisenhower administration, William Luers, then a junior Foreign Service officer on the Soviet affairs desk, set out for Macomber's seventh-floor office with a memorandum and letter for Macomber to sign and send to the Hill. These papers bore a deadline of 5:30 P.M., but as was often the case, they had been delayed in the clearance process. It was 6:45, or thereabouts, when Luers reached Macomber's office. As Luers stepped across the threshold and announced his purpose, the assistant secretary picked up the receiver of the telephone on his desk and flung it at his astounded visitor. The cord jerked the instrument back before it could strike its target, but Luers dropped the papers on a desk outside and turned and fled.

Macomber was very good at getting things done, however. Perhaps because of that, he survived into the Kennedy administration (he was not so much a Republican that he would not work for the Democrats), which sent him off to be ambassador to Jordan, and on into the Johnson administration, which, however, eventually demoted him to the job of deputy assistant secretary for congressional relations. With the return of the Republicans at the beginning of 1969, he sprang to the top rungs of the ladder. Deputy under secretary for management was the fourth-ranking job in the State Department. It was a powerful position, and Macomber made it even more so by his aggressiveness, and by taking on tasks that others did not want or were not able to handle. He became the Nixon administration's point man in Daniel Ellsberg's Pentagon Papers trial, marshaling evidence against Ellsberg and testifying for the administration at the trial. And when the office of coordinator for combatting terrorism was created at the end of September 1972, he had it put under his jurisdiction.

Around the State Department, Bill Macomber was feared. Crossing him could be fatal to your career.

In the Operations Center that afternoon of March 1, 1973, Macomber was in high dudgeon. His chin jutting from beneath glasses and a thick shock of black hair, he shouted orders and bawled out people right and left.

From the outset the main issue was whether Macomber should run the show from Washington or go directly to the scene, to Khartoum. It was really not an issue at all, for although Macomber proposed it for discussion and agonized over it for some time, others there felt he had already made up his mind. He wanted to fly to Khartoum, to be there on the spot, as he had been four weeks earlier in Port-au-Prince when Ambassador Clinton Knox was kidnapped. With Noel and Moore held captive, there was no American official of senior rank or experience in Khartoum—another parallel with the Knox case. Macomber argued that a strong hand would be needed to guide the rescue effort.

It was a valid point, but there were serious drawbacks. Port-au-Prince was less than a thousand miles from Washington; Macomber had been able to get there in three hours. Khartoum was more than seven thousand miles distant. It would take at least fourteen hours to get there, under the best of circumstances. In that time a lot could happen, and he would be out of touch, or largely so.

Macomber's presence in Khartoum was not the only conceivable way to restore strong leadership to the decapitated American embassy. John Gatch spoke up. Why not send Ambassador Nicholas Thacher over from Jidda to take temporary charge of the embassy in Khartoum? Thacher was an experienced career diplomat who knew the Arab world well. He could fly from Jidda to the Sudanese capital in no more than an hour.

It was an entirely reasonable suggestion, but it outraged Macomber. He turned on Gatch and cursed him. What had been proposed, Macomber shouted, was just plain stupid. He seemed to take it as a personal affront, as though the idea of sending Thacher was meant to say that Thacher could do a better job of running things in Khartoum than he.

His outburst ended the discussion. Macomber, accompanied by

Meyer, Newsom, and Roy Atherton, a deputy assistant secretary for Near Eastern and South Asian affairs, went off to confer with Under Secretary Kenneth Rush, in charge at the State Department in the absence of Secretary William Rogers, who was in Paris for talks with the North Vietnamese. When they came back a half-hour later, after Rush had spoken on the phone with President Richard Nixon, they announced that it had been decided that Macomber should fly to Khartoum.

*　*　*

The seizure of the ambassador and the deputy chief of mission had in fact thrown the U.S. embassy in Khartoum into considerable turmoil, though to what extent Washington had little idea at the time.

It was a small embassy, a tight little operation, one in which people forged close bonds. The staff were traumatized by the news that Noel and Moore were being held hostage by ruthless killers. Curt Moore was a man who inspired devotion among those with whom he worked closely, and though Cleo Noel had arrived at his post only recently, the staff had already developed enormous affection and respect for him. Margaret Thorsen, Curt's secretary, burst uncontrollably into tears. Sam Peale had to struggle to keep his composure, and Sandy Sanderson was visibly shaken. Ed Brawn, Sanderson's assistant, ran his car off the road as he drove to the embassy after learning that Moore and Noel had been seized.

The sudden disappearance of the two top men also spawned a dispute over who should be in charge. After Noel and Moore, George Thompson, the public affairs officer, was the senior American government official in Khartoum in rank. Thompson, a flamboyant figure, considered that he should be in charge. But when he tried to assert this claim, he found it ignored by the embassy's State Department contingent. Thompson was an official of the United States Information Agency. By tradition, if not by law, chain of command descended through the ranks of the State Department, and the senior State official was Sandy Sanderson. So even though Sanderson was junior in rank to Thompson, and his job was administrative officer—which involved a multitude of tasks, from counting out rolls of toilet paper to managing the local staff and paying the embassy's bill, but nothing political—State Department personnel now looked to him to lead them. Thompson, however, continued to maintain that he was in charge, and proceeded to conduct himself accordingly. But Sanderson controlled the embassy's communications, and as every ambitious third-world conspirator knew, he who controlled the means of communication held power.

*　*　*

Jim Blake, the director of the Office of Northern African Affairs, came late that day to the State Department Operations Center. He had been out of the building, at a long business lunch downtown. Less than three months earlier, Blake had given Cleo Noel a last briefing before Noel left for Khartoum. He had not seen Curt Moore since the visit he and Newsom had made to Khartoum in December 1971.

Now, as he surveyed the scene in the crisis room, Blake had the sinking feeling that he would never again see Moore or Noel alive. The rescue effort just was not going to work; they were going to be killed. It was all too chaotic. People were milling about in great confusion. Communications with Khartoum were unreliable; later that evening the teletype link went out for four hours, and efforts to reestablish the telephone connection yielded only unintelligible squawks. The government of the Sudan obviously had no influence with the terrorists, Blake reasoned, and the terrorists were not asking anything that it was in Nimeiry's power to grant. The United States also had little leverage, for it was clear that the terrorists' demand for the release of Sirhan Sirhan was not their real purpose.

Nobody who did have leverage seemed willing to help out. Washington's relations with Egypt were not such that much help could be expected from that quarter. The Israelis had, only a few months earlier, allowed nine of their people to die rather than release prisoners, so it seemed a reasonable bet that they were not going to let anyone go to save two Americans (Golda Meir's offer of a deal to the Black September at Munich was not known until several years later). The only possible exception was King Hussein of Jordan. Hussein held the people the Black September wanted released. He was a friend of the United States, one who received sizeable amounts of U.S. military and economic aid. He had in fact just left the United States after a state visit. He was in Morocco, having stopped there on his way back home. But so far as Blake could tell, no one in Washington was making any effort to get him to do anything.

So people started throwing out ideas. Blake suggested that Hussein should be asked to declare that if Moore, Noel, and the Belgian were not released, he would begin executing PLO prisoners he held in Amman. Harry Odell proposed that a secure telex link be set up between the American embassies in Khartoum and Rabat and that Nimeiry and King Hussein be invited to use it to work out a deal between themselves for freeing the hostages. Someone else came up with the idea that Nimeiry should be asked to go personally to the Saudi embassy to reason with the terrorists.

These and similar schemes went nowhere. They were unorthodox or impractical, but mainly they ran against the grain of the policy. Many of those in the middle and junior ranks who came to serve on the task force had not even known of the policy, and they were shocked when they learned of it.

For the policy seemed to foreclose all the realistic options for saving their two colleagues.

12

A New Terrorism Policy

The policy had descended from the White House, with the president's name on it, though many suspected that its real author was Nixon's national security advisor, Henry Kissinger. It had not been handed down for study or even for discussion. It had come engraved in stone, like the commandments Moses brought down from Mount Sinai. It was a brief, concise policy. It consisted of three noes: no negotiations with hostage-takers, no deals with them, and no concessions to them.

Many, including apparently both Nixon and Kissinger, thought the policy to be modeled on Israeli policy. The president and his national security advisor admired the Israelis' toughness, and they wanted the United States to be equally tough. This reflected a profound if rather common misunderstanding. The Israelis loudly proclaimed a policy of refusing to pay ransom. They put up a tough front, and in fact they often did refuse to pay ransom, but only when they saw a possibility of freeing their people through their own military action or in some other way; where there clearly was no such possibility, they almost always sought a deal, albeit for the most part secretly. They were ready to make close calls, and sometimes their people died because they miscalculated. But they never deliberately sacrificed anyone to the principle of "no deals" or "no ransom."

This policy of absolute refusal to make deals with hostage-takers had not always been American policy. When Charles Burke Elbrick, the newly arrived American ambassador to Brazil, was kidnapped on the afternoon of September 4, 1969, Washington responded quite differently. Elbrick was taken at gunpoint from his Cadillac limousine in a narrow street in Rio de Janeiro as he was returning to his office from lunch at his residence. Four young men jumped from a Volkswagen Beetle that had suddenly stalled in front of Elbrick's car. Brandishing .45 automatic pistols, they shouted, "We are Brazilian revolutionaries," forced Elbrick's driver aside, and drove off with him. The American ambassador spent the next days in a small, tightly shuttered room with a cot, a stool, and a single light bulb that burned around the clock. He was fed pizza and beans and passed the time by reading Ho Chi Minh's tracts on revolution. His kidnappers accommodatingly brought him a packet of Brazilian cigars.

The kidnappers were members of a communist student group. They issued a manifesto demanding the release of fifteen of their comrades who had been jailed and tortured by the Brazilian regime. Otherwise, the manifesto said, the U.S. ambassador would be executed. The Nixon administration, in office not quite nine months, pressed a reluctant Brazilian government hard to meet the kidnappers' demands and so avoid harm to Elbrick. The ambassador was a well-known and highly regarded personality. The Brazilian government decided to give in, though the decision almost provoked a revolt in the ranks of the military. Three days after Elbrick's kidnapping, the fifteen prisoners whose freedom the kidnappers had demanded boarded a Brazilian Air Force C-130 and were flown to asylum in Mexico. Elbrick was released into the street. He hailed a taxi and was driven home. He later said it was quite clear to him that had anything gone wrong, his abductors would have killed him.

Secretary of State William Rogers waxed rapturous in praise of the Brazilians for ransoming Elbrick. "The government of Brazil has not only shared our shock and revulsion at this terrible act but has also placed its concern for the life of Ambassador Elbrick above all other considerations," Rogers declared. "For this and all the many measures taken by the Brazilian government, we are most grateful."[17]

[17]"Ambassador Elbrick Kidnapped, Released after 78 Hours," *State Department Newsletter,* October 1969.

Elbrick was the first diplomat to be held and ransomed, but his kidnappers' success in getting their comrades out of jail encouraged others to imitate them. The following year, 1970, became a year of kidnappings of foreign diplomats in Brazil: in March, the Japanese consul general; in June, the West German ambassador; and in December, the Swiss ambassador. At the behest of their governments, the Brazilians ransomed each of them. The kidnapping of diplomats became a quick and easy way for underground movements to get their people out of jail and to fill their empty coffers. All told, in 1969 and 1970, to redeem the lives of kidnapped foreign diplomats, 129 political prisoners were released from Brazilian jails and sent to freedom abroad.

When the West German ambassador to Guatemala, Count Karl von Spreti, was kidnapped in March 1970, Bonn wanted the Guatemalan authorities to ransom him, too. The government of Guatemala, however, declined to meet the kidnappers' demands for the release of twenty-five political prisoners and a payment of $700,000, declined even to negotiate with the kidnappers. Von Spreti's body was found in an abandoned hut six days after he was seized. Bonn reacted angrily. It accused the Guatemalan government of abetting murder and withdrew its embassy.

The United States, which had been the first to ask another government to ransom one of its representatives, became the first to refuse to ask. When Tupamaro guerrillas in Montevideo kidnapped Dan Mitrione, an American police officer sent to advise the Uruguayan police under a U.S. assistance program, Washington made clear that it would not intervene; the decision was up to the government of Uruguay. The Tupamaros seized Mitrione on July 31, 1970, midwinter in the southern hemisphere. They claimed they had targeted him because he had been tutoring the Uruguayan police in methods of interrogation that involved, or bordered on, torture. Fifteen days later, after both the U.S. and Uruguayan governments had refused to deal with them, the Tupamaros shot Mitrione through the back of the head and left his body in the rear seat of a stolen car.

The Tupamaros later explained that they felt they had no choice. For the kidnapping-exchange method to be effective as a tool, they pointed out, it had to be carried to its logical consequence. If terrorists threatened to kill their hostages and then failed to do so once their demands were rejected, who would take them seriously? To be credible, they had to be ready to kill.

At the time, the Mitrione case was viewed in Washington as an isolated incident. The administration's refusal to ask the government of Uruguay to comply with the Tupamaros' demands in order to buy Mitrione's life was not seen as necessarily establishing any general policy. It had as much to do with the particular circumstances in Uruguay, where the Tupamaros had for some time been carrying out a campaign of terror and of kidnapping, as it did with the belief that bargaining was in and of itself wrong and would lead to more terror and more kidnapping. And—though no one would say this—Mitrione was an obscure official, not a highly placed and well-connected ambassador.

It was the Black September's capture and killing of Israeli athletes at the Munich Olympic Games in September 1972 that precipitated the change in U.S. policy. The kidnappings and killings in Latin America had made a few headlines, but basically they were something that seemed to happen on the margins of world events; kidnapping and killing were a thing, many felt, that could be expected in Latin America, a place with a reputation for violence. Munich and the Olympic Games were altogether different. They were center stage. The seizure of the Israeli pavilion by gunmen wearing ski masks, and the massacre of nine Israeli athletes in a failed rescue attempt, took place on camera, before the eyes of the entire world. Munich showed that hostage-taking and killing were not just something that happened in remote, secondary regions of the world. If it could happen in West Germany, it could happen anywhere.

Nixon and Kissinger felt strongly that terrorists had to be shown that hostage-taking would bring them no benefit. Three weeks after Munich, Nixon announced the establishment of a new entity, the Cabinet Committee to Combat Terrorism, comprising ten departments of the government and headed by Secretary of State Rogers. A week later, on October 2, Rogers announced the appointment of Ambassador Armin H. Meyer as chairman of the Working Group of the Cabinet Committee and as his own special assistant and coordinator for combatting terrorism.

Armin Henry Meyer was a prestigious name in the Foreign Service. Over the previous eleven years he had been ambassador first to Lebanon, then to Iran, and then to Japan, moving at each step to greater levels of responsibility. He was a tall, distinguished-looking man with a full head of white hair, but he was no Ivy League striped-pants diplomat. His parents were poor German immigrants. He grew up in poverty in the Depression years of the 1930s, but he was smart, ambitious, and determined, and he had immense drive. He worked his way through college, but not as most others did, with a part-time job. He had no money at all, and so to put himself through an obscure midwestern institution, Capital University, he worked full time—forty hours a week or more—while carrying a full course load. He was an inveterate optimist, and his energy was matched by his resourcefulness. He joined the State Department in 1946, near the bottom rung of the ladder. Fifteen years and a whole string of awards later, he got his first ambassadorial appointment.

The terrorism job was not a natural one for Armin Meyer. After his embassies in Beirut, Tehran, and Tokyo, it was a comedown, and he had no background whatsoever in the subject. But expertise on terrorism was not what the Nixon administration was looking for. It wanted a prestigious name.

The creation of the cabinet committee made it sound as though the Nixon administration were gearing up for a high-powered campaign against terrorism, as though the resources of the entire United States government were going to be mobilized. Palestinian terrorists, in particular, thought this to be the case. They imagined Meyer at the head of a massive American intelligence apparatus dedicated to tracking them down and killing them.

Nothing could have been further from the truth. Meyer himself quickly learned that he was to be a general without an army. He was responsible for coordinating everything the U.S. government did in regard to terrorism, and for giving direction and leadership to U.S. policy. He chaired a committee of mid-level representatives of the ten participating U.S. government agencies, and he was always enthusiastic about the cooperation he got from them. But the entire staff under his direct orders consisted of one middle-grade officer and one secretary. The job was so potentially immense, there was so much to be done, that the resources at his command were ridiculously small. Terrorism was a subject to which nobody in the U.S. government, with the exception of the Federal Bureau of Investigation, had theretofore given more than scant attention. Meyer had to build the whole structure, from the ground up, with very little idea even of its outlines.

Airport security became his first priority, for commercial airliners were being hijacked not only in the Middle East but even in the United States and Europe. The security of American embassies and personnel overseas was another priority, and Meyer and John Gatch, his deputy, were working on it when Moore and Noel were seized in Khartoum.

Meyer was also quickly to learn that he was to be the custodian of a policy which was still not formally ratified. After the Munich killings and the creation of the cabinet committee, the word from the White House was that there were to be no deals with and no concessions to terrorists. But there was no official announcement, nothing that categorically proclaimed that the United States had decided, at the highest level, to put the Elbrick precedent behind it and to forswear, once and for all, the paying of ransom in whatever form as a means of freeing its personnel.

And if the policy was not formally announced, neither was it debated or studied for its implications, to determine if it was the best policy, if it would accomplish the purpose that it was intended to accomplish— i.e., to discourage the taking of diplomats as hostages—or whether it was right and fair to demand a sacrifice of such magnitude from civilian personnel sent unarmed and unprotected to represent the United States abroad. The policy had a distinctly military flavor to it; soldiers knew and accepted that membership in their profession meant that their lives might be sacrificed. But they also knew that they would go into battle fully armed. Diplomats were now to be asked to accept that their profession, too, would require them to sacrifice their lives, but they would have to face the peril unarmed.

In one of the first of the weekly meetings that Meyer and Gatch held with officials of other U.S. government agencies assigned to their team, they learned that the no-negotiations, no-concessions policy was not the one followed in dealing with kidnappers in the United States. The FBI representative pointed out that in domestic kidnapping cases, his agency's policy was to negotiate, pay ransom, do anything to save people's lives. But, all agreed, the international arena was different. In kidnapping cases in the United States, once the hostage was freed or dead, the G-men would go after the kidnappers with everything they had, and their record of success in apprehending the criminals was almost 100 percent. In the world at large there was no FBI to track down kidnappers and terrorists and bring them to justice. That was the responsibility of each individual government, and many governments were very lax and very selective in the way they fulfilled that responsibility. Some even sponsored or abetted terrorism.

Word of the new policy did get around the State Department to some, but by no means to all. In staff meetings of senior officers of the Bureau of Personnel, where Cleo Noel was assigned before going out to Khartoum, people were asked their views about ransom, and all agreed it should not be paid. There may have been other, similar samplings of opinion as well. But no broader poll—nothing that could have been called a representative survey of State Department opinion—was ever taken.

The paradox that was later to emerge was that in the lower and middle ranks of the Foreign Service, there was considerable dissent from the policy, but the closer one got to the top ranks, the more general was its endorsement. Among the most senior officers, those who would be ambassador or deputy chief of mission and therefore were most likely to be its victims, practically everybody was ready to sign on to it. Some, like Cleo Noel and Curt Moore, saw it simply as their duty. For others, it was a matter of conforming to what was handed down from on high—the ability to do so, after all, being in most cases the price of a successful career—and hoping that the calamity would never happen to them. For still others, there was an element of bravado, of machismo, involved. Robert McClintock, the U.S. ambassador to Venezuela, sent the secretary of state a letter declaring that in the event he were taken hostage, he wanted nothing done to save him. He had made a copy of his letter, he wrote, and would carry it on his person at all times. He would rather go to his grave, he announced, than hand terrorists a success.

McClintock was fortunate. He never had to make good on his commitment to sacrifice himself, for he was never taken hostage. But even before the policy of no negotiations, no deals, and no concessions was publicly announced, another ambassador in Latin America was kidnapped. Late in the afternoon of January 23, 1972, Clinton E. Knox, the U.S. ambassador to Haiti and one of the few black Americans serving as ambassador, was seized at gunpoint by two men and a woman as his car was returning to his residence. The abductors took Knox into his residence and held him there, in the second-floor study. Identifying themselves as members of a Haitian opposition group, they demanded the release of thirty-one of their cohorts held in Haitian jails, the payment of one million dollars, and a plane to take them and the prisoners to asylum abroad. Otherwise, they said, they would kill the U.S. ambassador. To show that they were serious, they held a gun to Knox's head, not just for a few moments but for quite some time.

Knox, a career diplomat with a distinguished record behind him, was in his mid-sixties and had a heart condition. He was unaware of the new policy that had been adopted in Washington, and it evidently never occurred to him that his government might take the position that ransom should not be paid to save his life. His first action, in fact, was to call his consul, Ward Christensen, to join him at his residence, in the expectation that Christensen, who dealt routinely with the Haitian police on consular matters and had come to know the chief of police quite well, would be able to arrange for release of the thirty-one prisoners. When Christensen arrived at the residence, the abductors took him hostage as well.

Soon after seizing Knox, his abductors allowed him to put through a call to the State Department to convey their terms. The department's Operations Center switched the call through to John Burke, the office director for Caribbean affairs, at his apartment just a block away. It was 6:15 P.M. Burke had just gotten back from work and was showering before going out for dinner. As he stepped dripping from the shower, he found on the other end of the line a highly agitated Knox, who pleaded that the abductors' demands be met, and an even more agitated abductor, who threatened to kill Knox if they were not met speedily.

John Burke had served in Port-au-Prince from 1970 to 1972 as Knox's deputy. He admired the ambassador and had come to feel a deep friendship for him. Burke was aware of the new policy proscription against paying ransom, but he was not about to tell either Knox or, especially, the kidnappers that they should expect nothing from the United States, for to do so would almost certainly mean Knox's instant death. Burke decided to try to string things along. It would take time, he told the abductor, to locate the prisoners, get the money together, and find a plane. The man would have none of it: "Do it! Do it now!" he screamed into the phone. "Or shall I kill him?"

"No," Burke pleaded, "don't do that. Give us just a little time."

Burke rushed to the State Department's Operations Center, where shortly thereafter Secretary Rogers appeared along with Macomber and other senior officials. Amid much confusion, and after several telephone calls to the U.S. embassy in Port-au-Prince and to the Haitian foreign minister, at about midnight Rogers instructed Macomber to fly to Haiti to take charge of the rescue effort. The secretary of state admonished, however, that Macomber should hew strictly to the no-ransom line.

Macomber, Burke, Marvin Gentile (the State Department's chief of security), and a State Department doctor arrived in Port-au-Prince at daybreak aboard a White House executive jet. They were taken immediately to meet with President Jean-Claude Duvalier. Straight away, Macomber told "Baby Doc," as the younger Duvalier was known, that American policy was to pay no ransom and make no concessions, and that the United States advised other governments to take the same line. His objective, he said, was a Bangkok-type solution, in which the only thing the terrorists could expect to get would be safe passage out of the country in return for releasing their hostages unharmed.

Baby Doc had inherited the presidency some eighteen months earlier when his father, "Papa Doc," died. He was only twenty-one, less than half Macomber's age, but he had news for the American. "That may be what you say in the United States," he blurted out, "but this is Haiti. If we don't pay, they will kill them!"

Clinton Knox had been in Haiti for almost four years. During his time there, relations between Washington and the Haitian regime had warmed substantially; the United States had even launched a small economic aid program. All this had gained Knox the appreciation of the government and the Duvalier family, in particular Baby Doc's mother, who since the death of Papa Doc was the power behind the throne. The Duvaliers had no intention of letting Knox be killed. Baby Doc and his foreign minister, Adrien Raymond, had begun negotiations with the abductors through the Canadian chargé and the French ambassador almost immediately after Knox was seized. By the time Macomber arrived in Haiti, they had already agreed to release prisoners (although they said only twelve of the thirty-one the abductors had demanded could be located). They were upset and angry when Macomber told them that the United States would provide neither money nor an airplane to fly the abductors and the prisoners out of Haiti.

It was Burke who came up with ideas for solving these two problems. When the Haitians protested that they had no aircraft, Burke pointed out that he had seen an Air Haiti DC-6 cargo plane sitting on a runway at the airport that morning. Why not use it? As for money, Burke asked Baby Doc's mother, who was at the palace and was pushing the negotiations to free Knox, how much cash the family had immediately available. After conferring briefly with her son, she said they could pay $70,000.

The French ambassador was sent off to make the deal: the release of the twelve prisoners, payment of $70,000, and safe passage to Mexico for the abductors and the prisoners on the Air Haiti DC-6, in exchange for which Knox and Christensen were to be released unharmed. The French ambassador and the papal nuncio gave the abductors their governments' pledge that the deal would be honored to the letter, and the government of Haiti acceded to the abductors' demand that the terms be broadcast over the radio. By 9:30 that morning, just three and a half hours after Macomber's arrival in Port-au-Prince, everything was set and sealed.

Macomber did not try to stop Duvalier from making the deal—in an interview years later, he even claimed authorship of the $70,000 ransom figure—but he left the presidential palace upset that the kidnappers were getting both money and prisoners. He had, he told Burke, thought up a way to stop them: he would call the pilot of the DC-6, an American on contract to Air Haiti, and tell him to find a reason to abort takeoff. Burke argued strongly against this. The French government, the Vatican, and the president of Haiti, he pointed out, had all given their solemn pledge that the terms of the deal would be honored. Macomber, however, was not dissuaded. While Burke listened in on the conversation on another phone, Macomber explained to the pilot what he wanted him to do.

The pilot heard Macomber out in skeptical silence and then asked: "Are you giving me a direct order?"

Macomber backed off.

Just before noon on January 24, the three kidnappers and the twelve newly released prisoners boarded the DC-6 and were flown to Mexico City, where the Mexican authorities, alerted by the Mexican ambassador in Port-au-Prince, searched them and recovered $69,900 of Duvalier's $70,000 (had the prisoners managed to hide $100, or had Baby Doc shortchanged them by that much?). They sent the money back to Haiti.

Macomber, Burke, and the two others spent the night in Port-au-Prince. Before they departed the next day, Adrien Raymond, Duvalier's foreign minister, took Burke aside to confide a sinister suspicion. Raymond could not understand why the United States had been ready to sacrifice its ambassador.

"Was it not," Raymond asked, "because Knox is black?"

Clinton Knox emerged from his ordeal drained and shaken. At one point his captors had been quite genuinely on the verge of shooting him. "It was a helluva thing," he told reporters. "They threatened to blow my head off if they didn't get what they wanted."[18] It was a close call for the American ambassador to Haiti, closer than he perhaps realized at the time. Knox owed his life not to the actions of his own government but to those of Haiti's president and foreign minister, and also to the quick thinking and skill of his friend and former subordinate John Burke.

Back in Washington, Macomber got a mixed reception. Along with public satisfaction over Knox's safe release came ominous rumblings of dissatisfaction from the White House over its having been obtained through ransom. Macomber shot off a memorandum to Henry Kissinger to defend himself:

> Press accounts have not accurately reflected the position this government has taken in connection with the kidnapping of Ambassador Knox. While an important consideration from the start was the safe release of Ambassador Knox and Mr. Christensen, we also gave a very high priority to avoiding a solution which would encourage similar terrorist acts against other diplomatic officials in the future. For the latter reason, U.S. government officials (other than Ambassador Knox with a gun at his head) dealing with the Haitian government and with the terrorists never urged the Haitian government to release prisoners or to facilitate the exit of the gunmen from Haiti.[19]

It was literally true that U.S. representatives had never "urged" the government of Haiti to release the prisoners. But in fact the memorandum was misleading, for both Macomber and Burke were complicit in the deal that was made.

[18] *Washington Post,* January 26, 1973.

[19] "Kidnapping of Ambassador Knox in Haiti," memorandum from Theodore L. Eliot, Jr., Executive Secretary, Department of State, to Henry Kissinger, The White House, drafted by William B. Macomber, 1/26/73.

In Haiti, Macomber had gone out on a limb, beyond his mandate. The next time around he would be more careful.

*　*　*

But the Haiti precedent left no firm legacy. While Macomber was reassuring the White House that he had toed the official line, that line had still not been formally announced. After the Knox kidnapping, Armin Meyer drafted a message to correct this, to put the policy formally on record, to advise both U.S. overseas posts and Department of State personnel in Washington that thenceforth the U.S. government would refuse to make deals with or pay ransom of any kind to hostage-takers.

To his astonishment, Meyer found that none of the senior officials of the Department of State would sign it—neither Secretary of State William Rogers nor the under secretary nor Macomber himself. The new policy, they recognized only too well, declared forfeit the lives of American diplomats and other civilian officials serving abroad in the event they were taken hostage; it condemned them to death. It was just too callous. Nobody wanted to put his name to it, to take responsibility for it. Meyer withdrew the unsigned message and held it in his safe.

Several hours after Moore and Noel were seized, Armin Meyer was still in sufficient doubt of the policy that he would confer with the Department of Justice to see what possibilities there were for releasing Sirhan Sirhan. Justice replied that the federal government had no jurisdiction in the matter; it was up to the state of California.

Some time later Governor Ronald Reagan's office called, but by then it had become apparent that the release of Sirhan Sirhan was not really what the Black September was after. So it was decided to let the matter rest. Meyer told the California governor's people to sit tight. Along with this, he gave them other advice. They should keep quiet, he said. They should not publicly reject the Black September's demand for the release of Sirhan Sirhan; they should not say anything about it.

After all, Meyer pointed out, three men's lives were at risk. Nothing should be done that might needlessly antagonize those who held guns to their heads.

13

A Rescue Mission

In the early afternoon of March 1, 1973, Robert E. Fritts, Cleo Noel's new deputy chief of mission, was in one of the high-ceilinged offices in the stately old Department of Commerce building in Washington, meeting with the person there who handled the Sudan. Fritts, a former naval officer and a tall, slender, ramrod-straight man in his late thirties, was scheduled to leave Washington the next day for London and then on to Khartoum, to arrive there on the evening of March 5, just twelve hours after Curt and Sally Moore were scheduled to depart.

Fritts's meeting at Commerce was interrupted by a telephone call from the State Department's Operations Center. Something very serious had happened in Khartoum, the caller said; Fritts should come immediately to the department. Out on Constitution Avenue, Fritts hailed a taxi. When he got to State, he took the elevator straight to the seventh floor, checked in with the guard at the door of the Operations Center, and made his way down a narrow corridor to the task force room. There were two clocks on the wall. The hands of the one set to Washington time read 2:15 P.M., the one to Khartoum time 9:15 P.M.

* * *

By 9:15 on the evening of Thursday, March 1, the scene at the embassy of Saudi Arabia in Khartoum had assumed a new shape, one that it was to hold for some days to come. A little more than two hours after the storming of Ambassador al-Malhouk's reception, the sleek, polished sedans of the diplomatic corps had vanished from the street in front. Hassan, the driver of the American ambassador, was still there waiting—he was to remain devotedly there throughout the ordeal—but his white Chevrolet had been moved to a distance, out of the line of any likely gunfire. Sudanese police were in place around the embassy, and Major General Mohammed al-Baghir Ahmad, vice-president of Sudan and minister of interior, had come to make his first on-the-spot survey.

Baghir's official car stood in the middle of the street in front of the Saudi embassy. From behind it Baghir and George Thompson, the U.S. embassy's public affairs officer, studied the building. Through a megaphone Baghir called out to the Black September gunmen, urging them to release the hostages and give themselves up.

Thompson had rushed to the scene to take charge of the embassy's dealings with the Sudanese, a task he had taken upon himself. A slender, lively, articulate man, Thompson had been a newspaper reporter in the 1950s before joining the U.S. Information Agency. He remained a reporter at heart. Shortly after reaching the Saudi embassy, Thompson scrambled atop the hood of a Sudanese police vehicle to look over the wall to see if any of the terrorists were in the garden. A Sudanese policeman hurriedly beckoned him down.

Thompson had covered the taking of hostages by a gunman in Philadelphia and had watched as the police skillfully brought in friends and relatives of the abductor and gradually talked him into giving himself up. So Thompson felt he knew something about situations like this, and he freely offered his advice to the Sudanese vice-president. Over the coming twenty-four hours, Thompson was to spend much of his time at the command post in front of the Saudi embassy.

General Baghir had come from an emergency cabinet meeting called by Nimeiry the moment the Sudanese president had learned of the seizure of the Saudi embassy. Nimeiry had reacted with astonishment and outrage. He was indignant over the Palestinians' ingratitude for what he had done for them in the past, and over their abuse of the hospitality he and his government had extended them. In September 1970 Nimeiry had flown to Amman to help hammer out the agreement between King Hussein and the PLO that saved the Palestinians from annihilation at the hands of the Jordanian army; and it was Nimeiry himself who had authorized diplomatic status for the PLO and Fatah missions in Khartoum. He was persuaded that the Black September action was aimed mainly at embarrassing him and his government just as they were preparing to celebrate, together with Emperor Haile Selassie, the first anniversary of the signing of the agreements that had brought the civil war in the south to a close. He was also persuaded that the hand of Colonel Muammar al-Qaddafi, once his friend but now, since the signing of the autonomy agreements a year earlier, his sworn enemy, was behind the Black September.

But the Sudanese president's anger and his feelings of betrayal were tempered by a large dose of caution. Like all Arab leaders, he had always wanted to be considered a champion of the Palestinian cause—there was, after all, no cause more sacred to the Arabs—even if his interests at times led him in other directions. He did not want a fight with the Palestinians now, and his first instinct, concurred in by his closest advisors, was that the Black September gunmen could be persuaded to release the hostages. Accordingly, Nimeiry rejected two contingency plans for military action put forward by the Sudanese army; one called for an attack on the Saudi embassy if shots were heard inside it, and the other proposed an assault at dawn the next morning. Fear of endangering the hostages was one reason for ruling out recourse to force, but the belief that avoidance of confrontation was simply the wiser course was of at least equal weight.

As though to underscore this, Nimeiry announced that he would carry on with plans for the celebration of the Juba agreements. This meant that the president of Sudan would leave Khartoum at the very moment that a foreign embassy had been seized and foreign diplomats lay under threat of death. Nimeiry canceled the state dinner planned for that evening but decided that the ceremonies scheduled to be held in Juba, the capital of the south, on March 2, would be maintained. Early that morning he and the emperor of Ethiopia flew to Juba.

Nimeiry left the affair at the Saudi embassy in the hands of General Baghir, and he designated the minister of health, Major Abdul Ghassim Mohammed Ibrahim, to assist Baghir. Nimeiry himself would stay in radio touch with Baghir, and if his presence was required in Khartoum, he told his aides, he would fly back immediately. His instruction to Baghir was to keep things as calm as possible and maintain the status quo. Force was not to be used.

Before leaving for Juba, Nimeiry tried unsuccessfully to put a phone call through to Yasser Arafat in Beirut. The PLO leader was nowhere to be found.

The decision not to use force was reflected in the deployment in front of the Saudi embassy. Throughout the night of March 1 and through most of the day of March 2, only four police cars and some twenty policemen were stationed there—not a contingent likely to instill fear in the hearts of the Black September gunmen. But the Sudanese went even further. In one of his early contacts with the gunmen, Baghir told them that force would not be used. On the morning of March 2, the Sudanese radio made it a matter of public record. "The government," Radio Omdurman announced, "is absolutely not inclined to overrun the embassy or take any action that would endanger the lives of the hostages or the members of the [Black September] organization. Only the usual guard is now posted at the embassy."[20]

The gunmen were being assured that they were in no danger.

* * *

Mohammed al-Baghir Ahmad was an imposing figure. He was a sturdy, thick-set man of about fifty, of medium height with fierce, piercing eyes and a rough-and-ready appearance. He spoke directly and to the point, and he bore himself with a personal dignity that commanded respect. Martial attributes aside, he was also a man of sophistication and of quick and keen intelligence. He was Nimeiry's most trusted and capable aide.

Before going from the cabinet meeting to the Saudi embassy, General Baghir had already spoken by phone with Rizk al-Qas, the "political leader" of the Black September team and the one designated to handle contacts with the exterior. Al-Qas told Baghir that the gunmen were holding the U.S. ambassador, Cleo A. Noel, Jr., his deputy George Curtis Moore, Belgian Chargé d'Affaires Guy Eid, Jordanian Chargé d'Affaires Adli Nasser, and Saudi Ambassador Abdullah al-Malhouk. Al-Qas recited the Black September's demands—the release of Sirhan Sirhan, of Abu Daoud and other Palestinians held in Jordan, of Palestinian women imprisoned by Israel, and of the members of the Bader-Meinhoff gang in jail in West Germany. He announced a deadline for

[20]Omdurman domestic service, 0935 local, March 2, 1973; *Washington Post*, March 4, 1973.

later the same night—2:00 A.M. March 2—for fulfillment of these demands. If they were not met by then, al-Qas said, the two Americans and the Belgian would be killed.

But why, Baghir asked, was the Belgian, Guy Eid, being held? What did the Black September have against Belgium?

"Eid," al-Qas replied, "is a Jew and a spy for Israel."

Notwithstanding the government's assurances that force would not be used, al-Qas added a warning: the Black September team had wired the Saudi embassy with explosives. Any attempt to storm it would cause the structure to be demolished, and all those inside—not only the hostages but the Saudi ambassador's wife and her children—would be killed.

But during the course of the night of March 1 and the next morning, there were encouraging developments. Al-Qas asked for a doctor to be sent into the embassy to treat the hostages' wounds. This raised hope that the 2:00 A.M. deadline, at least, was not serious, for it made no sense to think that the gunmen would seek medical attention for the three men if they intended to kill them only a few hours later. At around 10:00 P.M. a Sudanese army doctor was admitted to the embassy. He dressed Eid's and Noel's wounds and gave them and Moore medication for the pain they were suffering. He came out and offered a reassuring report: the condition of the prisoners was good, and none of their wounds was life-threatening. Moore, the doctor reported, had only a minor contusion near his right cheekbone where he had been struck by a pistol or rifle butt. Both Noel's and Eid's wounds were minor, the doctor asserted. The American ambassador, he added, was reposing comfortably in a chair. The gunmen were "ferocious-looking," the doctor said, but they were also "humanitarianly inclined" toward their prisoners. They were in good spirits and confident that President Nixon would order King Hussein to release Abu Daoud and the others whose freedom they were seeking.

The doctor brought out a reassuring message from the gunmen for Mrs. Noel: "We have nothing against your husband. He is alright, but our cause is just and we will stay until our demands are fulfilled."[21]

Soon afterwards there was more good news. When General Baghir objected that the 2:00 A.M. deadline was unrealistic, that much more

[21]State secret telegram DTG 020328Z Mar 73.

time would be needed to contact those who held the prisoners the Black September wanted freed, the gunmen relented and set a new deadline of 4:00 A.M.

About fifteen minutes before the expiration of the 4:00 A.M. deadline, Minister of Health Ibrahim went to the Saudi embassy, was admitted, and spent over an hour talking with the gunmen. When he emerged, he advised that the gunmen had dropped all their demands except the one for the freeing of Abu Daoud and other prisoners held in Jordan, and they had agreed to another extension of the deadline, until 8:00 A.M.

Soon there was more encouragement. The story as written later by Western reporters was that a Sudanese woman doctor, Saida Abu Aboueila, a friend of the wife of the Saudi ambassador, had marched courageously into the Saudi residence and upbraided the Black September gunmen for holding Mrs. al-Malhouk and her children. The gunmen, overawed at the boldness of this woman, allowed her to take out the Saudi ambassador's wife and her five children, after which Mrs. al-Malhouk returned to be with her husband.

The truth of this episode, according to one who knew Saida Abu Aboueila well, was far more prosaic. She did not go to the Saudi embassy but only telephoned there. She did not demand the release of Mrs. al-Malhouk and her children; she pleaded for it. She did have a medical degree, but she was known less as a physician than as a society hostess, the mildly alcoholic wife of a wealthy Sudanese businessman. She told her friends of her call to the gunmen in the Saudi embassy, but later, when she saw the press stories, she preferred the media's more heroic version of the event and made it her own. For years afterwards, until she died in the mid-1980s, it became her claim to fame.

However it may be, the gunmen did release the Saudi ambassador's children, and they offered to let Mrs. al-Malhouk go, too, but she insisted on staying with her husband.

All this brought a sigh of relief at the American embassy. Maybe the Black September gunmen were not so bad after all, one staff member ventured; perhaps the whole thing was just a bluff. Hopes for a happy outcome mounted.

If others were cheered by these developments, Sam Peale was not. No one in the Khartoum embassy was closer to Curt Moore than Peale. Of Curt, Sam was later to write that he was "a true and close friend and would have remained so throughout life." Cleo Noel was a much newer acquaintance, but he was, Sam felt, "the epitome of a good man, a gentleman in the truest literal sense of the word." But Sam had concluded that Curt and Cleo were almost certainly going to die.

Two things led Sam Peale to this conclusion. The first was what had happened in Bangkok the previous December, when a Black September team had seized the Israeli embassy and then, when the Israeli government refused to meet their demands, freed the Israeli diplomats they held—let them go unharmed—in return for safe passage out of Thailand. Bangkok, Peale reasoned, was not an example that offered salvation. It was a Black September failure. Sam was sure that it would not be allowed to happen again, for if it did, the Black September would lose all credibility. If this time the Black September's demands were not met—perhaps not all its demands, but the essential ones—the gunmen would die rather than release their hostages. And before dying, the gunmen would kill the hostages.

The second was the cable that the embassy had received from Washington that evening, which decidedly contradicted the Black September gunmen's confidence that the United States would order King Hussein to free Abu Daoud. The cable set out the policy guidance to which Armin Meyer had theretofore been unable to get any top official of the State Department to put his name. It instructed the embassy to inform the government of Sudan that it was U.S. policy not to negotiate with hostage-takers and not to make any concessions to them. This was the first time the policy of no negotiations, no deals, and no concessions had been stated in an officially approved document. Intellectually, Peale was persuaded that there was no other answer to the problem of terrorism—"to give in once," he later wrote, "is only to ask for more"—but he realized also that it sealed Curt's and Cleo's fate.

Peale spent the night in the embassy, but he did not sleep at all. Among the many calls that came in that night—the phone rang constantly—was one he would never forget. At one o'clock Curt Moore called, and Sam took the call. Curt told Sam straight away and in a firm voice that his words would not be his own, that what he was about to say had been dictated to him by his captors. He had been told to report the specific details of the demands the Black September group was making. Curt then read off the text of the Black September's communiqué. It demanded the release of Abu Daoud and "his sixteen companions" held by Jordan, two Jordanian army officers imprisoned for collaboration with the PLO, Rifai al-Hindawi and Muhammad al-Khalili, "and all the military people who are kept in Jordan's prisons," together with another fifty fedayeen held by Jordan, and Sirhan Sirhan, whom the gunmen said must be released "quickly"; and then "our imprisoned sisters from the Zionist fascist prisons" in Israel. Peale could hear voices shouting in Arabic in the background.

The release of members of the Bader-Meinhoff gang had disappeared from the list of demands once the gunmen discovered that they had failed to snare the West German ambassador. The change was significant. It suggested a measure of realism on the part of the Black September; it also suggested that they had not seized the two Americans only as a publicity stunt or to kill them. They were in earnest in wanting to make a deal: the lives of their hostages in return for the release of Palestinians held in jail.

Curt gave Sam the same message the Sudanese doctor later brought out of the embassy: the Black September was sure that President Nixon could order King Hussein to release the prisoners in Jordan. "The Black September members here," Moore continued, "are determined to sacrifice themselves and refuse any semi-solutions. The demands must be carried out. The gentleman [evidently a reference to Rizk al-Qas] says I am to tell you that the demands are just and we want our government to do its best to press Hussein to obey these conditions before we lose our lives. I am also to tell you that the Saudi embassy is completely rigged with explosives."[22]

With that, the message ended and the line went dead.

* * *

Cleo Noel's choice of Bob Fritts to be his new deputy chief of mission was an act of faith in the Department of State's personnel system, one that said a good deal about Noel himself. In his last year in Washington before going out to Khartoum, Noel had been deputy director general of the Foreign Service, the second-ranking official in charge of the department's personnel system. In his years in Washington, Noel had made his way up the ladder not in the regional bureaus that handled America's relations with the rest of the world but in the personnel system. Until that time, most Foreign Service officers who got ambassadorial appointments won them on the basis of their work in the

[22]State secret telegram DTG 020326Z Mar 73.

regional bureaus, which were considered to be the ideal training ground for ambassadors. But after Bill Macomber became deputy under secretary in 1969, he decreed that senior officers working in administrative jobs were to be given preference for ambassadorial appointments. Macomber thought that ambassadors should not just be area specialists; they should be good administrators and managers as well. He also wanted to get competent people to agree to take jobs in administration. A good way to do it, he calculated, was to offer them the prize of an embassy. So Macomber, indirectly at least, had a hand in Cleo Noel's appointment as ambassador to the Sudan.

But Noel did not have to be enticed into personnel work by the prospect of an ambassadorship. He loved it, and he believed in the State Department's personnel system. When it came time for him to choose a deputy chief of mission, he did not look for someone he knew or had worked with earlier, as most ambassadors did. Instead, he called for the files of the half-dozen very best, top-ranked officers on the threshold between the middle and senior grades. Fritts was an East Asian specialist. He had trained in Japanese and had served in Japan and then in Indonesia. He knew no Arabic and had never worked in or on Africa or the Middle East. In Noel's view, that was less important than ability. Noel had never met or even heard of Fritts before, but he was very impressed by what he read in Fritts's file. For Noel, the notion of personal chemistry, the idea that two people might not work well together because their personalities did not mesh with one another, simply did not exist. The State Department's personnel system was built on the theory that everything one needed to know about an individual could be reduced to a piece of paper, and Cleo Noel was a part of that system. If the files said an officer was qualified, that was enough for him.

*　*　*

It was five o'clock that afternoon in Washington, midnight Khartoum time, before the issue of Macomber's flying to Khartoum was finally resolved. Four hours, four very precious hours, had passed since first word of Curt Moore's and Cleo Noel's capture was received in the U.S. capital.

But the decision to go was one thing; obtaining the means, quite another. One of the first things Macomber did after learning of the seizure of Moore and Noel was ask that the air force be alerted that he might need a plane. But there were no contingency arrangements for flying people, even senior officials, around the world to the scene of kidnappings. The United States Air Force was a separate branch of the government. It was not in the habit of snapping to upon request from deputy under secretaries at the State Department, even insistent ones. Macomber shouted at the air force. When that failed to have the desired effect, when it in fact seemed to cause the air force to dig in its heels rather than comply, he turned to his White House connections.

After he and the others returned from the meeting with Acting Secretary Rush, Macomber quickly began drawing up a list of the people he wanted to take with him. First on his list was Marvin Gentile, the head of the State Department's security unit. Gentile was also a sharp-shooter, and Macomber thought there might be a need for his skills in that area. (In this he turned out to be quite wrong; what he really needed, he was soon to discover, was someone with much more prosaic skills: a secretary to take dictation and type cables.) Curtis Jones, the director of the department's Office of Research for Near Eastern Affairs, volunteered and was enlisted; Jones had worked alongside Curt Moore in NE for two years in the mid-1960s. He and Moore both lived in Bethesda, and they had shared a carpool. Jones spoke Arabic and knew just about everything there was to know about the Arab world. Tom Scotes, another Arabist, was enrolled, along with Alan Bergstrom, a slender, handsome young man who had worked for Moore during those first two difficult years in Khartoum and who was now the department's research analyst for the Sudan. He was the junior officer of the group but the one who knew the most about the Sudan.

Fritts saw that the list was being completed, but that in the haste and confusion he was being forgotten. He decided that he must insert himself. "Look," he said, "I am assigned to Khartoum as DCM. I must go on that plane." Macomber readily assented.

Everyone was given forty-five minutes to pack a bag and report to the carpool station in the basement of the Department of State for transpor-tation to nearby Andrews Air Force Base in Maryland. Fritts was staying at quarters just a block away from the department. He rushed to his room and threw as much as he could into a single garment bag. Fritts called his brother, who lived in Washington, and asked him to come later in the day and pack the rest of his things and pay his bill. Other members of the team lived too far away to make it home and back in a mere forty-five minutes. Tom Scotes and Alan Bergstrom went to a drug store across the way, where each bought himself a set of toilet articles.

The party sped out the Suitland Parkway to Andrews, only to find that there was no plane awaiting it. The only aircraft there and ready to fly was a Boeing 707 Presidential Airborne Command Post, a plane kept constantly on standby and slated exclusively for use by the president in time of nuclear war. Macomber was furious. He got on the phone to the White House, and within less than half an hour he and his party were boarding the plane that was supposed to be used only to speed the president and the most senior officials of the U.S. government aloft to escape nuclear annihilation. It would have been the perfect craft to take them to Khartoum, for it was packed with the most sophisticated communications equipment—from its consoles a president could order into action the entire nuclear retaliatory force of the United States—and had comfortable executive quarters. But the air force was not about to let it fly to the Sudan. Instead, the plane circled out over the Atlantic, dumped the greater part of the full tank of fuel that it always kept aboard, and landed some twenty minutes later at an air base in New Jersey. There Macomber and his group changed to another craft that had been hastily ordered to fuel up to carry them across the Atlantic to Europe and on to Africa.

It was a C-141, a military jet transport plane that belonged to the U.S. Air Force Military Air Command. Its ordinary function was to fly soldiers and their equipment to faraway destinations. It had a large carrying capacity but was relatively slow, and it could not make the trip to Khartoum nonstop. It would require refueling in Europe, which meant the trip would take longer than the anticipated fourteen hours. Also, the plane had no windows and no evident acoustic insulation. Once in flight, the noise inside was overpowering. It was so loud that Macomber and the members of his party found it almost impossible to hold any kind of conversation. They tried everything. They stood in the center of the plane, in a circle, bent over with their heads crowded together, shouting at one another. Even with this it was so hard to make themselves understood that they soon gave up trying.

But the main handicap was the plane's lack of classified communications equipment. It had open-channel radio communication with the Military Air Command network, which could patch it through to State for voice communications. But it could not receive or send cables or hook up directly with the State Department. This meant that while he was in the air, Macomber could not keep abreast of developments in Khartoum. He was cut off from all but the most summary information.

It was not until 8:00 P.M. March 1 on the East Coast of the United States (3:00 A.M. March 2 Khartoum time) that the C-141 carrying Macomber and his team took off from the air base in New Jersey. Seven hours had now elapsed since first word was received of the seizure of the two American diplomats in Khartoum. Macomber's mission in flying to the Sudanese capital, as he himself saw it, and as it had been approved by President Richard Nixon and by Secretary of State William Rogers, whom Macomber had telephoned in Paris, was "to observe and assist in efforts to free the prisoners." That and only that. He was not going to negotiate with the Black September gunmen. He carried with him no secret authorization to make or propose a deal, to trade Sirhan Sirhan or Palestinians in jail in Jordan or the Israeli occupied territories for the lives of the two Americans.

At one point while the team was trying to confer over the din of the C-141's engines, Curt Jones understood Macomber to say something that suggested the administration might go for a deal in order to save Moore and Noel. Jones could not give up hope that if all else failed, a deal might be made; it was unfair, plain wrong, he felt, to sacrifice the life of his friend Curt Moore and his colleague Cleo Noel for a matter of abstract principle. So Jones picked up immediately on the opening he believed had been given him. He pointed out that the only Black September demand that was really serious was the one calling for the release of Abu Daoud and a few other Palestinians in jail in Jordan; all the others were so much window dressing. If King Hussein could be gotten to agree to it, a deal would not be hard to make.

Macomber instantly bristled. There was to be no negotiating and no deal, he shot back, not even any talk of negotiating or of a deal.

But Bill Macomber did not consider that "no negotiations" with terrorists meant no contact with them, or that "no deals" meant no talking with them. Much to the contrary, he felt it essential to make contact as soon as possible, albeit through the intermediary of others if at all possible, and to talk and talk and talk with them. Their demands should not be rejected outright; never should that be done, he felt. The proper tactic was to delay, to drag things out, and it was legitimate to use obfuscation or even ruses if doing so would advance that tactic. For the basic objective was to give the terrorists time to cool down, and after that to wear them down. All the studies, Macomber knew, showed that when terrorists first attacked, they were charged up and ready to die for their cause. After a while, however, they would look out the window and see the police and the army and begin to think about saving their own skins. That was the stage you wanted to get to.

Terrorists always set deadlines for the meeting of their demands. The whole art of dealing with them, Macomber felt, was to get them to break those deadlines. Once they did this, their determination would begin to wane, and they would be ripe for the only kind of deal the policy did not bar, the kind of deal that had been made in Bangkok: guaranteed safe passage for the terrorists to a country of their choice in exchange for freedom for the hostages. It was to the Bangkok solution that Bill Macomber and Armin Meyer looked for salvation. Bangkok showed that a Black September team could be broken, could be brought to the point of exhaustion and despair, where it would simply give up and go. And if a team of Black September killers could be persuaded to release a half-dozen Israelis, as they had done in Bangkok, why should it be impossible to get the gunmen in Khartoum to release two Americans and a Belgian? Bangkok was the model, the goal. It was the rallying cry.

*　*　*

The C-141 roared deafeningly across the Atlantic through the night, headed for Rhein Main Air Force Base at Weisbaden, Germany, where it would refuel. The flight took almost eight hours. It was just past 9:30 A.M. Frankfurt time, 10:30 A.M. in Khartoum, when it touched down. Robert H. Harlan, the U.S. consul general in Frankfurt, was at the air base waiting for Macomber with the latest cables from Khartoum and from Washington. Macomber read the cables but, Fritts noted with chagrin, did not share them with the members of his party.

Whatever the reason for this, the cables did bring good news. The terrorists had already broken three deadlines, the initial one set for 2:00 A.M. Khartoum time, a subsequent one of 4:00 A.M., and yet another of 8:00 A.M. These were three deadlines past which the gunmen had said they would execute the hostages, but the hostages remained alive. The Bangkok tactic appeared to be working.

But there was an important element of the Bangkok model that was missing in Khartoum, and Macomber was either unaware of this or did not grasp its significance. The government of Thailand had massed an intimidating show of force around the Israeli embassy. All the Black September gunmen had to do to realize that their lives were in danger was look out the window. This imposing military presence kept them on edge, and the Thai authorities did nothing to mitigate their fears that the embassy might be stormed at any moment. In Khartoum, this important psychological pressure was almost wholly absent. Far from making the Black September gunmen fear for their lives, the Sudanese seemed to be doing everything they could to reassure them: they had broadcast a statement promising that the embassy would not be stormed, and they had put only a token force at the embassy, one too small and too lightly armed to be intimidating.

These steps were taken in the name of avoiding provocation of the gunmen, who, it was said, might otherwise become nervous and kill their hostages—though avoidance of an open break with the Palestinians was surely also an important consideration for the Sudanese government. That giving assurances that no force would be used might also have the effect of making the gunmen bolder and less fearful of doing violence to their hostages appears never to have been considered. No one on the American side, it seems, ever questioned the wisdom of the Sudanese moves. Neither did any American official question Nimeiry's decision to absent himself from Khartoum following the seizure of the Saudi embassy, though it too could be seen as offering the kidnappers reassurance that forceful action would not be taken against them. U.S. policy dictated that saving hostages was the responsibility of the host government. So long as the host government seemed to be shouldering that responsibility in good faith, the Americans were not going to second-guess it.

And clearly the Sudanese were shouldering their responsibilities. General Baghir had proven himself to be reassuringly skillful in dealing with the gunmen. His tactic was exactly the one advocated by the Americans: drag out the talks, wear the Black September team down, and get them to break their deadlines, one after the other. Baghir's colleague Major Abdul Ghassim Ibrahim, the minister of health, was also impressive. He had shown much courage in going into the Saudi embassy to meet with the gunmen in the early morning of March 2. As a result of that meeting, the gunmen had extended their deadline once more and had let it be known that they were ready to drop all their demands except the release of Abu Daoud and others held in Jordan. These were important and encouraging accomplishments.

But there was an ominous side as well to the report that Major Ibrahim brought out with him from his talks with the Black September gunmen. The gunmen were quite determined, Ibrahim warned. He implored the Americans to press the Jordanians to accede to the Black September's demand for the freeing of Abu Daoud and his associates. Otherwise, he said, he had no doubt whatsoever that the gunmen would kill their three hostages.

For the Sudanese, the whole affair could not have been more frustrating. Terrorists were holding hostages in their capital and threatening to kill them unless their demands were met. Yet it was not in the power of the government of Sudan to grant any of the terrorists' demands; all were addressed to other governments, and the others showed no disposition to meet them. So if the Sudanese could not solve the problem themselves, why not export it?

In their early morning March 2 meeting with Major Ibrahim, the gunmen proposed to fly with their hostages to the United States if the government of Sudan would send along with them its ministers of foreign affairs and information. The proposal had ominous overtones (later the gunmen were to say their intention had been to kill Moore, Noel, and Eid in the United States if their demands were not satisfied, and then use the two Sudanese ministers to ensure their escape—a scheme vaguely reminiscent of the Sabena hijacking to Tel Aviv), and Baghir never seriously considered it. But it did give him an idea.

Would the United States agree to the terrorists' flying to Libya or Algeria with the hostages and releasing them there? Baghir asked George Thompson. If the Black September gunmen accepted this idea, Baghir said, he and the minister of health, Major Ibrahim (not the ministers of foreign affairs and information, whose names were associated with Sudan's restoration of relations with the United States and who had been sharply criticized for it by the Palestinians), would offer themselves as additional hostages. Thompson enthusiastically passed the idea back to the U.S. embassy, which cabled it to Washington.

The proposal to fly captors and captives out to an Arab capital was Baghir's idea alone. It had not been suggested by or, at that stage, even discussed with the Black September gunmen in the Saudi embassy. Still, it seemed possibly another indication that the will of the terrorists was weakening. With Macomber's approval, Armin Meyer in Washington fired off a message to the embassy in Khartoum instructing it to tell Baghir that the United States would agree to letting the terrorists fly out with the hostages, provided the destination was Egypt or Algeria, but not Libya.

It was the morning of March 2. Some sixteen hours had elapsed since the seizure of the hostages. With each new development, hope for their rescue was rising.

Then things began to go wrong.

14

Things Go Wrong

In fact, things had begun to go wrong even before the break of day on March 2.

It was in Amman, the capital of Jordan, that things first began to go wrong. When word arrived there that Moore, Noel, and Eid had been seized in Khartoum, and that the Black September was demanding the release of Abu Daoud and others being held in Jordanian prisons, King Hussein ibn Talal was out of the country. He had been in the United States, where he met with President Nixon early in February and then went on to Florida for vacation. On the morning of March 1 he took off from Miami, and at the moment of the event in Khartoum his plane was nearing Morocco, where he was to spend the next few days as a guest of his fellow monarch King Hassan.

In charge in Amman was Hussein's younger brother, Crown Prince Hassan ibn Talal. Some thought of Prince Hassan as a hard-liner, others as a young man of excessively trenchant views and frequently impulsive judgment. Hassan reacted immediately to the news from Khartoum, evidently without consulting his brother. He first tried to place a call to President Nimeiry. When the connection could not be made, he ordered the Foreign Ministry to send a cable to the government of Sudan to advise that under no circumstances would Jordan release any of the prisoners the Black September was demanding as the price for the lives of Moore, Noel, and Eid. The telegram was sent in the late evening of

March 1 but did not reach its destination until some twelve hours later, for Khartoum's telegraph office was closed for the night and did not open until 10:00 the next morning. In the meantime, either on Hassan's order or inadvertently, the text of the cable was broadcast over Jordanian radio. The broadcast was made just after 7:00 A.M. March 2, and the statement was tough and unyielding: "The government of His Hashemite Majesty will accept no bargaining with these criminals and will not under any condition allow any pressure or threat to achieve the aims of those exerting pressure or making threats."[23]

The Jordanian statement was the first public rejection by any government of the Black September's demands. When Armin Meyer cabled the U.S. embassy in Khartoum on the evening of March 1 to inform it of the no-concessions policy, he instructed the embassy to pass word of it to General Baghir, but to caution Baghir not to reveal it to the Black September gunmen. Even without this American word of caution, Baghir almost certainly would not have confronted the gunmen with the American refusal. To do so would have been at odds with his strategy of stringing things out and trying to wear the men down, which was also Macomber's and Meyer's tactic.

Washington either failed to take the same precaution with the Jordanians, or the message did not get through in time or was ignored by Crown Prince Hassan. Whatever the case, the Jordanian radio announcement badly undercut the joint U.S.-Sudanese strategy of trying to wait out the terrorists.

Amman was also the site of a second glitch, this one the result of an act of nature. Through much of the night of March 1, those on the task force in Washington groped for some means to oblige the Black September to abort its threat against the lives of Moore, Noel, and Eid. The officers on the task force had all served in the Middle East, and they all felt that only a policy of "an eye for an eye" would offer effective leverage. The United States could not be in the position of asking another government to put innocent people to death, but Abu Daoud and several of his co-conspirators had already been sentenced to death by a Jordanian court; all that stood between them and execution was King Hussein's approval for the sentences.

[23]Central Intelligence Agency transcript of Amman Domestic Service broadcast, 7:18 A.M., March 2, 1973.

Early on the morning of March 2, Armin Meyer ordered a call placed over the department's secure telephone network to Ambassador L. Dean Brown in Amman. Meyer was going to ask Brown to see if he could get the government of Jordan to announce that in the event any of the hostages in Khartoum were killed, Abu Daoud and others the Black September wanted freed would be executed. Meyer's call never went through. During the night of March 1 to 2, a heavy snowfall, a freakish occurrence in Amman, knocked the U.S. embassy's satellite communications equipment out of working order for the next twenty-four hours, making both voice and cable contact impossible.

Frustrated at this turn, Meyer authorized the U.S. embassy in Khartoum to suggest to Baghir, for the ears of the Black September gunmen inside the Saudi embassy, that if violence were done to the hostages, it could lead to the execution of Abu Daoud and others in jail in Amman whose freedom they sought. But without the public endorsement of the government of Jordan, the threat had no force.

The next thing to go wrong went wrong in Frankfurt. Macomber's C-141 developed engine trouble. The problem was minor, but takeoff was delayed for two hours. Macomber was in a rage; precious time was being lost. Meanwhile, other complications arose. General Baghir did not want the C-141 to land at Khartoum airport. The airport runway was in full view of the Saudi embassy. The gunmen would see the C-141 as it landed, and Baghir feared they would imagine that this large American military transport plane was carrying not half a dozen diplomats come to work behind the scenes to save the hostages but a contingent of troops to storm the Saudi embassy to free them. They might panic and kill the hostages. So to come into Khartoum, Macomber would have to switch to another plane, and this meant that he would have to land at some intermediate point.

State asked the U.S. interests section in Cairo to obtain overflight and landing clearance for Macomber's C-141 in Egypt. No answer came, so a cable was sent to the American embassy in Jidda asking for clearance for the C-141 to land there and for arrangements to be made for Macomber to proceed to Khartoum on a Saudi plane. The Saudis assented immediately, but Jidda was out of the way; making a connection there would delay Macomber's arrival in Khartoum. Cairo was by far preferable, and the Sudanese were offering to put Macomber and the members of his team on the scheduled flight of a Sudanese Airways plane from Cairo to Khartoum that afternoon. They would delay the flight's departure until Macomber reached Cairo.

Armin Meyer got on the telephone to Jerry Greene, the head of the Cairo interests section. Greene, Meyer learned, was having trouble persuading the Egyptian foreign minister, Mohamed Hassan al-Zayyat, to agree to let Macomber land in Cairo. Dealing with Zayyat could be frustrating under the best of circumstances. He was a difficult, mercurial individual, and he was personally reluctant to involve Egypt in the Khartoum affair. The request for permission for Macomber to come into Cairo had to go to President Anwar Sadat for decision.

If the Khartoum hostages were to be saved, Egypt's help would be critical. In Bangkok, despite the fact that those seized were Israelis and that Egypt and Israel were in a declared state of war with one another, the Egyptians had played a key role—really the major role—in averting a blood bath. The Egyptian ambassador in Bangkok had handled the negotiations that ended with the Black September gunmen's freeing the Israeli hostages, and President Sadat had offered Egypt as safe haven for the Palestinian gunmen. Would the Egyptians do less to save the lives of two Americans and a European than they had for six Israelis?

But at the beginning of March 1973, Sadat was at the tail end of a protracted effort to entice the Nixon administration into making a really serious try at breaking the deadlock in negotiations between Egypt and Israel and bringing about Israel's withdrawal from Sinai. Just two weeks earlier Sadat had sent his top aide, Hafez Ismail, to Washington for talks with Henry Kissinger. Ismail had come away with the feeling that the Americans were still stalling and still essentially backing the Israeli position. Disappointment over the outcome of Hafez Ismail's mission was to turn Sadat once and for all down the road to war, the road he had for the previous two years been proclaiming himself ready to take but that he had desperately wanted to avoid. It was from that moment that he gave the order to proceed with plans that were to culminate in the launching of the surprise Egyptian and Syrian attacks on Israel on the Jewish holy day of Yom Kippur, October 6, 1973.

So Sadat was not ready to make the kind of all-out effort required to get the Palestinians to call off the Khartoum operation. Neither, however, did he wish to be seen as condoning an act of terrorism. With a great show of reluctance, Zayyat informed Greene that Macomber would be permitted to land in Cairo, and that his government agreed to having the Black September gunmen and the hostages flown there as well. Zayyat cautioned that Egypt could offer no guarantees for the release of the hostages once they reached Cairo, or even for their safety there. Zayyat's caveat notwithstanding, this was heartening news. Clearly the Egyptians would not have Moore, Noel, and Eid brought to Egypt only to be killed there; implicit in the offer was a commitment that Egypt would do its best to avoid a tragic ending.

But the move to Cairo was not to be, and confusion over it was to complicate the rescue effort even further. Zayyat's notification to Greene that the government of Egypt would allow the gunmen and the hostages to be brought to Cairo came at 5:00 P.M. Cairo and Khartoum time—10:00 A.M. Washington time. By then, however, all prospect for it had long since vanished. Some three hours earlier, General Baghir had raised the idea with the Black September gunmen and they had turned him down. He had told this to the American embassy in Khartoum, and the embassy had transmitted the information to the task force in Washington via the telecon channel, in a message logged in at the State Department's Operations Center at 7:31 A.M. Washington time, 2:31 P.M. Cairo and Khartoum time.

The interests section in Cairo, however, was wholly unaware of this latest development in Khartoum. A little before 6:00 P.M., as he was leaving for the airport to meet Macomber, Greene sent off a cable to Washington reporting that the Egyptians had conveyed to the Sudanese their agreement to transferring the gunmen and hostages to Cairo but had no answer yet from Khartoum. The problem was that cables in the telecon channel went only to the task force in Washington. The Khartoum embassy was too overburdened to go through the more cumbersome process of putting its messages in the regular State Department communications channel. It had to rely on the task force in Washington to do that. To get Khartoum's message to Cairo, the task force had to retype the telecon message on the regulation green telegram form and send it to the communications center for retransmission. In most cases this was done promptly, but Khartoum's telecon message reporting the Black September's rejection of Baghir's proposal languished for almost four and a half hours before being retransmitted to Cairo. The task force cable conveying it was logged out at the State Department's communications center at 1700 hours GMT (7:00 P.M. Cairo and Khartoum time). No explanation for this delay was ever sought or given.

So when Jerry Greene met Macomber's plane at Cairo airport after it landed there at 6:30 P.M. local time March 2, he had every reason to believe that a change of venue was imminent, that the kidnappers and the hostages were about to move to the Egyptian capital.

Macomber's C-141, its engine trouble resolved, had taken off from Rhein Main just before noon local time. At the moment of takeoff, Macomber had not known whether he was going to Cairo or to Jidda. He was airborne for a little over an hour when he learned that the Egyptians had cleared him for landing in Cairo. In Frankfurt he had learned of Baghir's proposal. News of the Egyptian clearance led him to assume that it had been accepted by the Black September and that the scene of the action was about to shift from Khartoum to Cairo.

A large crew of newsmen were at Cairo airport to welcome the American deputy under secretary of state, in the hope—vain, as it turned out—that they could extract some statement from him. But Macomber was not saying anything. He and Greene had a hard time finding a place in the airport where they could talk without being overheard by the reporters who crowded insistently around them. Once they had conferred, however, Macomber realized he would have to make a quick call on whether to proceed to Khartoum or stay in Cairo. The Sudan Airways jetliner that had been kept waiting for him and his party was poised for takeoff. But everything Macomber learned from Greene seemed to argue for staying in Cairo. There was no word on how soon the Black September team and its hostages would transfer to Cairo, but the Sudan Airways flight to Khartoum might very well cross paths, without his even knowing it, with a plane carrying them in the opposite direction. If this happened, Macomber would arrive in Khartoum having left his C-141 in Cairo, and with no way of getting quickly back to the Egyptian capital.

So Macomber made his decision: he, Gentile, Jones, and Scotes would stay in Cairo to await the arrival of the terrorists and the hostages. Fritts would not be needed for the job that would face them in Cairo. He would proceed immediately to Khartoum on the Sudan Airways flight, to take charge of the embassy there. Bergstrom, the expert on the Sudan, would not be needed either. He would go with Fritts.

Fritts and Bergstrom proceeded to board the Sudan Airways flight. Macomber and Greene and the rest of the group piled into cars and drove through sparse traffic (Egypt was still at war with Israel, and even though there was no fighting, austerity remained very much in force) to the heart of Cairo, to the stately old American embassy compound just off Tahrir Square that had formerly been the U.S. embassy and now housed the U.S. interests section. Before leaving the airport, Greene dismissed the crew of the C-141. They needed a rest, and he was sure that their services would not again be required for some time.

State's cable advising of the Black September's turndown of the move to Cairo had just been put on Greene's desk at the interests section when he, Macomber, and the others arrived there.

15

"We Will Not Pay Blackmail"

Sam Peale and others in the Khartoum embassy were dumbfounded when they learned that Macomber had deplaned in Cairo in the expectation that the terrorists and the hostages would arrive there shortly. They could not understand how Macomber, or Jerry Greene in Cairo, could be unaware that they had, hours earlier, informed Washington that the Black September gunmen had turned down Baghir's proposal.

No one in the Khartoum embassy had slept the previous night. The tension was excruciating, and nerves were badly frayed. So when they learned that Macomber had stopped in Cairo, they fired off an angry, irreverent cable. "We screamed loudly, profanely and with limited respect," Peale was to write later. Afterwards Peale and others were to consider the Macomber mission utterly useless, even worse than useless, but at the time they were ready to grasp at any straw. They hoped desperately that Macomber might be bringing something that could save Moore, Noel, and Eid from tragedy, that his mere presence in Khartoum might win them a reprieve. So they implored him to proceed to Khartoum as quickly as possible.

By the afternoon of March 2, what optimism there had been was quickly draining away. The situation was beginning to look grim. At just after 4:00 P.M. General Baghir briefed the Americans on his latest talks with the gunmen. They had extended their deadline to 8:00 P.M. But otherwise Baghir found them rigid in their position. They had reiterated their demand for the release from jail in Jordan of Abu Daoud and Rifai Hindawi and a group of other Palestinian prisoners, and they had said the 8:00 deadline would be the last one. If it was not met, they said, they would kill the hostages.

Baghir pointed out to the Americans that this was the first time the gunmen had described a deadline as final. He had no doubt about the seriousness of their intentions. But he said he would be speaking with them again soon, and he still thought he could persuade them to break the 8:00 P.M. deadline.

If Baghir's report offered scant encouragement, the word from Saudi Arabia was hardly more promising. Soon after the seizure of the diplomats in Khartoum, the State Department had sent an urgent instruction to Ambassador Nicholas Thacher in Jidda: press King Faisal to get the Palestinians to call off the Black September operation. The Saudis, however, were incapable of acting either quickly or forcefully. It was not until the afternoon of March 2 that Thacher got a reply, and when it came it was a disappointment. The requested effort was being made, Minister of State for Foreign Affairs Omar Saqqaf told the American ambassador. But, Saqqaf added plaintively, his government did not have that much influence with the Palestinians. The Americans, he said, should not expect much of the Saudi effort.

Saqqaf's reply did not come as a surprise, for the Saudis had the reputation in Washington of having no backbone. They gave the PLO huge subsidies, and some of their money went directly to the Black September. But they were scared of the Black September and unwilling to threaten a cutoff of funds.

* * *

As night fell over Khartoum, it came more quickly and more darkly than expected. The reason was something quite extraordinary for the season: a haboob—a sandstorm—was beginning to envelop the Sudanese capital. It astounded everyone, for a haboob in the early months of the year was almost unheard of, really a freak happening. And this haboob was a particularly virulent one. The dust was thick and heavy. At watch outside the Saudi embassy with General Baghir, George Thompson put his handkerchief over his mouth and nose but found that it hardly helped; the dust clogged his nose and seared his lungs. It also blotted out visibility for more than a dozen yards. Years later Thompson, Joan Peale, Tim Wells, and Ed Brawn were all to remember the haboob and to recall that even at the time it had struck them with a sense of foreboding, had seemed an omen of tragedy to come.

Joan drove through the haboob that evening to the ambassador's residence to be with Sally Moore and Lucille Noel. Sally had gone there soon after she got news of Curt's and Cleo's seizure, to wait together with Lucille. The two women did not talk a great deal; they sat silently, hoping and praying. Neither cried or spoke emotionally. Outwardly, they remained entirely composed. They were, they felt, behaving as their husbands would want them to behave. Joan marveled at their composure. She wanted to be a comforting presence for them. She had two small children and could not be away from them for long periods, but she had shuttled back and forth between her home and the residence, spending as much of the previous twenty-four hours as she could with the two women.

* * *

Ambassador Armin Meyer did not go home the night of March 1. He stayed in the Operations Center at the State Department and slept for a few hours on a narrow bed in a small room down a corridor from the task force room, an amenity provided for the use of personnel engaged in monitoring a crisis.

One of the messages received from Khartoum the next morning disturbed Meyer. It reported that General Baghir had told the Black September terrorists that a senior official of the United States government, William Macomber, was on his way to Khartoum, and that Macomber's trip showed that the Americans were serious in wanting a solution that would avoid bloodshed. Meyer felt the disclosure was premature. Baghir should have waited longer, he believed, until the terrorists were worn out and would be more interested in saving their own skins, before letting them know that Macomber was coming. But Meyer was also concerned that Baghir himself might be under some misapprehension as to the import of Macomber's trip. Meyer sent off a cable to the Khartoum embassy instructing it to reiterate to Baghir that Macomber was coming only to observe and assist, not to negotiate.

General Mohammed al-Baghir Ahmad had in fact already been told by American representatives in Khartoum that U.S. policy precluded concessions of any sort to terrorists. He was aware that Macomber would be coming only to observe and assist, that he was not bringing anything with him for the Black September. But by the afternoon of

March 2, Khartoum time, the Macomber mission was just about the only card Baghir had left. It was all well and good to talk about stringing things out and wearing the abductors down. It was a fine theory. But you needed more than just theory; you had to have something palpable to work with. There were no magic words to cast a spell over the Black September gunmen, and they were not morons. Terrorists too had read the terrorism experts' studies, and they knew that stringing them along and exhausting them was one of their opponents' prime tactics. Baghir could pretend only so many times, without losing all credibility with the Black September gunmen in the Saudi embassy, that he was trying to reach King Hussein to work something out but that communication was delayed because Hussein was in Rabat, or flying from Rabat to Marrakesh, or in the air on the way back to Amman.

The Sudanese themselves had nothing they could offer the Black September in return for the lives of the three Western hostages. Baghir's effort to export the problem to Egypt had failed. He and his colleagues continued to try to reach Arafat, to get him to call off the Black September operation. They tried also to contact King Hussein, to see if he would be willing to release Abu Daoud. Arafat remained unavailable, and Hussein's counselor Zaid al-Rifai, who was traveling with the Jordanian monarch, was unreceptive to Sudanese appeals.

So finally all General Baghir could do to gain time was to play the Macomber card. As Rizk al-Qas threatened to kill the Western hostages if he had no satisfaction by the 8:00 P.M. March 2 deadline, Baghir argued that he should await Macomber's arrival, to see what the American was bringing with him. Baghir evidently did not say outright that Macomber was coming to Khartoum to strike a deal, but he led al-Qas on and on in this hope—himself hoping in this way to gain time and prolong the lives of the three men under threat of death inside the Saudi embassy.

It was Baghir's impression that the news of Macomber's coming aroused Rizk al-Qas's interest. So it was on Macomber's impending arrival, and the Black September's curiosity to see what he was bringing, that Baghir based his hope of gaining a postponement past the "final" 8:00 P.M. deadline.

*　*　*

Osborne Day, one of the National Security Council representatives on Armin Meyer's cabinet committee working group, phoned Meyer early on March 2. He told Meyer that President Nixon would be holding a press conference at 11:30 that morning. "What," Day asked, "should the president say about the events in Khartoum?"

Meyer immediately recognized danger. He replied to Day with the same advice he had given the governor of California the previous evening: the president should say nothing; he should decline comment. The situation was just too delicate to take any chances. People's lives are at stake, Meyer admonished the White House aide. The fact that Israeli Prime Minister Golda Meir had just been in Washington made it particularly important, Meyer felt, that the president say nothing. Any suggestion that the United States was coordinating with Israel could precipitate the killing of the hostages.

Day agreed emphatically with Meyer's recommendation. So Meyer considered the matter settled. The president would avoid comment on the Khartoum kidnappings.

The same advice was given to Secretary of State William Rogers, who was still in Paris. Rogers had finished his talks there on the morning of March 2 and was preparing to fly back to the United States. Before boarding his plane, he answered questions from the press, one of which was about the kidnapping of the two Americans and the Belgian in Khartoum. Rogers replied circumspectly:

> I don't want to make any comment on that matter at the present time, for reasons which I think the press will understand. I merely point out that the government of Sudan is now actively negotiating on this whole tragic event and we have a team in Washington working around the clock in close contact with our people in the Sudan. I would not want to make any comment beyond that.[24]

Rogers did not mention the Macomber mission.

Owing to the six-hour time difference between Paris and Washington, Rogers's press conference took place well ahead of the president's.

The events in Khartoum were the subject of one of the first questions put to Nixon that morning. "Mr. President," a reporter declared, "we have a crisis in the Sudan where a U.S. ambassador is being held hostage and one of the ransom demands is that Sirhan Sirhan be released. I wonder if you have any comment on this, on that particular demand?"

Nixon replied casually, as though telling a good story:

[24]*Department of State Bulletin*, Volume LXVII, No. 1761, March 26, 1973, p. 342.

Last night I was sitting by the wife of Mr. Rabin [Yitzhak Rabin, ambassador of Israel to the United States] and we were saying that the position of ambassador, once so greatly sought after, now in many places becomes quite dangerous. As you know we had a problem in Latin America last year. We have one here this year. I don't mean to suggest that it is that hazardous everyplace, but it is a problem and it is a risk that an ambassador has to take.

As far as the United States as a government giving in to blackmail demands, we cannot do so and we will not do so. Now, as to what can be done to get these people released, Mr. Macomber is on his way there for discussions. The Sudanese government is working on the problem. We will do everything that we can to get them released but we will not pay blackmail.[25]

Nixon had ignored the advice of his staff and of the State Department. He had said everything he should not have said. He had rejected the terrorists' demands outright. This was something no U.S. official had done to that time. For it was one thing to decide in one's own inner councils not to make deals or concessions, but it was quite another to flaunt one's refusal in the face of armed killers who were holding defenseless hostages. Nixon's reference to the wife of the Israeli ambassador was less serious, but it did make an Israeli connection, and it could easily be taken to suggest consultation and coordination with the Israelis. And the president, unlike the secretary of state, had spoken of the Macomber mission.

It was a few minutes after 11:30 A.M. in Washington, 6:30 P.M. Khartoum time, when Nixon answered the reporter's question. His remarks were on the airwaves and news tickers around the world almost instantaneously.

Armin Meyer could not understand what had happened. He was appalled, and so was David Newsom, the assistant secretary for African affairs. Both men feared that what the president had said now placed the hostages in real danger. Bill Macomber and his team learned of Nixon's statement in Cairo as they were scrambling madly to get back into the air after receiving the Khartoum embassy's angry cable telling them that the Black September gunmen and Moore, Noel, and Eid would not be coming to the Egyptian capital. Years later Macomber was to describe

[25]Ibid., p. 350.

himself as having been "very upset" when he learned of the president's remarks. Curt Jones had the same recollection of that moment: Jones, Macomber, and all those with them had felt that Nixon had committed a grievous error, and that his remarks had put the hostages' lives in even greater jeopardy.

George Thompson heard Nixon's words rebroadcast over shortwave radio at about seven o'clock that evening Khartoum time. Thompson was briefly at home resting, but Nixon's statement alarmed him. Fearing that the terrorists might now kill their hostages, he rushed back to the watch post in front of the Saudi embassy.

*　*　*

Nixon's statement was a clear disavowal for Baghir. The Sudanese vice-president had based his hope for getting past the 8:00 P.M. deadline on keeping the Black September gunmen in the dark about Macomber's intentions, on leading them along in the expectation that Macomber might be bringing an offer of a deal. Now, however, the American president had said there would be no deal. And then the State Department made it even more explicit.

At the department's noon press briefing, held just a half-hour after the president's press conference began, a reporter asked spokesman Charles Bray about the Macomber mission. Bray pulled out guidance that had been prepared for him by the Operations Center task force. Macomber's role, Bray replied, would be "quite limited—he is going to observe, not to negotiate."[26] Macomber would lend whatever assistance he could to the Sudanese government, but that was all. He carried no authorization to make a deal, the spokesman emphasized.

Bray was a strong supporter of the no-ransom, no-deals policy; he had advocated it ever since the Mitrione killing in 1970. But his remarks at the noon briefing on March 2 appear to have been the product of sheer bureaucratic routine. Every morning, offices all around the State Department drew up guidance for the spokesman on events that might prompt questions at the daily noon briefing. The spokesman gathered these together and took them with him to the briefing. There he would pull each out and read it off as questioners came forward.

The rationale for drawing up the guidance on the Macomber mission was something like this: that Macomber was en route to Khartoum was

[26]"Nixon Demands the Killers Be Punished," *New York Times,* March 3, 1976.

now known to the media. It could be expected that reporters would ask about it at the noon briefing, and so Bray had to be given something to say. Apparently, it occurred neither to those who drafted and approved the guidance, nor to Bray when he used it, that a less explicit and candid statement regarding Macomber's instructions would have been advisable, that proclaiming to the Black September gunmen that Macomber was not coming to offer them anything or even to talk with them would be seen by them as a challenge, one that could precipitate tragedy.

Earlier in the day, the government of Jordan had already publicly rejected any deal with the Black September. Evidently, however, the gunmen in the Saudi embassy had not taken the Jordanian statement as the final word; they counted on Nixon to "order" King Hussein to release the people they wanted. Now, in the face of the two statements coming out of Washington, they could hardly be under the illusion that this was likely to happen.

King Hussein himself had no quarrel with the position so precipitously announced by his brother. Hussein was the Black September's number one target. The Black September's original plan, it seems, had been to seize Moore and Noel while Hussein was in Washington conferring with Nixon, a move that would have added immeasurably to the drama of the affair, and also to the pressures on Nixon and Hussein. If the Americans were not pressing the Jordanian monarch to buy the lives of their people by releasing Black September terrorists held in his jails, he had no reason to volunteer to do so. In fact, he had every reason to let the Black September show themselves to the world as wanton murderers, should they carry out their threat to kill the hostages.

The Israelis, too, made it known that they were not disposed to meet the Black September demands for the release of Palestinians held in their jails. They had, after all, made no deal with the Black September a few months earlier when the lives of their own Olympic athletes were at stake. So why should they do so now, to save the lives of two Americans and a Belgian, when the American government was not even asking it of them?

* * *

The unconscionable delay in retransmission to Cairo of the Khartoum message and the mindless press guidance on Macomber's mission suggested that the attrition the crisis-management theoreticians hoped to impose on the Black September terrorists in Khartoum was being felt as well by those on the task force in the State Department's Operations Center. Harry Odell was to recall later that the task force had been, from the very outset, a chaotic operation. Macomber had left for his long flight to Khartoum without, so far as Odell was aware, issuing any clear instruction leaving Armin Meyer in charge of anything more than the routine running of the task force. Those who served on the task force recognized that Meyer was the senior person there, but there were lines of authority that stretched outside the task force—to the Bureau of African Affairs, and to the offices of the under secretary, the deputy under secretaries, and the assistant secretaries—that left things unclear. A few of those who served on the task force stayed on the whole time it was in existence, but most came and worked in shifts. When they left, those who followed frequently did not know what had happened a few hours earlier.

The screen on which were projected the latest messages from the U.S. embassy in Khartoum and other posts, which at first had seemed a boon, soon turned into a terrible burden. It attracted a crowd of people from around the department and from other agencies, people who had no business in the task force room, who came merely to satisfy their curiosity about the latest developments, and whose presence distracted those working there from doing their job.

Amid the tension and the frustration there were, nonetheless, moments of mild comic relief. Toward noon on March 2, an air force lieutenant general, resplendent in uniform with three stars glistening on each shoulder and rows of medals sprouting from his chest, stalked angrily into the task force room. Harry Odell was on duty.

"If the State Department has complaints about our airplane," the general announced in a very loud and belligerent voice, "I want to hear what they are."

Odell knew what it was all about. Macomber had sent a cable from Frankfurt bemoaning the deficiencies of the C-141. It was too late now to do anything about this particular problem. Odell gave the general a hearty handshake, assured him that everything was just fine, and sent him away with a pat on the back.

*　*　*

At 6:10 P.M. Khartoum time, some twenty minutes before President Richard M. Nixon met the press in Washington, the phone rang in the

American embassy in downtown Khartoum. Ambassador Cleo Noel was on the other end of the line. He asked to speak to Sanderson or Peale. Sanderson took the receiver.

"Is there any word from Washington on the demands?" Noel asked.

"Negative," Sanderson replied.

Sanderson asked if the conversation was being overheard.

"Yes," Noel replied.

The ambassador repeated his question: had any information been received concerning the Black September's demands?

Overheard by the Black September gunmen, Sanderson realized, a straight answer to this question would be a death sentence for Noel, Moore, and Eid. Sanderson well knew that Washington was not prepared to meet any of the Black September's demands. He knew Macomber was not coming to negotiate about the Black September's demands. But Sanderson, like General Baghir, also knew that the only hope for gaining time was to leave open the prospect that Macomber might be bringing something.

"We expect somebody from Washington later tonight," Sanderson said cautiously.

"That will be too late," Noel replied.[27]

The line then went dead.

*　　*　　*

A half-hour later, at 6:40 P.M., not long after night had begun to fall, the Sudanese and Americans watching the Saudi embassy saw all the lights in the upper part of the building suddenly go off, go on again, and then go off and on again briefly. A moment later the lights went off for the third time, and those observing the embassy building saw figures—they thought they counted nine—emerge in darkness onto the fourth-floor patio and look toward the airport. After a brief appearance, the figures retreated into the building and the lights went on again.

But at 7:20, the lights inside the building again went off, at least all those that could be seen through the shuttered and heavily curtained windows, and this time they stayed off. Only the bulb over the front doorway remained burning. It cast a sickly yellow light that paled almost into obscurity as the haboob closed in.

At about 8:15, General Baghir spoke again by telephone with al-Qas.

---

[27]State Department telegram to Cairo, secret, DTG 021658Z Mar 73.

The news Baghir received evidently alarmed him, for afterwards he ordered his forces to begin clearing vehicles and evacuating houses from a two block area surrounding the Saudi embassy. It was a move intended to give Sudanese forces the option of storming the embassy. Quickly and efficiently, the Sudanese went about their task. A detachment of heavily armed troops in armored cars deployed in the street facing the embassy.

At the scene, Sudanese police told Americans that the situation was now "hot." The Black September, they said, was insisting that the 8:00 P.M. deadline was final.

16

Cold River

The Sudan Airways flight from Cairo rocked and bucked savagely as it began its descent to Khartoum. Bob Fritts looked to the window next to his seat and tried to pierce the blackness outside. There was nothing to be seen; the fierce sandstorm—the haboob—made the night impenetrable, like a wall. But Fritts could tell that the aircraft was making its way down. There was the familiar sensation of descent, the grinding of metal as the landing gear swung out of its cowling, and the rasping rush of air as the wing flaps were lowered into landing position.

Suddenly the engines bellowed a terrific roar, and the craft jerked violently upward, flinging Fritts and the other passengers hard against the backs of their seats. In the obscurity of the haboob, the pilot, Fritts learned later, had mistaken the lights of the control tower and the arrival lounge for those of the runway. He was headed straight for the tower and the lounge when, just in time, he discovered his error. The pilot brought the plane around for a second approach and by some miracle landed it safely.

It was just after 9:00 P.M. when the plane touched down. A howling wind thick with swirling sand and dust greeted Fritts and Bergstrom. Ed Brawn quickly escorted them through immigration and customs. Brawn had been at the airport awaiting Fritts's and Bergstrom's arrival since just after 8:00, so he had no late word on developments. All he could tell them was that the terrorists' 8:00 P.M. deadline had passed quietly.

Jim Hoagland, the *Washington Post* correspondent who had visited Khartoum a little less than two years earlier, in May 1971, who had met Curt Moore then and had struck up a friendship with him, was on the plane with Fritts and Bergstrom. Hoagland was the first of dozens of American and European journalists to arrive in Khartoum following the storming of the Saudi embassy.

*   *   *

Another passenger on the plane was Theo L. R. Lansloot, counselor of the Belgian embassy in Cairo. Lansloot's mission was to rescue Guy Eid. When officials at the Foreign Ministry in Brussels first learned that Eid had been seized along with the two Americans, they tried to put a telephone call through to Khartoum, to talk with someone in the Sudanese Foreign Ministry. The Belgians could not get a line, so they sent a cable to their embassy in Cairo instructing Lansloot to proceed as quickly as possible to Khartoum.

The Belgians had no policy barring the payment of ransom to terrorists. Their Foreign Ministry evidently never considered following the American lead. As the Black September had made no demands on Belgium, the ministry instructed Lansloot to attempt to negotiate Eid's release in exchange for a promise of payment of a sum of money.

By the time Lansloot received these instructions, it was almost midday of March 2 in Cairo. The next flight to Khartoum was the Sudan Airways plane, scheduled to depart at 5:00 P.M. but delayed pending Macomber's arrival. While waiting for the late-afternoon flight, Lansloot prepared himself by gathering evidence to counter the gunmen's allegation that Eid was a Jew. A quick search of the embassy's files turned up Eid's birth certificate, and a relative in Cairo, the Reverend Xavier Eid, furnished a copy of Eid's baptismal certificate. Both showed Eid to be a Greek Catholic.

*   *   *

For Shigeru Nomoto, the Japanese chargé d'affaires, the two and a half hours that he spent inside the embassy of Saudi Arabia after its seizure on the evening of March 1 were a time of such terror that they would remain forever engraved in his memory.

After Moore and Noel were dragged up the stairs and left on the carpet of the second-floor living room, the man Nomoto called "the boss" ordered an aide to cut the bindings on the hands of the half-dozen Arab diplomats with whom he was seated. The boss announced that he was releasing them all; all, including Nomoto, were ordered to stand and walk single file to the staircase, down it, and out the front door of the residence. Nomoto was last in the line. As he neared the staircase, he heard the boss shout: "Japanese, stop! Don't go!" The words sent a shiver of fear through Nomoto. He had been on the threshold of deliverance. Now, he was sure, he was being brought back to be held with the two Americans, possibly to be killed with them.

Nomoto returned to the living room. The boss sat him down in a chair next to a table with a telephone on it and commanded him to call the Sudanese minister of information. He was to convey the gunmen's demands to the Sudanese official. Nomoto dialed repeatedly but got no answer, and after a while the line went dead. During this time the boss stood over him, the muzzle of his rifle pointing straight at Nomoto's head. The muzzle was so close that the Japanese could see inside it.

As Shigeru Nomoto pondered what this might mean for his fate, he again heard a heavy thumping on the stairwell. This time he saw gunmen dragging the Belgian chargé d'affaires into the room. They laid Eid next to Noel. The Belgian's trousers were soaked in blood. His hands and feet were bound. In a pathetic, feeble voice he called repeatedly for a doctor.

A bit later the chargé d'affaires of Jordan, Adli Nasser, was brought in, escorted by a gunman but walking and unharmed, with only his hands bound. Nasser was ordered to sit on the floor. A few minutes later the Saudi ambassador appeared, unaccompanied and unbound. It was the first time Nomoto had seen Ambassador al-Malhouk since the storming of the embassy. He had not been harmed, but his face bore a look of profound anguish and confusion; he paced to and fro and then left the room, evidently free to come and go as he pleased.

At about 9:30, the boss told Nomoto he was released, that he could leave the building. Nomoto walked quickly, pursued by his own fright, down the stairs, through the front door, and across the street to the police post on the other side.

* * *

Curt Moore was still in a state of semi-consciousness when Shigeru Nomoto left the embassy of Saudi Arabia. Cleo Noel seemed to have regained full consciousness, but he did not move. Nomoto thought the American ambassador looked like a Zen monk in meditation.

If we are to credit the account given afterwards by the Jordanian chargé d'affaires, Adli Nasser, the condition of the two American hostages improved markedly later that night. Moore and Noel revived, and the gunmen, so Nasser said, did not abuse or mistreat them. After a while the gunmen loosened the Americans' bindings and allowed the Saudi ambassador's wife to serve them tea and sandwiches left over from the reception. The bullet fragment that had hit Noel in the ankle during the first moments of the capture was still lodged there, but the wound was a minor one. The Sudanese army doctor who came in just after 11:00 P.M. cleaned and dressed it and, as he later told U.S. embassy officials, left the American ambassador reclining in a comfortable chair, his feet elevated. Occasionally, Nasser later related to Macomber, the gunmen even joked with the two Americans.[28]

But even if the two Americans were no longer being mistreated, their wait through the night of March 1 and the day of March 2 had to be an ordeal of terror. It is hard to believe that there could have been any humor for them in the gunmen's "jokes," for from the beginning Moore and Noel had been told that they would die if their government did not satisfy the Black September's demands. After what they had just experienced, neither man could have deluded himself that this threat was not real and immediate.

Adli Nasser was probably the only one among the diplomats present at the Saudi ambassador's reception who had been alert to the possibility of a terrorist attack and, when it came, could instantly guess who the attackers were and what they wanted. Some two weeks earlier, not long after Abu Daoud was arrested in Amman, the Jordanian Foreign Ministry had sent a cable to all its embassies warning of a threat by the Black September. So while others tried to hide in bathrooms and behind curtains or shrubs—ineffectual places—Nasser knew where the surest sanctuary lay, where even an Arab terrorist would hesitate to trespass. He dashed up the stairway to the al-Malhouk family quarters and locked himself in the Saudi ambassador's bedroom, along with Mrs. al-Malhouk and three of her children. From there Nasser could hear the gunmen calling out his name as they searched for him. They came and pounded on the door, demanding that it be opened, but the Saudi ambassador's wife shouted at them to go away, there were only women and children in the room. And they did.

[28]Khartoum telegram 430, Secret/Exdis, DTG 041237Z Mar 73.

Adli Nasser was on the Black September's list, but because of his skillful evasion, he escaped the gunmen's fury in the first minutes after the storming of the embassy. After about half an hour, when the gunmen had calmed down, the Saudi ambassador brought Nasser out from his hiding place.

Nasser was the head of the Jordanian embassy in the Sudan—there was no Jordanian ambassador resident in Khartoum—and he was therefore the representative of King Hussein. As such he had reason to fear for his life. He was a tall, slender man, about forty, with thinning hair and a somewhat aloof manner. Some thought he was himself a Palestinian; others believed him to be a Circassian, a descendant of peoples native to the northern coast of the Black Sea whom the Ottoman Turks had settled in their Arab dominions at the height of their empire. Whichever the case, he was married to a good-looking and very spirited Palestinian woman who was in no way overawed by the Black September gunmen. Throughout the night of March 1 and into March 2, Mrs. Nasser bombarded the gunmen with telephone calls, demanding that they release her husband, screaming at them, telling them that they should be fighting the Israelis, not Arabs or friends of the Arabs. Salah Khalaf, the head of Black September, later wrote of her that she was "close to the [Palestinian] resistance."[29] Her connections and her vigorous intervention very likely saved her husband's life.

The Saudi ambassador was in yet another category. Ambassador al-Malhouk was never bound or threatened by the Black September gunmen, nor was he otherwise treated as a prisoner. He was kept in the embassy—he probably would have stayed there in any case, for to leave would have dishonored him in his own code—but he was not confined with the others. Mrs. al-Malhouk could have left had she wished, but she chose to stay with her husband; she herself was of Palestinian origin, and she must have felt that her presence there would be a guarantee of safety for him.

The fact that the gunmen did not bind Ambassador al-Malhouk and allowed him to move about freely must have raised a shadow of suspicion in Adli Nasser's mind. The Jordanian asked one of the gunmen why no restrictions were placed on the Saudi ambassador and was told that

[29]Eric Rouleau with Salah Khalaf, *My Home, My Land* (New York: Times Books, 1981), p. 102.

the Black September team had received special instructions regarding al-Malhouk's treatment.

This explanation was not further elucidated. Presumably it meant only that Black September headquarters in Beirut wanted no harm to come to the Saudi. There was ample reason for this. The Palestinians did not like Saudi Arabia's friendship with the United States and its support for King Hussein. They were not, in particular, afraid of the Saudis, but it was not in Fatah's interest to throw down an outright challenge to them, for they contributed a hefty annual subsidy to the PLO and Fatah, and even paid directly into the Black September's coffers.

There were things about Ambassador al-Malhouk's reception for Moore that did raise questions. One of these was the invitation to Fawaz Yassin. The Saudi ambassador had to be aware that American diplomats were strictly forbidden from social or professional contact with Fatah or any other element of the PLO, that they could not invite a Fatah or PLO representative or attend any function hosted by one, and that they could not even engage in conversation with them. So why should Ambassador Abdullah al-Malhouk have invited the head of the Fatah office in Khartoum to his farewell party for the counselor of the American embassy? Those who knew al-Malhouk could not imagine that he would knowingly have collaborated with the Black September in a plan to harm his American guests. He and Curt Moore had become good friends during their time together in the Sudan.

Then had al-Malhouk somehow been the dupe of the Palestinians, led along in the belief that he could bring them together with the American for a talk that might help bridge the gap between the two parties? Conceivable, but unlikely, for by all description Abdullah al-Malhouk was not a naive person or one inclined to venture into unconventional initiatives. The most commonplace explanation would seem to be the most plausible one: the Fatah office in Khartoum enjoyed full diplomatic status, and Fawaz Yassin, its director, was on the diplomatic list. The reception was a diplomatic corps function, and the Saudi ambassador's secretary unthinkingly sent invitations to all chiefs of diplomatic missions.

But this explanation runs up against a problem, which is that Cleo Noel, the American ambassador, was not originally invited to the Saudi ambassador's reception for Moore. Noel had expected to be on a trip to southern Sudan on March 1, 1973. When he changed his plans and decided to stay in Khartoum, he felt he should attend the reception. He asked Margaret Thorsen, his and Moore's secretary, whether he had received an invitation from the Saudi ambassador. She told him he had not. Noel assumed that he had been left off the list either inadvertently or owing to his travel plans. This sort of thing happened from time to time, so the American ambassador had no hesitation in asking his secretary to call the Saudi embassy and request an invitation for him. This she did, but she did not get immediate satisfaction. It took Margaret Thorsen two or possibly three calls before the Saudis finally sent over the requested invitation card, only a day or so before the event.

As people in the international community in Khartoum later talked about the seizure of the three diplomats—and for months they talked of nothing else—the suspicion emerged that someone among the staff of the Saudi embassy had been in collusion with the Black September. Had Cleo Noel deliberately been left off the Saudi ambassador's guest list because Curt Moore was the only American originally targeted, because, as the gunmen said in the message they sent Lucille Noel via the Sudanese doctor on the night of March 1, "we have nothing against your husband"? Very likely there was nothing more to it than bumbling on the part of the Saudis, but suspicion lingered, like a shadow somewhere on the periphery.

* * *

The case of Guy Eid was a truly bizarre one. Eid was not on the list of intended hostages that the Black September gunmen had brought with them from Beirut. Yet from the very beginning Eid was told that he would be killed, and evidently it was intended that he should die regardless of whether Abu Daoud and the others whose freedom the Black September sought were released.

Guy Eid was born to a Lebanese family that had settled in Cairo generations back, and that somewhere along the line had obtained Belgian nationality, which made him Belgian at birth. He went to Brussels for his university studies, and most of his family moved to Belgium in 1961, after President Gamal Abdul Nasser began expropriating foreign holdings in Egypt. Guy's elder brother George became a businessman. Guy used his fluency in Arabic to gain entry into the Belgian Foreign Ministry, through a kind of side door. He was not a regular career diplomat. He joined the diplomatic service as an "auxiliary," as the Belgians called it, a temporary status and one ordinarily used for the recruitment of personnel with hard language or special technical skills.

The flock of Western newsmen who descended on Khartoum after the seizure of the Saudi embassy puzzled briefly but with no great success or sustained interest over why Eid was being held. Some thought it was simply that Eid had had the bad luck to be with Noel when the Black September gunmen stormed the Saudi reception. Others suspected the motive to be recent Belgian collaboration with Israel in military co-production ventures. Plans were afoot for a joint Belgian-Israeli-American aeronautics factory near Liège that would produce an Israeli-designed light transport plane, the Arava, capable of either military or civilian use, and a business jet, the Commodore. The project also included the production of guided missiles and military electronic equipment.

Yet the Black September never mentioned this, never demanded that Belgium revoke its firms' contracts with Israel, never, in fact, made any demand of the government of Belgium.

Guy Eid was an enigma. Although he was Belgium's resident diplomatic representative in the Sudan (the Belgian ambassador in Cairo was accredited in Khartoum but visited there only occasionally), he was not much seen around the Western diplomatic circuit. He attended the national day receptions, but few Western diplomats knew him other than through an occasional sighting or handshake. Eid did, however, socialize frequently with the members of the PLO and Fatah missions in Khartoum. Other NATO governments did not have as strict rules on contacts with the PLO as the Americans, but it was highly unusual, indeed strange, for a Western diplomat to be seen regularly with them. The Palestinians in Khartoum, it seems, knew Guy Eid much better than did most of his Western diplomatic counterparts. Perhaps, it was later said, they felt he knew too much about them. Was there some dark game going on there? Was Eid spying on the Palestinians? Or was he being used by them in some way?

People found Eid's behavior more than a little suspicious. Once, out of the blue, Eid telephoned one of the officers of the American embassy (who, though not publicly identified as such, was in fact the CIA station chief in Khartoum). Eid hardly knew this American official, but he asked if he could come to his home to take a picture of his dog. Eid explained that he had heard that the dog was a beautiful animal; he loved dogs, he said, and he simply had to have a photograph of this one.

So when people thought back on the sequence of events in the storming of the Saudi embassy, they remembered that it was Eid who had stopped Cleo Noel and delayed him from reaching the street gate just before the Black September's attack. Had Eid been used by the Black September to catch the American ambassador? Had he been made a dupe in his own murder? Nothing in the testimony that Adli Nasser or Abdullah al-Malhouk gave later bore witness to any kind of verbal exchange between Eid and his captors that would corroborate this hypothesis. Yet suspicion persisted that Eid was involved in some way.

Whatever the truth of Eid's relationship with the Palestinians, the Black September gunmen clearly had it in for him, even more than for Curt Moore, for they continued to treat him with great cruelty even after the initial moments of the capture. The diagnosis of the Sudanese doctor notwithstanding, Eid's leg wound was not minor. It caused him much pain, and it bled profusely. Yet the gunmen refused him water, and despite his wound, they continued to abuse him, kicking and beating him to the point where finally, Adli Nasser later told one of the Americans in Khartoum, Eid cried out pathetically to be killed. Rizk al-Qas cursed Eid, said he was a Jew, and accused him of being a spy for Israel. The Saudi ambassador, according to his own later testimony, tried to defend the Belgian chargé, but his pleas were ignored.

There had to be a reason for such cruelty, and it may have been far more prosaic than all the suspicions about his spying on or complicity with the Black September. Rizk al-Qas held a personal grudge against the Belgian. The two lived only a block apart, knew each other—and had quarreled over a woman. Later, people in Khartoum's diplomatic community talked a lot about this quarrel, but they seemed to have only very sketchy information, to know only that it had developed into a nasty feud between the two men, and that the woman in question, a Frenchwoman named Dominique, eventually became Eid's fiancée. They were due to be married in the summer of 1973.

Al-Qas was not someone you would want to tangle with. He was twenty-seven, of medium height and build, with dark hair, a mustache, and a kind of wild good looks. But he was a firebrand, a crazy, a man whose anger spewed in every direction, a man who would say or do anything. He called himself a journalist, and he was well known to listeners of Radio Omdurman, for he did the nightly half-hour broadcast that the official Sudanese radio allotted to the PLO. In the vitriol of his denunciations of

Israel, the United States, King Hussein, and other assorted imperialists or imperialist tools, Rizk al-Qas was second to none.

Rizk al-Qas, it appears, was determined that Eid should die. At about noon on March 2, General Baghir telephoned al-Qas to say he had proof, in the form of Eid's birth and baptismal certificates (Eid's French fiancée held these documents in preparation for the wedding, and she delivered them to General Baghir as soon as she learned that the gunmen were saying he was Jewish), that Eid was not a Jew but a Greek Catholic Christian. It didn't matter, al-Qas replied. Eid would still have to die, to atone for the killing of the Palestinian commandos in the Sabena Airlines hijacking in May 1972.

*　*　*

All through the night of March 1 and the day of March 2, the telephone rang incessantly in the embassy of Saudi Arabia. Except for a brief interruption early after the seizure of the Saudi embassy, the Sudanese authorities kept the embassy's telephone service working. They listened in on the gunmen's conversations but did not cut them off. People called in continuously, some to rebuke the Black September gunmen, or curse them, and some to plead for mercy for the hostages. So many calls came in that one of the gunmen turned to the hostages and asked: "Do you know everybody in town?"

The news media called in, too. Reporters from several national and international wire services claimed to have spoken by telephone with the gunmen.

And all through this time the gunmen listened avidly to the radio, to the major international stations, the BBC and the VOA, to Radio Omdurman (the Sudanese government station), Radio Cairo, and the Voice of Palestine stations in Cairo, Tripoli, Beirut, and Baghdad. The gunmen had brought a shortwave radio with them into the Saudi embassy, and they found additional sets there. They also had access to the embassy's powerful radio communications equipment on the fourth floor of the residence but were unable to use it; they asked General Baghir to allow either the Fatah office radio operator or the Saudi embassy's communicator to join them, but Baghir refused. Even if they were unable to send messages, they were able to receive them from broadcasts by the various Voice of Palestine stations, and they listened with particular attention to these stations.

During the night of March 1 to 2, the Black September gunmen dictated a statement to the two Americans. It was the usual kind of statement that abductors require of their hostages. It proclaimed the justice of the Palestinian cause, and declared the two Americans' support for it and their endorsement of the Black September's demand for the release of Sirhan Sirhan, Abu Daoud and his confederates, and Palestinian women imprisoned in Israel.

Commanded at gunpoint to write, Moore and Noel wrote. But this was to be the limit beyond which they would not go. When Curt Moore spoke with Sam Peale a few hours after his abduction, he was careful to make clear that he was saying only what he had been ordered by his captors to say.

In doing this, Moore was letting Peale know discreetly but unmistakably that he and Noel were not endorsing any of the Black September's demands, that whatever their pain and their fright, they were not prostrating and humiliating themselves, and that their strength and their pride were intact. He was telling Peale that they had not capitulated.

Those few seconds of the storming of the embassy of Saudi Arabia just after 7:00 P.M. on March 1 had caught each of the three men at a peak in his life and had brutally pitched each into a terrifying abyss. Cleo Noel had just entered upon his first appointment as ambassador, an attainment that only a small number of those who took up the career of diplomacy in America could expect to achieve. Curt Moore was a man for whom life itself was an enthusiasm, and who had had a rich and fulfilling life; like Noel, he had come to a breakthrough point in his career, the career he had dreamed of from boyhood.

Curt Moore in particular felt a deep affection for the Arabs. He loved them as people. He savored their language and their culture, and he truly believed in—and worked hard for—better relations between the United States and the Arabs. Cleo Noel was more reserved; he appreciated the virtues of the Arabs but was troubled by their obsessive preoccupation with their conflict with Israel—on his second tour of duty in Saudi Arabia, in 1957 and 1958, it had colored everything—and their tendency toward fanaticism. And even in the Sudan, a country he loved, he had been disappointed to find himself forsaken after the break in relations in June 1967 by Sudanese he had thought were true friends.

Curt Moore had never had any premonition of the fate that awaited him. He had never suspected that he might die a violent death, or that he might be killed while still in the prime of life. But years earlier he had asked himself what he would do if his courage were ever put to the ultimate test. He had talked about it with Sally and had pondered it, as he did so many things in life. Now as he faced the prospect of death, those thoughts must have returned to him. For at the moment of testing, Curt Moore made a decision. He and Cleo Noel made a pact with one another, perhaps in words spoken surreptitiously, perhaps in silence. They would not humiliate themselves. Whatever happened, they would not plead for their lives.

They were not resigned to dying. Clearly they still hoped that their government would find some way to save their lives; there could be no other meaning to Noel's telephone call to Sanderson. But they were not going to beg either their captors or their government. If they were going to die, they would die with dignity.

* * *

But as their captivity entered its second full day, at 7:00 P.M. on March 2, it was not at all clear to them that they were going to die. They certainly knew that they remained under threat of death; Cleo Noel's ominous remark to Sanderson, during his call to the American embassy at 6:10 P.M., that Macomber's arrival later that evening would "be too late" is evidence of that. But when General Baghir spoke with the gunmen around 6:00 P.M., he later said, he found them divided over what to do, and he was persuaded that he could get them to break their 8:00 P.M. deadline.

But an item broadcast over Cairo radio soon afterwards gave the Black September gunmen a fright. Egypt's Middle East News Agency reported that an American military plane had been flown to Khartoum but had been refused landing clearance there and was being flown back to Cairo. The story was a garbled version of Macomber's arrival in Cairo, but according to Adli Nasser's later testimony, it made the gunmen fear that the Macomber mission was actually some kind of military operation.

Still, right up until approximately 8:00 P.M. the gunmen remained undecided. Then, Adli Nasser later reported, their attitude suddenly changed. Rizk al-Qas left the second-floor hall area where the gunmen were holding the hostages. He was gone for about fifteen minutes. When he returned, he appeared shaken. He announced in English that the three Western diplomats were to be executed.

The change in the gunmen's attitude was so sudden, Adli Nasser later said, that this announcement took the hostages by surprise. Al-Qas explained to them the reasons they had to die: the gunmen had heard Nixon's statement over the radio; they had heard State Department spokesman Charles Bray's statement that Macomber would have no authority to negotiate; they had heard also that Macomber was to arrive momentarily in Khartoum, and they feared that his plane would be carrying a team of American commandos to assault the embassy.[30]

These may, in fact, have been the reasons for the decision to kill the Western hostages. But the order to kill came from outside, via radio broadcast—perhaps from more than one broadcast, in these or similar words, around 8:00 P.M. on March 2: "Why are you waiting? The people's blood in Nahr al-Bard cries for vengeance." Nahr al-Bard— Cold River—was the code word that triggered the killings, according to John Barry, the London *Sunday Times* correspondent who covered the Khartoum events.[31] But in his own later investigation, Barry was unable to pinpoint the source of this broadcast.

"What are you waiting for? Do it now!" is the message the Sudanese authorities reported having intercepted. The Sudanese first thought it had been broadcast from Baghdad radio but later decided it came from Tripoli.

And then there were these words, broadcast at around 8:00 P.M. on March 2 by the PLO Voice of Palestine station in Cairo: "Greetings. Your message has been received. Do what is required quickly because the blood of the martyrs is a revolution."

At 8:15 P.M. the telephone rang in General Baghir's office. On the line was one of the Black September gunmen. His message was terse: they were going to kill the three Western hostages.

*　　*　　*

On hearing al-Qas's pronouncement, Curt Moore is said to have cried out: "Untie my hands. If I am going to die, I want to talk with my wife first." Cleo Noel too asked to speak with his wife.

The gunmen denied Moore's and Noel's requests but gave them paper and pen and told them they had twenty-five minutes in which to write their wills and farewell letters to their families. Guy Eid was offered this same opportunity, but he was unable to write. He had lost a great

[30]Khartoum telegram 430, Secret/Exdis, DTG 041237Z Mar 73.
[31]*Sunday Times* (London), March 11, 1973.

deal of blood, had been savagely beaten, and had been in unremitting pain since the beginning of the ordeal. He broke into tears.

Moore and Noel wrote and then handed their letters to Ambassador al-Malhouk, who pledged that he would see to their delivery.

Curt Moore wanted Sally and their daughters Lucy and Cathy to know that he had been strong, that he had not failed in this last moment when his courage had confronted its supreme test. "Cleo and I," Curt wrote in the closing sentence of his letter to his wife, "will die bravely and without tears as men should."

Noel asked if he could make one last telephone call to the U.S. embassy, to see if there was more news, but the gunmen would not permit it. The delay they had allowed the three men for the writing of their last letters had already brought an impatient reproach from Beirut: why, a message asked, has the job not been completed; why are they still alive?[32]

Mrs. al-Malhouk, her husband later told *Washington Post* reporter Jim Hoagland, pleaded tearfully with the gunmen not to kill Moore, Noel, and Eid. Ambassador al-Malhouk asked al-Qas to wait at least until Macomber arrived; perhaps the American envoy was bringing a proposal to avoid bloodshed. "We already know the Americans' answer," al-Qas replied, "and besides we have received our final orders."[33]

Adli Nasser and Abdullah al-Malhouk marveled at the two Americans' composure. As the gunmen took them away, Cleo Noel stopped momentarily beside al-Malhouk. Graciously, Noel thanked the Saudi ambassador for the hospitality of the reception. He assured al-Malhouk that he and Moore did not hold their host responsible for what had befallen them.

It was such an extraordinary gesture that it stuck in the imagination, and when the Saudi ambassador later told reporters about it, they all wrote it up in their stories. Some of the Americans in Khartoum conjectured that there must have been more to it than al-Malhouk had revealed, that the words must have been spoken in defiance, or that they must have been loaded with a bitter irony that al-Malhouk and Nasser, who were not native speakers of English, might not have grasped. But others who knew Cleo Noel well found it wholly characteristic that he

[32]Khartoum telegram 428, Confidential/Exdis, DTG 041143Z Mar 73.
[33]*Washington Post*, March 9, 1973.

would seek to console his Saudi host for the tragedy he himself was about to face.

The men were taken downstairs to the basement. All eight of the Black September gunmen went with them.

* * *

All night March 1 and all day March 2, Sergeant Timothy Wells had been at the observation post in the Triplex Apartments just down the street from the Saudi embassy, periodically calling the U.S. embassy to report some development, or to report nothing new. Wells was too keyed up to sleep. He was alert and did not even feel tired—that was to come later.

Just before five o'clock, two members of the Black September gang had come out on the third-floor veranda and made obscene gestures in Wells's direction. Wells wished he had had a rifle with him; he would have found it a relief to shoot the two terrorists down, like mad dogs.

At a few minutes after 9:00—the moment was later fixed at 9:06—Wells and other U.S. embassy personnel in the darkened apartment heard five bursts of automatic weapons fire and then some additional shots. The bursts were muffled. From his Marine Corps training, Wells knew the sound. He was sure the shots had come from inside the Saudi embassy.

* * *

Khartoum's telecon report number 36 came off the teletype ticker in the task force room of the State Department's Operations Center at just before 3:00 P.M. Washington time. The room was crowded, as it had been for much of the day. The projector operator quickly put the Khartoum message on the screen so that all could read it. It began: "Embassy observers in a darkened house about a block from the Saudi embassy have reported about 5 bursts of sub-machine gun fire at about 8 shots each." And it ended: "We frankly now fear the worst." A collective gasp arose from the group.

* * *

The office building in downtown Khartoum that housed the American embassy was surrounded by a guard of heavily armed Sudanese police when the car carrying Fritts, Bergstrom, and Brawn pulled up in front of it. The Sudanese were taking no chances.

Carrying his garment bag draped over his shoulder, Fritts climbed the stairs to the ambassador's office. The dust of the haboob lay almost as thick in the air inside the building as it did in the street outside. As Fritts came up the last turn in the stairwell, he saw Sandy Sanderson standing silently at the top, silhouetted in the blaze of a klieg light over the entryway. Sanderson's glasses lay on his chest, strung from a chain around his neck. Tears were running down his cheeks. He did not greet Fritts.

"We've heard gunfire at the Saudi embassy," he said. "We think they're dead. You're in charge."

17

The End of a Siege

But there was no proof that Moore, Noel, and Eid were dead. At about 9:30 Ambassador al-Malhouk telephoned Fadl al-Obeid, the under secretary of the Foreign Ministry, to advise that the three Western diplomats had been executed. But the Saudi ambassador was only acting on the instruction of his captors; he himself had not seen the bodies or even (it later became known) heard the shots.

Al-Obeid passed the word along to Sanderson. A Sudanese military officer went to the door of the Saudi embassy, just after 11:00 P.M., to ask the gunmen to give up the bodies. He came back and reported that Moore and Noel were dead and Eid was wounded but still living. But it soon was learned that he was only repeating what he had been told; he had not been allowed to see the bodies of Moore or Noel and had not seen Eid either, and he had not even been inside the building. So all that could be said for sure was that shots had been fired and the gunmen were claiming that Moore and Noel were dead but were refusing to give up the bodies or even to allow anyone to verify their claim.

The gunmen's refusal to hand over the bodies caused much puzzlement. Islamic law required burial within twenty-four hours, and in the 100 degree heat of the Khartoum day, decomposition would come quickly. There were several plausible explanations. One was sheer callousness on the part of the Black September; this was something everyone was prepared to believe. Another was that the killers hoped to use release of the bodies to bargain for their own safety. But it was also just possible that the announcement of the killing was a ruse, and that the three men were still alive.

Nonetheless, despite this glimmer of hope, the Nixon White House hastened to announce (at 4:30 P.M. Washington time, 11:30 P.M. Khartoum time, March 2) the deaths of Moore and Noel, to trumpet the news almost proudly, and to use it as the occasion to issue a call to all nations to stand firm against "the menace of international terrorism." The words the president had spoken a few hours earlier and those the White House used in making the announcement left the impression that the administration was intent on wringing every bit of political profit it could from the event.

Either just before or just after the White House announcement, Sandy Sanderson put in a call to his German-born wife Ilsa at their home. Sanderson was worried about how Sally Moore and Lucille Noel would take the report of their husbands' deaths. He knew of an American doctor in Khartoum, Dr. Donald Francis, an epidemiologist from the Centers for Disease Control in Atlanta, Georgia, employed on a project in the Sudan. At her husband's request, Ilsa drove to a nearby hotel, roused Dr. Francis from his sleep, and then drove him to the U.S. ambassador's residence. Ordinarily the trip would have taken ten or fifteen minutes. In the obscurity of the haboob, it took all of an hour. Rather than drive back home, Ilsa spent that night at the residence, dozing fitfully on a sofa in the reception room, waiting to see if she could be of further help.

* * *

Within a few minutes after the shots were heard, the Sudanese army began closing in on the Saudi embassy. A tank appeared out of the blackness and drove to within a short distance of the front gate. It was followed by an armored car, and then came a second armored car. Five heavily armed soldiers were seen standing immediately in front of the embassy. High-powered searchlights were moved up close to the building, where they could cut through the haboob's opaqueness, and were played across its exterior. More troops were coming in, and soldiers or police armed with rifles were positioning themselves on the balconies of surrounding buildings. A Land Rover equipped with a heavy machine gun pulled up in front of the embassy. The army and the police now had the building sealed off. The haboob had reduced visibility to no more than fifteen or twenty yards, but even with this it would be impossible for anyone to slip out of it unnoticed.

This deployment completed, the Sudanese settled in to wait.

* * *

In Beirut that same evening, the newspaper *Al Muharrir* (The Liberator), known for its connections with Fatah and other Palestinian organizations, readied a story for its edition the next morning. The story said the paper had received a phone call from an unidentified spokesman of the Black September Organization who had announced the execution of the three Western diplomats held in Khartoum. According to the story, the Black September spokesman added: "This operation will teach the world to respect what we say. We will not allow ourselves to be deceived again or subject our demands to bargaining."

Some thirty-six hours later, the Iraqi news agency in Beirut reported a call from a Black September spokesman. The caller declared that one of the American diplomats executed in Khartoum, George Moore, was "the mastermind of the United States Central Intelligence Agency in the region and one of those who are directly responsible for the September [1970] massacres."

* * *

On learning that there would be no switch to Cairo, Macomber had rushed back to the airport and taken off for Khartoum, ignoring General Baghir's injunction against a landing there by the C-141. He arrived over Khartoum at about 10:00 P.M. The haboob had cut visibility even further since the Sudan Airways flight had landed an hour earlier.

Back at Military Airlift Command headquarters, at Scott Air Force Base in Illinois, Ted Tremblay, Curt's USC classmate, hooked into the communications between the pilot of Macomber's plane and the MAC air controllers. The pilot was worried about trying to land in the sandstorm. Ted asked whether the pilot thought he could make it in. The pilot said he believed he could; he could see the runway lights. Ted Tremblay was political advisor to the MAC. He had no command authority, but he injected himself anyway. He told the pilot to go ahead.

But hesitations prevailed. The plane flew on to Asmara. Macomber and the members of his party spent the night at the American consulate general, where Curt Moore had served a decade and a half earlier.

The day before, on March 1, the day Curt was seized, Ted and his wife Harlan had received a letter from Curt and Sally. They were departing Khartoum on March 5, the letter announced, and would be in the Chicago area soon afterwards. They wanted to arrange an evening with Ted and Harlan.

*   *   *

At six o'clock the next morning—it was now March 3—Baghir and Minister of Health Ibrahim were at the military command post near the Saudi embassy. Police were continuing to evacuate civilians from the area. President Nimeiry was still in Juba; he had intended to return to Khartoum the previous evening, but the haboob had made that impossible.

The sandstorm continued thick and heavy on the morning of March 3. Sandstorms ordinarily passed in a few hours, half a day at most, but this one unaccountably lingered. Everyone remarked on the sandstorm and remembered it later, because it was so unusual and because it seemed so ominous.

At a little after 8:00 A.M., Macomber's C-141 was again over Khartoum. But again, visibility was too poor for it to land. The C-141 flew back to Asmara.

At mid-morning General Baghir spoke once more by telephone with Rizk al-Qas. Al-Qas asked when the American envoy would be arriving, and what offer he would be bringing with him.

"What is the meaning of this question?" Baghir shot back. "I do not understand; you say you have killed the Americans." Al-Qas did not reply.

Baghir called on the gunmen to give themselves up. They were surrounded and had no choice but to surrender, he told them. Al-Qas demanded an airplane and safe passage out of the Sudan to Libya for himself and his group. Otherwise, he said, they would kill the two remaining hostages, the Jordanian and the Saudi.

At about ten, foreign newsmen who had stationed themselves at the limit permitted by the Sudanese security forces saw the troops begin hitching up their belts and readying their equipment, as though preparing for an assault. But after a short while the troops returned to resting position. The Sudanese, it appeared, were playing a game of nerves with the gunmen.

Just before 1:00 P.M. Baghir and al-Qas again spoke, this time by bullhorn. Al-Qas threatened to kill one or both of the remaining hostages if by 2:00 P.M. the Black September group was not allowed to leave the country. But Baghir would not budge. "You must surrender," he replied.

The Black September gunmen were beginning to find their situation highly uncomfortable, and not just because of the menacing Sudanese military deployment. During the night of March 2, the Sudanese had cut off the supply of water and electricity to the Saudi embassy, which up to then had been maintained. Moreover, the gunmen had brought no food with them other than a few biscuits and sweets. They were surprised to find the embassy's larder poorly provisioned, too poorly to sustain eight unexpected guests. Fear and hunger were beginning to take their toll. At a little after 2:00 P.M., four of the gunmen appeared on the third-floor veranda; one shook his fist in the air in an apparent gesture of frustration.

General Baghir stepped up the pressure. At 2:40 P.M. Radio Omdurman broadcast the text of a statement approved that morning by the Sudanese government. Laconically, it rejected the gunmen's request for a plane to take them out of the country and reiterated Baghir's demand that they surrender:

> Since the leader of the operation has stated that three of the hostages have already been executed, meeting the previous requests is no longer a subject of negotiation. . . . Sudan sees no justification for taking this problem to another Arab state and abandoning its own responsibility. Therefore, the Cabinet asks the leader of the operation and his group to release the hostages and to turn themselves over to the Sudanese authorities.[34]

At 6:15 P.M., with darkness falling but the haboob finally clearing, five of the gunmen appeared on the third-floor veranda. One lifted the bullhorn and began to make a speech. "We will not surrender," he declared. "We demand a plane to take us to Libya." The Sudanese soldiers must not make any further moves, or that would be a provocation. The speaker became emotional and seemed to break into sobs. He ended his speech with the words "ma assalama"—goodbye. Another took the bullhorn from him and made a speech of his own, and so did a third, who also closed with "ma assalama."

The Black September killers' nerve was beginning to break.

[34]CIA transcript of Omdurman Domestic Service broadcast.

Just before 7:00 P.M. on March 3, Macomber's C-141 again appeared over Khartoum. This time it landed.

Macomber went straight to General Baghir's office. Macomber's most immediate fear was that the Sudanese might yet strike a deal with the Black September gunmen in the Saudi embassy, that despite the government's statement earlier that afternoon, it might still allow them to leave in exchange for a promise to spare the lives of the Saudi ambassador and the Jordanian chargé. On this point, Baghir gave the American firm reassurance. The Sudanese government would not make any deal with the killers, Baghir said, and it would take no initiatives. It would simply wait for them to give up. Baghir said he hoped that this would not lead to the death of the Saudi or the Jordanian, but if it did, the responsibility would lie with the Black September. The Sudanese vice-president spoke calmly, in a reassuringly matter-of-fact way.

Macomber was much relieved. But what Baghir had to say next was not at all pleasing to the American envoy. Baghir described how he had tried to use Macomber's impending arrival in the Sudan as well as King Hussein's reported hurried return to Jordan to get the Black September to extend their deadline. He said he had thought this was working, but then the gunmen had told him they had heard on the radio President Nixon's statement that the United States would make no concessions. This, they had said, made further waiting pointless.

Macomber himself had been upset when he learned of Nixon's statement, for he had feared that it would put Moore and Noel in greater jeopardy. But if he was anything, Bill Macomber was a company man. He rallied angrily to Nixon's defense.

"Absolutely unacceptable," Macomber declared. The explanation given Baghir by the Black September was "absolutely unacceptable"— as though by calling it unacceptable he could deny it validity.

In the cable he sent to Washington that same evening, Macomber devoted half a page to recounting his response to the allegation that Nixon's statement had brought on the execution of the hostages. The position taken by the U.S. president, he told Baghir (so he reported to Washington), was not at all new; it was very well known. Any terrorist thinking of taking Americans would be familiar with the U.S. government's firm refusal to pay ransom, which had been reiterated not only by the president but by many other U.S. government officials on many occasions. It was a well-known fact, Macomber asserted, that U.S. policy was not to give in to blackmail, or to urge other governments to do so. Certainly, he added, the Black September specialists in terror would be well aware of this.[35]

In the comment he appended to his report to Washington, Macomber explained that he had felt that "Baghir's unfortunate reference to the President's statement . . . required my vigorous rebuttal."[36]

In Washington, too, people were worried that Nixon would be blamed for the killing of the hostages. On the evening of March 3, the State Department sent a flash cable to the U.S. embassy in Khartoum:

> Request Embassy opinion whether there [is] any possibility that statement made by President at press conference three hours earlier could possibly have been conveyed to terrorists by the apparent time of shooting at 2105.[37]

The answer that came back was not the one the senders of the department's cable quite obviously had hoped to elicit. In fact, it seemed to support the contention that Nixon's remarks did trigger the murders. "Possibility exists," the Khartoum embassy's reply stated, "that BSO terrorists heard at least paraphrase of President's statement since they have radio and reportedly monitor it." Then the cable added:

> Director General [of the] Ministry [of] Interior previously told EmbOff that terrorists gave three proximate reasons for their decision to kill the three diplomats: a) President's statement; b) Jordanian position [word garbled] negotiation; c) announcement that Macomber not empowered to negotiate. Director General also said it obvious that terrorists were carefully monitoring radio.[38]

* * *

Through the night of March 1 and all day on March 2, Yasser Arafat had been unavailable. The governments of both the Sudan and Saudi Arabia had tried repeatedly, and always unsuccessfully, to reach him to plead with him to call off the Khartoum operation.

Now, however, on the evening of March 3, after the murder of the

---

[35]Khartoum telegram 419, Secret/Exdis, DTG 040002Z Mar 73.
[36]Ibid.
[37]State telegram 397544, Confidential, DTG 031734Z Mar 73.
[38]Khartoum telegram 416, Confidential, DTG 032215Z Mar 73.

three Western diplomats had been proclaimed, and after it had become clear that the government of Sudan was not going to let the gunmen go, Arafat emerged from his clandestinity. The PLO chairman spoke over the telephone with Sudanese authorities and worked out terms for the surrender of the gunmen. The Sudanese held fast to their refusal to let the killers go. The best Arafat could obtain was a promise that they would not be summarily executed, and that they would be dealt with according to the law. The order to surrender was broadcast over Fatah's Saut al-Asifa radio. "Your mission is over," it read. "Release the Saudi and Jordanian ambassadors." And then:

> Present yourselves to the Sudanese authorities with courage so you may explain your just cause to the great Sudanese people, the Arab masses and to world public opinion. . . . Glory to the victims of the Zionist-imperialist aggression against Baddawi and Nahr al-Bard [camps] and the martyrs of the Libyan plane.[39]

At about 10:00 P.M. the gunmen signaled to General Baghir that they would surrender. But they would not surrender that night. They did not want to give themselves up in darkness. They had not feared to take life, but now they feared for their own lives, and they were not taking any chances. They would give themselves up only in the safety of the light of day.

* * *

The siege of the embassy of Saudi Arabia came to its end just after daybreak on March 4, fifty-nine hours after it began. By then several dozen journalists from major news organizations in the United States and Western Europe had swarmed into Khartoum. They were there to record the scene.

It came in stages, and it played like a silent movie with only time captions. At 6:10 A.M., two of the Black September men went out the front door of the residence, unarmed, and crossed the circular inner driveway to the street gate. One of them stayed there, speaking with someone on the outside, presumably a Sudanese official. The other returned to the building. At 6:35 Ambassador al-Malhouk appeared in the doorway. Three Black September men were now outside the building, unarmed, near the street gate. A few moments later others

[39] *Arab World*, Beirut, March 5, 1973.

emerged, carrying two stretchers covered with blankets; soon afterwards came a third stretcher. By 7:05 all eight of the Black September terrorists had given themselves up. They filed out the street gate, their arms raised not in a token of surrender but in the sign of victory, the fingers of each hand extended to make a V.

The Sudanese did not handcuff them and did not even take them away in police vans. They put them in unmarked Hillman passenger sedans and drove off, a convoy of five vehicles altogether. A Red Crescent ambulance whisked away the three blanket-covered stretchers.

The Sudanese police then entered the Saudi embassy. After a time, they emerged carrying the weapons the Black September had left behind: four Kalashnikov assault rifles, four pistols, eight hand grenades, 352 rounds of live ammunition, and 44 spent cartridges. Contrary to expectation, they found no explosives, only a tangle of wires. The Black September's threat to blow up the Saudi embassy in the event it was stormed had been sheer bluff.

18

To Protect a President

The siege was over and the men were dead, but this did not mean that the episode was closed. It was not to be closed for a very long time thereafter, for many more things had to be done. The first was to identify the bodies.

This task was assigned to Carol Roehl, because she was the U.S. embassy's consular officer. Roehl was the only one of the staff with whom Curt Moore had not been on good terms, so it seemed an irony that she should be the one to identify him in death. Sergeant Timothy Wells was detailed to go along with Roehl because, Wells later said, Roehl had never before seen a dead body. The two drove together in silence to the Sudanese military hospital where the bodies had been taken.

Wells had seen many a corpse in Vietnam, but he was shocked when he and Roehl were led into the room. The three whose remains were laid out on tables were unrecognizable, their bodies smashed by the bullets that had been fired into them. A medical autopsy would be conducted later, in the United States, but in Khartoum on the morning of March 4, only their heights gave a clue to the three men's identities. The tallest had to be Cleo Noel and the shortest Guy Eid. And so the other could only be Curt Moore.

On a table nearby lay a wallet with calling cards engraved in the name G. Curtis Moore, and below the name the title: Counselor of Embassy of the United States of America. A bullet had torn a hole clean through the wallet, piercing one edge of the cards on its way. Roehl and Wells took the wallet and the cards and other personal items found on the two Americans and delivered them to Bill Macomber, but Wells could not resist the temptation to keep one of the cards. The card with the bullet-pierced edge was so poignantly symbolic; it seemed to tell the whole story.

It was left to Macomber to tell Sally Moore and Lucille Noel that their husbands were dead. No one else wanted to do it, and Macomber was the senior-ranking person there, so it was a duty he could not escape.

The two women took the news quietly. They remained composed, as they had been throughout the ordeal. By then they already knew, intuitively, that there was no hope.

It was, Macomber felt, the most heart-rending moment of his life. He could not bear to present Sally the wallet and the cards; the bullet hole was too vivid and distressing a reminder of the monstrous way Curt and Cleo had died. He gave the wallet, the cards, and the two men's other personal effects to an aide, with instructions to deliver them to the widows after the funeral.

Throughout the afternoon of March 4, Lucille Noel and Sally Moore received callers in the reception room of the U.S. embassy residence, Sudanese and members of the international community who came to offer their condolences. Years later, many of the Sudanese were to remember Lucille Noel on that day and to marvel at the way she had turned the roles around, not allowing them to console her but consoling them in the grief and the guilt they felt that such a terrible thing could happen on their soil—just as her husband had sought to console his Saudi host moments before his own death. Was it, many wondered, simply her way of coping with the shock and pain of tragedy, or was it only a habit, a mannerism so deeply ingrained that not even tragedy could bring her to throw it off?

As the day wore on, the two women anxiously awaited arrival of the letters the gunmen had allowed their husbands to write them, but the letters did not come. Inquiry revealed that Ambassador al-Malhouk, after having spoken briefly with the press following the close of the siege of his embassy, had taken to his bed and forgotten them. Appalled by this and overcome by grief at what had happened to Moore and Noel, one of the Western diplomats with whom Moore had been friendly drove to the Saudi residence, stormed into Ambassador al-Malhouk's bedroom, and shook him awake.

An hour or so later, a messenger arrived from the Saudi embassy bearing the two letters. The messenger also brought another missive, this one for Sally Moore alone: the engraved silver plate presented to her husband by the diplomatic corps at the Saudi ambassador's reception on March 1.

*　*　*

The remains of the two men were brought to the U.S. embassy. Cleo Noel and Curt Moore lay there in state through the night of March 4, their coffins draped in American flags, in the chief of mission office that each had occupied for so many years. Sergeant Timothy Wells put his Marines in their dress blues and had them stand honor guard by the coffins. Sam Peale, Sandy Sanderson, and others kept vigil with their slain colleagues until dawn.

At daybreak the coffins were taken to the airport, where an aircraft from the presidential fleet, dispatched at the order of the White House, stood on the tarmac waiting to take the two men's remains, and their widows, back to the United States. There, before a Sudanese army honor guard smartly presenting arms, and a Sudanese bagpipe band outfitted in highland Scotch kilts, the Marines carried the coffins to the plane. Over and over again, endlessly it seemed, and very slowly, the bagpipes squealed out the notes of "Auld Lang Syne." Almost two decades later, after other memories had faded, the sound of the bagpipes playing "Auld Lang Syne" remained indelibly imprinted in the minds of those who witnessed the scene.

A large crowd of friends and mourners, Sudanese officials and private citizens, members of Khartoum's international set and of the diplomatic corps, turned out to offer their condolences and to bid Lucille and Sally farewell. Among the diplomatic corps, the Arab envoys were notable by their absence. Only the Egyptian ambassador and the Saudi first secretary, representing his ambassador (al-Malhouk remained bedridden for over a week afterwards), came. The killings and the Black September's claim that Curt Moore was a CIA agent responsible for the massacre of Palestinians in Jordan in 1970 had done their work. The other Arabs, intimidated, stayed away.

It was eight o'clock on Monday morning, March 5, 1973, when the

President Jaafar al-Nimeiry
(*Al Sahafa,* 3/1/73).

Guy Eid's fiancée being given condolences at Khartoum airport
(*Al Sahafa,* 3/6/73).

184

Deputy Under Secretary of State William B. Macomber in 1973.

Caskets of George Curtis Moore and Cleo A. Noel, Jr., lying in state at the National Presbyterian Church, Washington, D.C., March 5, 1973 (*State Department Newsletter*, 3/73).

President Richard M. Nixon standing beside the State Department memorial plaque on which Moore's and Noel's names are freshly engraved, State Department diplomatic entry lobby, March 6, 1973 (*State Department Newsletter,* 3/73).

President Richard M. Nixon addressing State Department employees on the assassinations, State Department diplomatic entry lobby, March 6, 1973 (*State Department Newsletter,* 3/73).

Secretary of State William Rogers with Sally Moore and Lucille
Noel at their husbands' burial at Arlington National Cemetery
(*State Department Newsletter*, 3/73).

presidential Boeing took off from Khartoum bearing the bodies of
George Curtis Moore and Cleo Allen Noel, Jr., and their widows and
children back to the United States. It was the day, and almost the hour,
that Curt and Sally Moore had been scheduled to fly home together in
a happy ending to what Curt had called, in his letter to Bob Fritts four
days earlier, "three and one-half of the finest years of my life."

* * *

Bill Macomber flew out on the presidential aircraft with Lucille and
Sally and the two men's remains. But before leaving, Macomber had
business to do in Khartoum. He had to make sure that President Jaafar
al-Nimeiry understood the importance the United States government
attached to ensuring that the killers were brought to justice.

The president of Sudan had been held up in Juba by bad weather and
had made it back to Khartoum only in the late afternoon of March 4.
Nimeiry summoned Macomber to his office at military headquarters that

187

evening. What the American envoy heard from the president of Sudan gave him ample satisfaction.

Nimeiry said that he was truly shocked by what had happened. The Black September, he said, were "a group of crazy savages." It had all been "simply senseless," and he was very, very sorry about the outcome. He had known both Moore and Noel personally, he remarked, and he had consulted each many times. They were sincere men, he said, and they were honest in their desire to improve relations between the Sudan and the United States. He knew their efforts were based not just on the instructions they received from their government but on their own personal convictions.

Unlike his vice-president the evening before, Nimeiry made no mention of Nixon's press conference remarks or of the State Department spokesman's announcement of Macomber's circumscribed mandate. Instead, he thanked Macomber for the support his government had received from the American embassy and from the State Department. His government, he said, had expected help from other governments in the area, but help had not been forthcoming. Nimeiry did not mention names, but obviously this was his way of expressing disappointment that Egypt and Saudi Arabia had not weighed in more energetically to prevent tragedy.

Nimeiry vowed that the killers would be tried and punished according to Sudanese law. Macomber welcomed this, but he probed for more assurance. In every case of Arab terrorism to that time, Arab and Western governments had let the killers go unpunished. The Egyptians had released Wasfi Tal's killers, the French had let go the gunman who had tried to kill Zaid Rifai, and the Germans had freed the three surviving Munich gunmen.

Macomber broached the issue with uncharacteristic indirection. He had noted, he said, that some newspaper reports had implied that the terrorists would be set free in a little while. Would the president comment on this? Nimeiry paused a moment, as if to reflect, and then asked that what he was about to say be held in strictest confidence. The killers, he confided, would be tried by military tribunal. A civil court, Nimeiry said, would not be appropriate, for it would become a front for political propaganda. He implied that the trial would begin very soon and would be speedy; he expected the evidence to be ready for presentation to the military tribunal within a week.

Macomber was gratified, but it seemed just a little too good to be true. In the comment that he appended to his cable to Washington, he added a word of caution. "I believe he meant what he said," Macomber wrote. "However Department should bear in mind that he spoke under the immediate impact of events which represent a stain on his government and, because he knew and liked the men involved, a personally felt tragedy as well. The pendulum which has moved very far in the direction we would like may swing somewhat back in the weeks ahead."[40] It was to prove a prescient forecast.

Earlier in the day Macomber had met with Omar al-Haj Musa, the Sudanese minister of information. Musa had come to the American embassy at noon on March 4 to convey President Nimeiry's official condolences, but in the discussion that followed, he had things to say that Macomber eagerly noted.

Musa told Macomber that he was persuaded the Black September had from the very beginning intended to kill the Western diplomats. He based this belief, he said, on the fact that the Black September gunmen had turned down all Sudanese proposals to give them safe passage out of the country in return for their commitment not to harm the hostages. The gunmen had insisted that they were going to kill the Western hostages. President Nixon's statement, the State Department's announcement that Macomber was coming with no authority to negotiate, the timing of Macomber's arrival, Jordan's refusal to release Abu Daoud—all these things, Musa maintained, at best affected only the timing of the killing.

In support of this view, Musa recounted that the Fatah radio station in Beirut had broadcast a message on the evening of March 2 chiding the gunmen, asking why the job had not been completed, why Moore, Noel, and Eid were still alive.

Macomber said he too had come to the conclusion that the Black September intended to kill the Western hostages, at least if the demand for the release of Abu Daoud was not met. But did Musa not think the release of Abu Daoud would have saved the three?

The Sudanese minister of information was skeptical. Perhaps, he said, but he was not sure.

Here was a view of the events of the previous days that would

[40]Khartoum telegram 440, Confidential/Exdis, DTG 042137Z Mar 73.

exculpate President Richard Nixon of responsibility for the three men's deaths. Macomber quickly cabled a report of Musa's remarks back to Washington.[41] That Musa's role had been secondary to those of Baghir and of Ibrahim, the minister of health, and that Musa himself may have been a target of the Black September (he was considered one of the architects of Sudan's policy of rapprochement with the United States, and the Black September gunmen had asked for him as a hostage in their proposal to fly to the United States, evidently with the intention of killing him there), was not mentioned in Macomber's cable.

*   *   *

Back in Washington, Macomber's cable came as a windfall for the State Department's spokesman, Charles Bray, as he faced the press at his daily noon briefing on Monday, March 5. A reporter asked if Bray had any comment on a statement issued by the Black September the previous day that attributed the killing of the hostages to "the arrogance and obstinacy of American imperialism represented by Nixon's statement and by the attitude of the hireling tools in Jordan."

The Black September statement, Bray shot back, was "sickening." Then he continued: "Our debriefings of those who were very much involved in this indicate to us an equally sickening fact. And that is that by their assessment it appears to have been the case that the terrorists planned from the outset to execute the three Western diplomats."

The reporter persisted. "Who were these people that you were debriefing, that you said were more directly involved?"

Bray went on background to answer the question. "They include not only Sudanese government officials involved but the Jordanian chargé d'affaires as well."[42]

The rallying to protect the president had begun in Washington, and it had begun in a way typical of such things. The opinion expressed by one Sudanese official, Minister of Information Omar al-Haj Musa, had become that of "Sudanese government officials." And the Jordanian chargé, Adli Nasser, had been brought in to bear additional witness to the inevitability of the killings, although the report Macomber sent in on his conversation with Nasser did not touch on this issue.[43]

[41]Khartoum telegram 428, Confidential/Exdis, DTG 041143Z Mar 73.
[42]State telegram, unclassified, DTG 052949Z Mar 73.
[43]Khartoum telegram 430, Secret/Exdis, DTG 041237Z Mar 73.

* * *

Even before the siege of the Saudi embassy ended, the Sudanese police raided the Fatah office in Khartoum. They found papers scattered everywhere. Whoever among the Fatah group had been charged with covering the tracks had not done his job. Police discovered an eight-page document that set out in detail the plans for the seizure of the Saudi embassy, together with drawings of the embassy and role assignments for the members of the Black September team.

The plans for the operation were in the handwriting of the head of the Fatah office, Fawaz Yassin Abdul Rahman. The Sudanese police also found a cable instructing Fawaz Yassin to fly to Tripoli on the morning of March 1.

The Palestine Liberation Organization maintained an office in Khartoum, separate from the Fatah office, and it too enjoyed diplomatic status. Ignoring his diplomatic immunity, the Sudanese police arrested the head of the PLO office, Abdul Latif Abu Hijle, questioned him, released him, and then arrested and released him once again. Abu Hijle had not taken part in the operation, but he could not have been ignorant of it. The Fatah office and the PLO office were located in the same building, the Blue Nile Insurance Building, on Qasr Street in downtown Khartoum.

On March 13, the Sudanese government expelled Abu Hijle and closed the PLO office in Khartoum.

* * *

George Thompson was perhaps the busiest member of the American embassy staff during the siege of the Saudi embassy and the days immediately afterwards. All the Western newsmen who came to Khartoum to cover the story headed straight for Thompson's office the moment they stepped off the plane. They all wanted a briefing, and they all wanted help of one sort or another. Thompson helped them all, and the newsmen repaid him by passing along tidbits of information they had gathered. A West German film crew that had managed to set up its cameras in a building in view of the Saudi embassy provided Thompson with pictures of the Black September gunmen as they filed out of the Saudi embassy; others gave him accounts of the surrender and of what the Saudi ambassador and the Jordanian chargé had told the press about their captivity.

The day after the presidential aircraft left Khartoum, John Barry of the

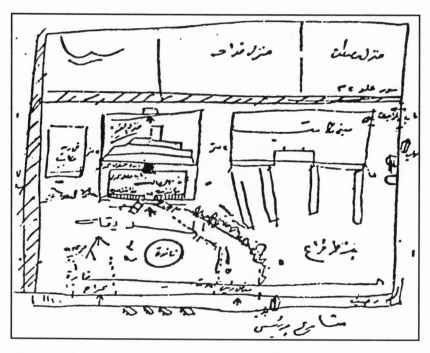

Map 3. *Top:* Crude sketch of the Saudi embassy in Arabic, drawn for the guidance of the terrorist squad by Al Fatah representative in Khartoum, Fawaz Yassin Abdel Rahman. Found in the Al Fatah office in Khartoum after the Black September's seizure of the embassy. *Bottom:* Redrawing and English-language translation. Source: the U.S. Central Intelligence Agency.

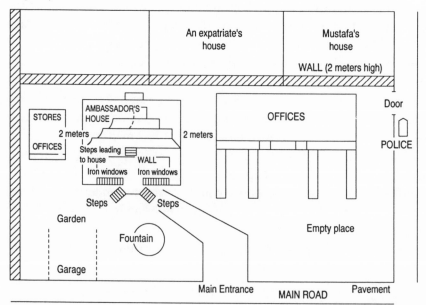

London *Sunday Times* came to speak with Thompson. He handed Thompson a packet of papers, all in Arabic. Thompson, an accomplished Arabic speaker, glanced briefly at the papers and realized that what he had in his hands were copies of the notes and plans for the Black September's seizure of the Saudi embassy. Barry asked for Thompson's help in translating the documents, in exchange for which, he said, Thompson could copy them. He explained that he had been given the papers by a senior Sudanese police official, a friend of his from an earlier time when he himself had been stationed in the Sudan in British government service.

Also among the papers was a transcript, prepared by the Sudanese government, of communications between the Fatah radio in Beirut and the Black September team in the Saudi embassy.

Thompson immediately handed the papers over to the CIA station chief, who sent them off to agency headquarters. Fritts sent a cable to the State Department reporting the find. To his cable Fritts added one further bit of information. It was worth noting, he wrote, that

> terrorists were apparently under external control from Beirut and did not murder Ambassador Noel and Moore nor surrender to GOS until receiving specific codeword instructions. GOS also reported attempting [to] buy Abu Daoud from Jordan (King Hussein refused) and contacting BSO in Beirut (who assumed full responsibility for attack).[44]

* * *

Washington Post correspondent Jim Hoagland stayed in Khartoum for ten days piecing together the story of what had happened in the Saudi embassy during the first three days of March. Afterwards, Hoagland flew to Tripoli to cover a press conference that Qaddafi held. For some reason the Libyan leader chose Hoagland to ask the first question, but the question Hoagland asked was not one that Qaddafi expected.

"Where is Fawaz Yassin?" Hoagland called out.

Qaddafi pretended he didn't know who Hoagland was talking about.

"Sure you do. You know," Hoagland insisted angrily. The Libyan leader, Hoagland was persuaded, knew all about the Khartoum opera-

[44]Khartoum telegram 471, Confidential, DTG 071215Z Mar 73. "GOS" refers to the Government of Sudan.

tion, and knew very well that Fawaz Yassin, the head of the Fatah office in Khartoum, had fled to his capital the day it took place.

Qaddafi passed on to the next questioner.

*　*　*

One of the first things King Hussein of Jordan did on returning to Amman after his stopover in Morocco was confirm the death penalty that had been issued at the end of February against Abu Daoud and his confederates.

For a moment, it looked as though the deaths of the three men in Khartoum would be avenged in the blood of the man the Black September had sought to ransom with their lives. But then protests quickly began to pour in from around the Arab world. The ruler of Kuwait, the president of Lebanon, and many others pleaded for mercy for Abu Daoud.

Hussein was a cautious man, one who was ready to bend with the wind. He had never executed any Palestinian terrorist, though many had plotted against him. The pleas for mercy offered him a way out of a situation he found distinctly uncomfortable. A few days later, the king of Jordan commuted Abu Daoud's death sentence, and that of the others, to life imprisonment.

19

No Rush to Justice

President Jaafar al-Nimeiry was genuinely aggrieved over the killing of the three Western diplomats. It was a heinous crime, he felt, and on top of that it was an insult to him and to his government. He was furious at the Black September and at Fatah. And he was furious at Yasser Arafat for having failed to come forward when there was still time to prevent tragedy.

Arafat publicly denied that the PLO or Fatah had had anything to do with the Black September's seizure of the Saudi embassy and the killing of the three Western diplomats. Despite this, the PLO leader refused to condemn the operation.

Nimeiry went on television on March 6, the day after the bodies of the three Western diplomats were flown out of Khartoum, to deliver a scathing denunciation of the murders and of the Black September. The president of the Sudan usually appeared in public in military uniform, but this time, in an appeal to national sentiment, he wore the traditional Sudanese flowing white robe. He spoke for over half an hour.

"What happened, I cannot describe other than being a criminal, irresponsible, unrevolutionary and cowardly act," Nimeiry declared. "There was no daring or risk in entering a country whose doors were open. . . . It was not heroic or manly to detain unarmed men while fully armed, to blackmail asking impossible demands, to slaughter these men like goats, or to keep their bodies for more than twenty-four hours in a way contrary to religion and morality."

Nimeiry reviewed the evidence:

The director of the Fatah office in Khartoum was deeply involved in the operation; he left plans in his own handwriting in his office before escaping to Libya the day of the incident. A telegram ordering him to be in Tripoli no later than March 1 had been found in his office.

The leader of the operation was the second in command at the Fatah office.

The vehicle that had carried the eight members of the operation belonged to Fatah.

But that was not all, Nimeiry declared indignantly. Documents discovered in the Fatah office showed that Fatah had been spying not only on certain embassies in Khartoum, but also on Sudanese government officials, following them, recording their movements, and conspiring against the Sudanese government and army. Nimeiry called on Arafat to return Fawaz Yassin, the director of the Fatah office, to Khartoum to stand trial along with the eight gunmen.

He closed his speech with an angry vow not to forget or forgive. "I am determined never to be lenient or forgiving. . . . September alone will not be black for them, but the government has the power to turn all the days of the year very black for them. . . ."[45]

As Sahafa, one of Khartoum's two daily newspapers (both controlled by the government), ran a long article telling the story of the operation—the arrival of the young Palestinians, the flight of Fawaz Yassin, the role of Rizk al-Qas, the use of a diplomatic-licensed Fatah vehicle to transport the gunmen to the Saudi embassy, General Baghir's efforts to dissuade the gunmen from killing the hostages, and the gunmen's cowardly surrender.

The regime proceeded to whip up a show of public solidarity with its leader. The official Sudanese media reported that telegrams of support were flooding into the presidential palace from every corner of the Sudan. They came from the Sudanese Women's Association, the Blue Nile Province General Trade Union, the workers of the Department of Posts and Telegraphs, the Gezira and Managil Tenants' Union, the Union of Workers of the Veterinary Department, the General Secondary Schools, Khartoum Province, the Sudanese Youth Union Committee, and on and on. Radio and television announcers spent hours reading

[45] *Nile Mirror,* March 9, 1973.

excerpts from the cables, to prove, as it were, that the whole nation was behind Nimeiry in his outrage over the killings. One hundred thousand workers were reported to have demonstrated in the provincial city of Atbara. They chanted "No Black September in the Sudan," called the Black September an "arrogant enemy," and demanded the death penalty for the killers. President Nimeiry was reported to have been greeted in Wad Madani by a massive demonstration of support from farmers who promised to back him "all the way." The Khartoum trade unions announced that a massive demonstration and parade would be held on March 10.

But there was less to all this than met the eye, and by March 10 even the government's ardor was beginning to fade. The demonstration and the parade announced for that day turned into a mere "rally." General Baghir delivered a short address to a relatively sparse crowd of no more than five thousand. The demonstrators carried banners and chanted slogans—"Long Live Nimeiry," "Down with the Enemies of the Revolution," "Death for the Plotters," "Criminals, Criminals, Black Septembrists"—but the affair bore all the marks of official sponsorship and few of genuine public emotion.

While Nimeiry and his associates denounced the Black September and the murderers, they were careful to proclaim their support for the Palestinian people and the Palestinian cause. Whatever Arab leaders thought, none could afford to appear less than fully committed to the Palestinians. A great many Sudanese were shocked and grieved by the murders, and many felt guilt that such a thing could happen in their country. But there was also much public sympathy in the Sudan for the Palestinians. People were already beginning to say that the killers really should not be blamed; they were young men who had grown up in the bitterness and misery of the refugee camps. They had known only misfortune, and so they should be dealt with leniently.

But there was no similar feeling of public sympathy for Libya or for its leader, Muammar al-Qaddafi. The extent of Qaddafi's involvement in the Black September operation in Khartoum was unclear, but the fact that Fawaz Yassin had fled there was well known. And so was Qaddafi's backing for the Black September. Unlike the Palestinians, Qaddafi was a real threat to Nimeiry and to his regime. So increasingly the Sudanese government turned its ire against Libya and Qaddafi and spotlighted Libya's real or presumed role in the operation. Among the banners carried at the March 10 rally were several that denounced Qaddafi and implied that he had had a hand in the killings.

Nimeiry's own barbs against Qaddafi were veiled; in public the president of Sudan never mentioned Libya and Qaddafi, but his allusions to them were unmistakable. Privately Nimeiry was much more candid. On March 12, speaking on deep background to Henry Tanner of the *New York Times*, Nimeiry declared himself "furious with Qaddafi." The Libyan leader, he said, was trying to drive a wedge between Sudan and the rest of the Arab world. The reason? "Libya is angry with us," Nimeiry said, "for reestablishing relations with the Americans and for settling the southern problem which of course has brought us closer to the Ethiopians. This is something Libya doesn't want."[46]

Qaddafi, like Arafat, disclaimed any link with the Khartoum operation but also refused to condemn it. In fact, the Libyan went even further than Arafat; he made a statement condoning it.

Sudanese government spokesmen put out word that the Fatah office in Khartoum had actually been doing Qaddafi's work by supporting the Eritrean rebels against both the government of Sudan and that of Ethiopia. General Baghir told the press that the Black September gunmen had tried to lure the Ethiopian ambassador to the Saudi reception so as to seize and execute him—this being the reason for the mysterious telephone calls insistently inviting the Ethiopian—and that they had also hoped to seize the Iranian ambassador, the Shah of Iran being another of Qaddafi's enemies of predilection.

* * *

Nimeiry had told Macomber that the killers would be tried by a military tribunal. This meant a quick, no-nonsense trial and a practically guaranteed death penalty. But by mid-March the U.S. embassy in Khartoum learned that trial by military tribunal was in question. A debate was underway within the ruling circle between those who still insisted on a military trial and those who argued for trial by civilian court, and a growing number were on the latter side. It was a contest between those who wanted stern punishment for the killers and those who advocated leniency.

Prospects even for the early trial that Nimeiry had promised were fast fading, too. When Fritts went to call on Foreign Minister Mansour

---

[46]Khartoum telegram 528, Confidential, DTG 131115Z Mar 73.

Khaled on March 14, he found Khaled evasive. Khaled had little to offer in response to Fritts's inquiry about the investigation and the trial. When would the trial begin? Fritts asked. It was not possible to say, the foreign minister replied. The investigation was proceeding, and the trial would be held under judicial auspices. The Sudanese judiciary, Khaled added with more than a little self-righteous bombast, was "properly jealous" of its prerogative to pursue justice under Sudanese law without external or even Sudanese government pressure. Fritts was soon to find that he rarely got a straight answer from Foreign Minister Mansour Khaled.

The independence of the judiciary was a refrain that American officials were to hear frequently in the months ahead: the matter was in the hands of the judiciary, its independence must not be infringed, and any pressure would be "counterproductive," might even cause the government of Sudan to release the killers.

This talk of the independence of the Sudanese judiciary should have been enough in and of itself to set off alarm bells in Washington. A judiciary with a strong sense of its own independence and integrity was one of the legacies of British colonial times, but in the years since 1956 the judiciary, like the country's other institutions, had been severely buffeted. The Sudan still had a judiciary that wanted to maintain the appearance of independence, and many of its officers were men of considerable integrity; but in actual fact it operated under governmental direction and did what the government wanted it to do. The talk about the independence of the judiciary signaled that the Sudanese were having second thoughts about how, when, and perhaps even whether to prosecute the killers.

In Washington, however, people still relied on Nimeiry's promise to bring the killers to justice, and there was little inclination to pound the table. Fritts himself counseled prudence. The American position, he cabled the State Department, "should continue to be one of watchful observation." Fritts advised against "approaches supposedly designed to strengthen the [Sudanese] commitment."[47]

The Sudanese foreign minister made another remark that showed a change in attitude. The government of Sudan, he told Fritts in their March 14 meeting, distinguished between Palestinian organizations that were political in orientation and those that were terrorist. On that basis,

[47]Khartoum telegram 558, Secret/Exdis, DTG 151300Z Mar 73.

it had decided that the Palestine Liberation Organization should be allowed to continue its presence in the Sudan. A day earlier the PLO representative in Khartoum, Abdul Latif Abu Hijle, had left Khartoum, reportedly under order of expulsion. Now the foreign minister was saying there was no expulsion, that the PLO would stay and that it was exculpated from complicity in the murders. Fritts remarked that he had understood that relations with the PLO had been suspended. "Yes," Khaled replied disingenuously, "but the suspension will only be for a short while."[48]

The PLO moved quickly to exploit these Sudanese hesitations. Its first objective was to dissociate itself from the murders. On March 18 Abu Hijle returned to Khartoum together with Jamal al-Sawrani, the PLO representative to the Arab League in Cairo. The two PLO officials came with honeyed words. On arrival at Khartoum airport, they announced that they wanted reconciliation. "What happened in the Sudan is . . . a summer cloud which has passed and gone," al-Sawrani told the press. "What happened in Khartoum," he protested, "had nothing to do with either the PLO or any PLO units." Al-Sawrani and Abu Hijle met with Foreign Minister Khaled and with General Baghir. They left the Sudanese capital singing the same tune they had arrived with. The operation, they assured, had had nothing to do with any of the Palestinian organizations; it was a rogue operation, and responsibility for it lay only with those who had carried it out.

The Sudanese knew this to be false, but they wanted to avoid a confrontation with the Palestinians, so they let the claim stand. When Fritts got in to see General Baghir on March 28, Baghir told him straight away that the Sudanese government was no longer challenging the PLO's and Fatah's public stance of dissociation from the killings, even though it was well aware of the Black September's links to both organizations.

In April, the Sudanese government allowed the PLO to reopen its office in Khartoum. In June they even let Fatah come back in, though after a short while they obliged it to merge its office with that of the PLO.

While responsibility was being lifted from the shoulders of the PLO

[48]Ibid.

and Fatah, Nimeiry pursued his campaign to transfer it to Libya. In a long, rambling interview published on March 17, the Sudanese president declared that "another Arab state" had "planned and financed the [Black September] operation." Sudanese and other Arabs were accustomed to these elliptical formulas. Everyone knew that "another Arab state" was Libya.

* * *

In Washington, another exculpation was underway. Richard Nixon was exculpating himself of responsibility for having triggered the murders of the two Americans and the Belgian.

The day before Moore's and Noel's funeral, Nixon came to the State Department to deliver a speech that turned out to be mainly a defense of his no-concessions policy. Standing on a dais erected in the main lobby, in front of a marble plaque on which Moore's and Noel's names had been freshly chiseled, Nixon suggested that the policy of "not paying blackmail" to those who took American personnel hostage had enjoyed the unreserved prior approval of the Foreign Service. Secretary Rogers, Nixon declared, had told him that a survey had been made of members of the service a few months earlier, and that the unanimous reply had been that "the United States government should not submit to demands for blackmail or ransom" in the event they were taken hostage.

This came as news to the crowd of State Department employees who had gathered to hear the president speak, for few if any of them had ever been asked to express an opinion on the matter. There had been no general survey, only a sampling of opinion among some senior officers at staff meetings in the State Department.

Then Nixon addressed the issue head on.

I was noting a well-intentioned comment by one individual who raised a question as to whether the United States, in this instance, might have been better advised to bring pressure on another government to release 60 who were held in prison in order to save the lives of two. I disagree with that. All of us would have liked to have saved the lives of these two very brave men, but they knew and we knew that in the event we had paid international blackmail in this way, it would have saved their lives but it would have endangered the lives of hundreds of others all over the world, because once the . . . terrorist . . . has a demand that . . . is satisfied, he then is encouraged to try it again.[49]

In one way, at least, it was a candid statement, for Nixon acknowledged what his State Department spokesman had sought to deny: "in the event we had paid international blackmail in this way, it would have saved their lives." Here Richard Nixon said it plainly. The two men had not been doomed from the outset. The Khartoum operation was not solely a killing operation. A deal could have been made.

But the deal, Nixon said, was sixty for two. Where Nixon got the figure sixty, he never explained. The Black September gunmen did not cite a specific number they wanted released from prison in Jordan; they had, quite likely, deliberately left the number vague. They had quickly set aside their demands for the release of Sirhan Sirhan, the Bader-Meinhoff gang in Germany, and Palestinian women prisoners in Israel. The total in the various categories they specified in their demand for release of prisoners in Jordan amounted to more than seventy. But since negotiations were ruled out, neither the United States nor Jordan ever tried to find out what final number the Black September would have settled for. In fact, in the Black September's second communiqué, only two were mentioned by name, Abu Daoud and Hindawi. So the number sixty cited by Nixon had no basis in fact. It was pure invention, intended evidently to suggest that the price for saving the two men's lives would have been too high.

Nixon declared that the two men had died so that others could live in safety. There was a large measure of sophistry in this argument too. A deal probably would have encouraged terrorists to try again, but that would not necessarily have entailed more deaths. And condemning the hostages to die was not the only possible response to hostage-taking.

Three days after Nixon spoke, the State Department sent a cable to all its overseas posts citing his words. The cable was the first formal State Department directive in announcement of the no-ransom policy, but it was couched in language that suggested that the policy was not being announced for the first time but merely reiterated. The only hint of acknowledgment that this was in fact a new directive that had never been formally communicated before was a stipulation that the president's

[49] *State Department Newsletter,* March 1973, pp. 6–7.

statement was to be brought to the attention of all American personnel.[50]

*   *   *

In Khartoum, as the weeks passed Fritts was getting more signals that an early trial was not in the offing. When Fritts saw General Baghir at the end of March, Baghir acknowledged that the Sudanese government was, as he put it, in "no hurry" to proceed. There was another trial, Baghir said, that the government wanted to get out of the way first, that of a retired general who had been arrested for plotting a coup. In mid-April the story was much the same. The debate between the partisans of "leniency" and "firmness" was still going on, a senior Sudanese official told Fritts, and it had not yet been decided whether the trial would be by civilian or military tribunal. This person thought the trial might begin in May, but he said no decision had been taken.

Now Fritts's patience began to wear thin. He warned that the United States' public silence should not be mistaken for indifference; Washington expected that justice would be done.

But May came and there was still no trial.

American efforts to learn the identities of the killers were not meeting with much greater success. The Sudanese media gave the names only of Rizk al-Qas and Karam Ahmad Aram, the two members of the Fatah office identified as having taken part in the operation. After several insistent American requests, the Sudanese handed over photos of the Black September gunmen, mug shots taken after their arrest, but the names attached to the pictures were those carried in the men's passports. They were almost certainly cover names. The Sudanese claimed these were the only names they had for the killers.

In this matter as with the trial, the State Department hesitated to press vigorously. The reason, it appears, was Washington's concern that to do so could annoy or offend the Sudanese. "We have asked our Chargé [in Khartoum] to suggest possible tactics for obtaining this information without offending the Sudanese government," read a memorandum prepared by the State Department's Office of Northern African Affairs on May 23.

And in May, Washington began to move ahead with plans to appoint a new ambassador. Some argued that a replacement for Cleo Noel

[50]State telegram 043544 DTG 092037Z Mar 73.

should not be named until his killers had been brought to justice. But this was a minority view. As one official put it later, the predominant view was that Nimeiry was not responsible for what had happened, and that he had done some positive things that merited recognition: he had renewed relations with the United States, he had reached agreement with Ethiopia, and he had brought peace to the southern Sudan for the first time since the Sudan became independent. So it seemed axiomatic that the right thing to do was send a new ambassador without waiting for a trial to be held or even insisting on one as a condition.

But there was another side to it as well. Bureaucracies, if they do anything well at all, do only what they are created to do. The Department of State was created to conduct the nation's diplomacy. Diplomacy, for most of its practitioners, meant the promotion of better relations between the United States and any given country. There was always a tremendous push in this direction, for better relations were equated with success. And the stronger the impetus for better relations, the more likely were other considerations to be brushed aside.

The apprehension and punishment of criminals was not something the State Department was set up to do. There was no bureaucratic entity within the department specifically charged with this function, none to champion its cause and do battle with others who had conflicting agendas. And since officials moved from one job to another with considerable frequency, no one individual could be relied upon to take on such a task himself.

Bill Macomber had been personally touched by the tragedy of the two men's deaths. With his fighter's instinct, he might have been the one to see to it that the natural impulses of diplomacy did not prevail over the moral duty to ensure that Moore's and Noel's killers were punished. But two months after the Khartoum killings, Macomber was sent off to be ambassador to Turkey. Armin Meyer was another who might have played that role, but Meyer retired in July and moved on to academia, glad to leave a job that he found the most thankless of his career. Meyer was replaced as head of the terrorism office by Lewis Hoffacker, a Foreign Service officer who was a former ambassador to Cameroon. Hoffacker was serving as political advisor to the naval command in Norfolk, Virginia, when one day in June 1973, a few weeks before Meyer's retirement, a call came from Washington asking if he would take the terrorism job. The call caught Hoffacker wholly by surprise. He knew nothing about terrorism, but as he later remarked, he was in the habit of taking jobs that were offered him, so he accepted. He had no idea why he had been chosen.

Hoffacker, however, did not consider that responsibility for ensuring punishment of Moore's and Noel's killers lay with his office. That, he felt, was the job of the Bureau of African Affairs, which office was, of course, the one designated to handle America's diplomatic relations with African countries. David Newsom, the assistant secretary of state for African affairs at the time of the Khartoum murders, was strongly committed to bringing the killers to justice, but Newsom had other priorities as well, and he too eventually left the job—in January 1974, on appointment as ambassador to Indonesia. William Schaufele, a career official who became assistant secretary for Africa in 1975, also had other concerns. Michael P. E. Hoyt, a Foreign Service officer who had been taken hostage and brutally mistreated during the troubles in the former Belgian Congo in 1964, later admonished Schaufele for wiping the slate clean for the Sudanese. "He [Schaufele] said that was not his responsibility," Hoyt recalled.

So Curt Moore and Cleo Noel, who were required to sacrifice their lives in Khartoum to sustain a principle of U.S. policy, found neither an institutional nor a consistent personal advocate at the State Department in Washington, no one whose prime and overriding responsibility it was to ensure that the government of Sudan honored its commitment to bring to justice the eight men who had murdered them. And none elsewhere in the United States government either, for the crime had occurred outside the United States, and the Department of Justice had no jurisdiction over it. From time to time, a congressman or senator wrote the State Department to inquire testily why the killers had not yet been brought to trial, and to ask what the administration was going to do about it. But they were fobbed off with routine replies, and even the most outraged among them did not persist.

In August a new secretary of state was appointed. Richard Nixon fired William Rogers, the man who had declined to sign the directive on the no-negotiations, no-deals, and no-concessions policy because he found it too callous (this, it should be noted, had nothing to do with Rogers's firing), and replaced him with Henry Kissinger, the man many thought to be the true author of that policy.

*　*　*

The appointment of the new United States ambassador to Sudan was announced on June 26, 1973, just a few days short of four months after the murder of his predecessor. The trial of the murderers had not yet begun, but the State Department was at pains to deny that there was any linkage between it and the appointment of the new ambassador. No assurances had been demanded, Washington declared, in counterpart for the sending of a new envoy.

The new ambassador was William D. Brewer. A man of medium height and build with coal-black hair, Brewer sported a bushy mustache and thick-lensed glasses that made his eyes seem to bulge from their sockets. He had a keen and ready wit that some thought a bit on the acid side, but he was an exceptionally astute and shrewd person and as able a diplomat as any in the American career service. The job of seeing to it that the Sudanese government brought Curt Moore's and Cleo Noel's killers to justice was to fall to Brewer, and he was to pursue it with skill and single-minded determination.

Brewer had no part in Washington's debate over whether to send a new ambassador in advance of a trial. He was ambassador to the Indian Ocean nation of Mauritius (a job well beneath his qualifications but one that afforded delightful opportunities for leisurely weekend sailing and snorkeling in the island's clear blue-green waters) when he was notified that he had been selected for the Sudan. In the course of his career, Brewer had known Curt Moore and Cleo Noel, but his relationship with both was simply that of a colleague; there was no close personal friendship between Brewer and either Moore or Noel. If there was an irony in Brewer's appointment as ambassador to Sudan in June 1973, it was that he had narrowly missed finding himself in Noel's shoes. In the summer of 1972 he had been a prime candidate for the job of ambassador to the Sudan. He had lost out to Cleo Noel, apparently because Noel enjoyed the potent support of William Hall, the director general of the Foreign Service and Noel's boss, and the advantage of extensive prior service in the Sudan.

* * *

Brewer did not arrive in Khartoum until September 1973. Early in June the Sudanese government announced that the trial would be by civil court, and that a preliminary phase called a magisterial inquiry, set to begin June 16, would precede the actual trial. Magisterial inquiry was the Sudanese equivalent of a grand jury hearing, intended to establish whether the charges had sufficient validity to warrant trial. On the face of it, this seemed quite unnecessary; neither the fact of the murders nor the identity of those who had committed them was in question. What it clearly showed was that the Sudanese authorities were still very hesitant about bringing the Black September terrorists to justice.

But the Sudanese were coming under increasing pressure from the PLO and from radical Arab states to let the Black September killers go, and they were frightened. They were frightened first of all of the Palestinians. The PLO and its various offshoots were playing a double game with them. Publicly the PLO continued to disavow the killings, to take the position that neither it nor any of its components had had any part in the seizure of the Saudi embassy and the murder of the diplomats, and that those who did these deeds had acted entirely on their own. Privately, however, they rushed to the defense of the killers and threatened reprisal if the Sudanese continued to hold them or put them on trial. In mid-March, hardly more than two weeks after his arrival in Khartoum, American intelligence discovered that Bob Fritts was under surveillance by individuals linked to the Black September. The Sudanese security authorities quickly moved to head off danger, but what did it mean? Had the Black September been planning to seize Fritts and ransom him for the eight imprisoned gunmen? In May there were intelligence reports that the Black September was plotting a coup in Khartoum, or threatening to seize a Sudanese embassy abroad. Thinly veiled threats of reprisal were made against the prosecutors and the judiciary, against members of the government, and even against Nimeiry if the eight gunmen were brought to trial.

The regime was also, to a lesser extent, afraid of its own public. Unless it was handled carefully, the prosecution of the eight young Palestinians could become a rallying point for the opposition. Leftist, pan-Arab circles in the Sudan were organizing in support of the imprisoned Palestinians. The Sudanese bar association fielded a defense team of twenty-two lawyers, headed by none other than the association's president, a certain Mirghani el-Nasri, who was on record as fully supporting the Black September's murder of the three diplomats as well as any similar act against Israel or the United States. The bar associations of Egypt, Algeria, Iraq, Syria, and "Palestine" also dispatched lawyers to Khartoum to assist in the defense.

So two days before the magisterial inquiry was to begin, the Sudanese prosecutor announced that it was being postponed—at the request of the defense attorneys. Fritts cabled Washington that he did not think it would be an extended postponement. But when Fritts asked the Sudanese authorities to tell him what specific charges would be filed against the defendants, he found himself rebuffed. The charges, he was told, were "strictly a judicial matter" and could not be disclosed. The Sudanese, Fritts found, were also stalling on his request for permission for a U.S. observer to be present at the trial.

July and August passed with no word on a date for the magisterial inquiry. When Brewer arrived in Khartoum in mid-September, Sudanese officials were saying privately that it might be postponed until the following year.

* * *

In the early 1970s, September was always a dangerous month in the Middle East. The problem was that it had too many anniversaries. September 1973 was the third anniversary of the massacre of Palestinians in Jordan. It was the first anniversary of the Munich operation. And now it was to take on a connection to the Khartoum murders of the previous March.

On September 5, 1973, the actual date of the first anniversary of Munich, five Arab gunmen stormed the embassy of Saudi Arabia in Paris. They took thirteen hostages and threatened to kill them if their demand was not met. That demand was the release of Abu Daoud from prison in Jordan—the same Abu Daoud whose release had been at the top of the list of the Khartoum Black September gunmen.

This time, however, it was not a Black September operation. The gunmen called themselves "the punishment group," and their aim in demanding the release of Abu Daoud may have been to get hold of him and make him pay for his embarrassing confession after his arrest in Jordan the previous February. The gunmen were very likely renegade elements of the Black September and the PFLP. These two organizations quickly dissociated themselves from the operation. Yasser Arafat spoke up to condemn it, and so even did Qaddafi. Finding no support for their action, the gunmen accepted an offer to fly out of France to Kuwait with five of their hostages. After holding out in Kuwait for a while, they capitulated and released the hostages.

Abu Daoud was still in jail in Jordan, but not for long. Two weeks later King Hussein flew to Cairo to meet with President Sadat and

President Hafez al-Assad of Syria to discuss "reactivation" of the eastern front against Israel. The meeting was the final step in Sadat's and Assad's secret preparations for the October 1973 war. It also marked Jordan's full reconciliation with its major Arab partners. The slate was wiped clean of the stains of September 1970. To show that this was so, Hussein returned home and amnestied all Palestinian prisoners. More than a thousand went free, most prominent among them Abu Daoud. It was said that Hussein went to the prison and took tea with Abu Daoud before releasing him.[51]

When Sam Peale learned of this, he thought back to the three lives that could have been saved if Abu Daoud had been freed only a few months earlier. He found Hussein's action "more than a bit sickening."

*　*　*

Making sure that the Black September killers were tried and punished was at the top of Bill Brewer's agenda when he arrived in Khartoum. Before he left Washington for Khartoum, Brewer let it be known that if the Black September killers were set free, he wanted to be recalled immediately.

Brewer saw that the time for caution had passed. Further postponement of the magisterial inquiry risked causing the whole process to collapse and the Black September killers to end up being freed. He was determined that this should not happen. Unlike the many diplomats who preferred to tiptoe around a confrontation, Brewer could be blunt when the occasion demanded it. But he also had a talent for saying hard, blunt things in a way to which few could legitimately take exception.

Brewer decided to raise the issue in his first meeting with Nimeiry, just after the ceremony in which he presented his credentials. By tradition it was not a meeting in which business was discussed, but Brewer considered that all the more reason to do so, for to bring the matter up then would show what importance the United States attached to it. Brewer told Nimeiry that the American people expected the Black September killers to be brought to justice "within a reasonable period." He made the same point publicly in remarks to the local media following the meeting with Nimeiry.

In Washington, David Newsom's patience with Sudanese foot-dragging was also running out. The assistant secretary for African affairs felt

---

[51]Dobson, *Black September,* p. 160.

it was time to move more energetically. A few days after Brewer's arrival in Khartoum, Newsom called in the Sudanese ambassador in Washington and laid it on the line: any "unreasonable delay" in the prosecution of the Black September killers would have serious repercussions on U.S. relations with the Sudan. This was language the Sudanese were not used to hearing. Fadl al-Obeid, the Foreign Ministry under secretary, sought to take Brewer to task for Newsom's bluntness. Obeid called Brewer in and observed testily that he hoped Newsom had not said what the Sudanese ambassador had reported him to have said.

Brewer was not one to be intimidated. He coolly deflected Obeid's objections. The United States, he said, was in no way seeking to instruct the Sudanese in this matter. But at the same time there was no question that an unreasonable postponement of the trial would have a serious impact on relations between the two countries. Borrowing a metaphor from the PLO, Brewer said the issue was "like a cloud on the horizon that might either pass away or develop into a real storm." Which happened, he added pointedly, was up to the Sudanese. For its part, the United States wanted to alert the government of Sudan to the danger while hoping that a downpour could be avoided.[52] The message got through. The magisterial inquiry convened for its first session on September 25.

The first session lasted only an hour and was largely symbolic, aimed merely at launching the inquiry. The accused—the eight gunmen who were in the Saudi embassy, plus the driver who had delivered them there and the Fatah office's radio operator—filed into the courtroom flashing a V-for-victory sign. They drew noisy applause and shouts of support from some three dozen Palestinian students massed in the public gallery. The main event was a rambling speech by Rizk al-Qas, who, after having shared leadership of the gunmen in the Saudi embassy with Tariq, was now, in court, assuming the role of sole leader and spokesman. He and his colleagues were innocent of any crime, al-Qas declared. Their act was a "revolutionary deed," warranted by America's support for Israel.

Al-Qas even found a precedent for it in Sudanese history. He likened the Black September's killing of Moore, Noel, and Eid to that of Gordon by the Mahdi's forces.

With that the magisterial inquiry adjourned, at the request of the

---

[52]Khartoum telegram 2147, Confidential, DTG 241110Z Sep 73.

defense, whose legal team was in disarray. Early in September several of its members had been jailed for taking part in a demonstration against the government.

Ten days after the first hearing, the Middle East was rocked by war as Egypt and Syria struck at Israel, seeking desperately to drive Israel out of its 1967 conquests. The Israelis suffered heavy losses in equipment and in men. In mid-October the United States launched a massive airlift to resupply the Israelis with tanks, artillery, aircraft, and ammunition, and it coincided with a successful Israeli campaign to push the Egyptians and the Syrians back.

If the Sudanese wanted a political excuse for releasing the Black September killers, the American airlift for Israel would have been it. In fact, on October 17 the Sudanese did release Karam, the Fatah office employee who had met the gunmen on their arrival in Khartoum and who the next day had driven them to the Saudi embassy, and Hassan Ahmad Hussein, the radio operator at the Fatah office. Both were deeply complicit in the crime and should have been tried and punished as such, but neither was actually in the Saudi embassy.

By early November, however, the United States and Egypt were launched on talks that were to save the Egyptians from the humiliation of defeat and would soon lead to a resumption of diplomatic relations between Washington and Cairo. Brewer saw that the moment was right to give the Sudanese a push. On his own initiative, with no instruction from Washington, he urged them to proceed with the magisterial inquiry without further delay.

When Assistant Secretary David Newsom stopped in Khartoum a few days later, in the course of a trip through East Africa, he made a point of letting the president of Sudan know that the United States wanted justice done. Nimeiry assured Newsom that the trial would go forward.

Brewer's and Newsom's insistence on raising the matter put things back on track. The magisterial inquiry resumed in mid-November.

20

Trial and Release

But the resumption of the magisterial inquiry and Nimeiry's commitment to carry through with the trial did not solve all problems.

The defense used every tactic imaginable to string out the proceedings. It claimed that the government of the Sudan, by its prior declarations of support for the Palestinian cause, had forfeited the right to prosecute the defendants for an act aimed against Israel and its supporter the United States. It argued that because the act had occurred inside the embassy of Saudi Arabia, the Sudanese government had no jurisdiction over it. When the court rejected both these contentions, the defense sought to overturn the ruling through appeal to another court. But this too failed.

Rizk al-Qas continued his theatricals and his diatribes. The defendants, he proclaimed at one session, were revolutionaries and heroes. They were not killers at all, and anyone who said they were was either "a Zionist or a U.S. agent." Al-Qas tried one tactic after another. He contended that General Baghir had promised the Black September group during the surrender negotiations that they would not be prosecuted. In the hearing on November 17, al-Qas read a long prepared statement in which he accused both Noel and Moore of being CIA agents, and of being responsible for the deaths of twenty-five thousand Palestinian fedayeen in Jordan and Syria; and he alleged that Eid had been involved in smuggling arms to rebels in southern Sudan. The defendants' only purpose was the recovery of Palestine, al-Qas said, and all Arab governments approved the use of force to that end. The Black September men had been wrongly detained in the Sudan for an extended period. They should have been released early in October so that they could fight alongside the Egyptians and Syrians against Israel. Al-Qas closed this declaration, and other later ones, with shouts of "Death to Israel and the USA" and "Long Live Palestine."

If all this showed that al-Qas and his associates were becoming a bit desperate, so did another statement the Black September team leader made. At the November 17 hearing, al-Qas publicly contradicted the PLO's denial of involvement in the Khartoum operation. The PLO, he said, had instructed them to carry out their act. If they were to be tried, it should be by the PLO, which would judge whether or not they had done their duty.

Al-Qas's antics irritated the court but might have succeeded in intimidating it, had it not been assured of higher backing. Nimeiry stepped in to shore up the court's determination. The Sudanese president, a "good source" told the American embassy, made it known to the chief magistrate and to the prosecution that he did not want "political elements" to intrude into the judicial process. The court and the attorney general, he said, had a responsibility to uphold the reputation of Sudanese justice.[53]

For the PLO itself, al-Qas was coming to be regarded as a liability. The PLO representative in Khartoum—a new one, named Abu Kheir, had been appointed—attended the sessions and was frequently seen trying to shut up the vitriolic young Palestinian. Al-Qas was said to be complaining about Abu Kheir, accusing him of doing nothing to help the Black September defendants, and of being absent from the Sudan during critical periods in the trial. Al-Qas and the other defendants also complained frequently about their defense lawyers, even treated them insolently, despite the fact that the members of the defense team were ardent supporters of their cause.

The hearings brought out a grisly detail: during interrogation following their arrest, the defendants confessed that all eight of them had taken part in the killing of the three diplomats, that they had fired Kalashnikov assault rifles and pistols at the three men as they were lined up against

[53]Khartoum telegram 2488, Confidential, DTG 161235Z Nov 73.

the wall of the basement of the Saudi embassy, their hands and feet bound.

Among the evidence brought forward by the prosecution was the confession made by al-Qas following the surrender. In it he said that the Black September action was directed primarily against Moore and (contradicting his public statement at the magisterial inquiry) that the gunmen had nothing against Noel. He repeated the story that Moore was a CIA agent who had masterminded the massacre of Palestinians in Amman in September 1970. The other members of the Black September team said the same thing in their confessions: it was Moore they were out to get, and the reason they wanted to get him was that he was a CIA agent and was responsible for the killing of Palestinians in Jordan in 1970.

* * *

The magisterial inquiry ended in March 1974, but it ended, to the great relief and satisfaction of the U.S. embassy in Khartoum and of the Department of State, with the announcement that the defendants were to be tried on charges of murder.

Under Sudanese law, a murder conviction carried an automatic penalty of death, although if it wished, the court could recommend life imprisonment. If it did so, however, it was required to submit a brief outlining the mitigating circumstances that justified the lesser punishment.

Ambassador William Brewer did not believe the Sudanese would execute the Black September killers, but he saw the indictment issued by the magisterial inquiry as a kind of Rubicon for Sudanese justice. Having crossed it, the Sudanese would not now be able to turn back, and since guilt was established, the sentence could not be less than life imprisonment.

But March passed into April and April into May, and still no date was set for the trial to begin. Brewer prodded and cajoled and here and there let drop veiled threats about the impact on the U.S. aid program of further delay. Sudanese officials reassured the American ambassador that the trial would go forward and the killers would be punished. But plainly the Sudanese were scared of Palestinian retaliation. And the local rumor mill was disquieting. On the street, and in the salons, people were saying that Nimeiry would release the eight Palestinians.

The trial finally began on June 1. Two days later the U.S. radio broadcast monitoring service picked up a dispatch filed by the Khartoum correspondent of the Beirut newspaper *Al Muharrer* reporting that the Sudanese had assured the PLO that the eight defendants would be released on June 16. Brewer considered this unlikely but wanted to be armed to counter pressures on Nimeiry for leniency. He sent off a cable to Washington asking for instructions that he could use with Nimeiry as soon as the verdict was issued, on the assumption that the court would convict. Brewer would go to Nimeiry and express the U.S. government's great satisfaction. He would say the United States was confident that the sentences would be carried out, and he would make clear that if they were not, relations would be adversely affected.

The State Department approved the line Brewer proposed. Satisfied that he was now prepared for any eventuality, Brewer put the department's reply in his safe and waited for the verdict.

The trial moved along smartly. Rizk al-Qas delivered another of his diatribes charging that Moore was a notorious CIA agent responsible for the killing of Palestinians in Jordan in September 1970 (the head of the defense legal team told a Sudanese lawyer the U.S. embassy hired to monitor the trial that the Black September gunmen did not believe this and had never believed it),[54] that Noel was "an important imperialist," and that Eid was an Israeli spy. But the defense had only political arguments: that the Black September action was a "new and glorious page to commando deeds for the liberation of Palestine," and that the eight young men were representatives of the whole Palestinian nation and their act represented its collective will. The prosecution had the facts, the confessions of the gunmen, and the law on its side. The chief prosecutor, Abdel Moneim Mustafa, presented a forceful and detailed closing summation. Rizk al-Qas was observed to be sweating heavily during much of the hour and three-quarters the prosecutor spoke.

The trial ended on June 24, 1973, just short of sixteen months after the murder of George Curtis Moore, Cleo Allen Noel, Jr., and Guy Eid. The court convened at 10:00 A.M., and at noon it announced sentences of life imprisonment for all eight of the Black September killers. At the American embassy there was jubilation. Sam Peale came home for lunch that day elated that at long last justice had been done.

The elation was to be short-lived, however. Unbeknownst to the

---

[54]Khartoum telegram 8273, Confidential, DTG 041245Z Jun 74.

Americans, the sentences were rushed to the Supreme Court, which immediately confirmed them, and then on to Nimeiry, who commuted them to seven years' imprisonment and remanded the prisoners to the custody of the Palestine Liberation Organization. At midafternoon, some three hours after the announcement of the life sentences, the prisoners were on a plane headed for Cairo.

The Sudanese made no move to inform the U.S. embassy. The Americans were stunned when they learned the news late that afternoon, from a BBC shortwave newscast. Brewer telephoned the Foreign Ministry and was told that a statement explaining Nimeiry's move had been prepared and was available at the ministry. He sent Sam Peale to pick up a copy of it, and he cabled it back to Washington. It read:

> The Court has today pronounced its judgement against the accused in the case of the Saudi Arabian Embassy's incident in Khartoum on lst March 1973. The court found all the accused guilty and sentenced them to life imprisonment. The sentence was later confirmed by the High Court who recommended to the President the remission of sentence for the special circumstances of the case. With a view to those considerations and the sufferings of the convicted and that of their families and relatives caused by the barbaric Israeli aggression which resulted in the assassination of some high ranking Palestinian leaders in Beirut and in the death of tens of innocent children and women living in refugee camps in southern Lebanon and the persistent Israeli persecution of Palestinians everywhere, and in order to sustain the genuine efforts recently made to maintain peace in the region and the world at large, the President of the Democratic Republic of the Sudan has decided to commute the life sentence to seven years of imprisonment. . . . The eight condemned persons will be handed over to the Palestinian Liberation Organization to execute the sentence passed against them, being the legitimate representative of the Palestinian people.[55]

The American ambassador was outraged. The instructions he had were now worthless. He cabled frantically for new instructions, for to make the kind of demarche he envisaged, he would need to be able to say that he was speaking not just personally but on orders from his government. Brewer expected an immediate reply to his cable, but hours passed and none came. The cause of the bottleneck, he later learned, was

[55]Khartoum telegram 1503, Limited Official Use, DTG 241855Z Jun 74.

Secretary of State Henry Kissinger. The Bureau of African Affairs had prepared instructions for Brewer, but Kissinger insisted on seeing them before they were sent. The secretary of state, however, was busy with other things. He took the cable home with him that evening, but he came to the office the next morning without having read it. Finally, just before leaving for a trip to Brussels with Nixon, Kissinger approved the cable and it was sent.

As soon as he received Washington's cable, Brewer got on the phone to the foreign minister's office. The official on the other end of the line guessed Brewer's purpose in calling, and he tried to stall.

"The minister," the official said, "is not available."

Brewer was in no mood to be put off. "Well, then, please make him available."

A short while later, Foreign Minister Mansour Khaled called Brewer back.

"I have urgent instructions to see President Nimeiry," Brewer told the Sudanese foreign minister.

There was a brief pause on the line. "Regrettably that will not be possible," Khaled replied, "because the president is going to Wad Madani."

"Then I will go to Wad Madani too."

Khaled realized that the American ambassador was not going to take no for an answer. He phoned back a few minutes later and told Brewer that an appointment had been arranged for nine o'clock the following morning.

Brewer had developed good relations with Nimeiry, but now he had a hard message to deliver. Sending the guilty out of the country was wrong, Brewer told the Sudanese president. He could not understand how the Sudanese government could have done it. The Sudanese were a proud people, a brave people. Now, however, they had violated their commitment to see that justice was done. There would be serious repercussions on relations between the Sudan and the United States, Brewer warned. He could not say what steps would be taken, but he was sure some would be.

Nimeiry took it quietly, as though he expected it. He did not apologize. He said simply that what he had done he had done in the interests of the Sudan. Sudanese interests everywhere would be threatened if the

Black September men were permanently jailed in the Sudan; Sudanese diplomatic missions abroad might be attacked and Sudanese diplomats killed. He could not afford to take that risk.

Later that morning Brewer went by to see Fadl al-Obeid, the under secretary of the Foreign Ministry, to give official notification of his recall to Washington. He took the occasion to register his surprise and disappointment that the Sudanese would act so deviously—sneaking the killers onto a plane to Cairo within hours of the issuance of the verdict, creating a fait accompli.

"We had to do it that way," Obeid replied. "We were afraid you might have shot the plane out of the air if you had known about it."

Brewer and his wife spent the rest of the day packing. Early the next morning they flew out of Khartoum, back to Washington.

* * *

Lucy Moore Wyatt does not remember the exact date that she was called to the presidential palace in Khartoum to meet with Nimeiry. But it must have been the day of the sentencing itself, June 24, 1974.

Lucy was Curt's and Sally's elder daughter. She had interrupted her undergraduate studies to spend 1972 with her parents in Khartoum and had gone back to college in the United States only toward the end of January 1973, just a little more than a month before her father's murder. In the course of the year in Khartoum, Lucy had met a young Englishman, David Wyatt, who during the day taught English at Khartoum Polytechnic and at night changed into a flaming yellow shirt to play the saxophone in a rock band at the city's main hotel. Lucy had joined the band and played the organ, and she and David had seen a lot of one another. When Lucy flew into Khartoum on March 4, 1973, on the presidential aircraft sent to bring back her father's remains, she was surprised to find David at her mother's side, helping her pack. David came to Washington that summer, and he and Lucy were married there.

After the wedding they went back to Khartoum, David to resume teaching at the Polytechnic and Lucy to work at Khartoum University, and both of them to play once more in the band. They were not part of the diplomatic crowd, so they did not see much of the people at the American embassy, or even of Curt's and Sally's Sudanese or other foreign friends. They got their news about the magisterial inquiry and the trial mainly from the Sudanese newspapers.

The invitation to see Nimeiry came without explanation of its purpose. For a moment, Lucy hesitated. The only means of transportation she and David had was a small, battered motor scooter. Her father had represented the United States in the Sudan. She wondered if it would not seem strange for her to arrive at the presidential palace on a motor scooter. She asked people at the American embassy if they could provide a car to take her to the appointment, but the embassy refused; they said they did not want to put an official imprimatur on the visit. Lucy decided to go anyway. If her father were alive, she told herself, he would never have understood if she had not gone. So she pulled up to the palace gate on her motor scooter. Once inside, she was told that Nimeiry could not see her after all, but that the vice-president, General Baghir, would meet with her. She waited a while and then was taken to Baghir.

Very quickly it became apparent what was desired of George Curtis Moore's elder daughter. "Basically," Lucy Moore Wyatt said, years later recalling the meeting, "he [Baghir] told me that they were going to send the terrorists out of the Sudan to Egypt. And he was asking for my okay. It was very clear what was happening. I was supposed to say that's all right, I understand, I accept it, you can tell everybody that I accept it. I know you're in a terrible position."

She was only twenty-three, and she was acutely conscious of her youth and of the fact that she was merely a private citizen, and an unimportant one at that. But she had her father's spunk. And now it was falling to her to speak for her family and for her father. And so she spoke, in the way she knew her father would have wanted her to speak. She told Baghir straight away that she was not going to do what she was being asked to do. She was not going to give her family's blessing to this act. She knew there was a lot of pressure being put on the Sudanese, and that even in holding a trial the government of Sudan had gone well beyond what other Arab governments had done in similar cases.

"But my father was a friend of your people," Lucy reminded the Sudanese vice-president. "He worked hard to help them, and he certainly would not have felt that it was right for you to do this. There's no question what these men did, and I'm not going to tell you that what you propose is right. It isn't. It is wrong."

With that Lucy Moore Wyatt got up and left the office of the vice-president of the Sudan.

* * *

By June 1974, Hermann Frederick Eilts had been the United States ambassador to Egypt for only a few months. In January of that year, American diplomacy had engineered a disengagement agreement between Egypt and Israel that cleared Israeli forces from the west bank of the Suez Canal and pushed them back some miles behind the canal's east bank, setting the stage for Egypt to reopen the waterway. The U.S.-Egyptian relationship was fast developing, and it held out the prospect of substantial amounts of American aid for Egypt. Cultivation of that relationship was at the top of President Sadat's agenda.

A short while after the Black September killers arrived in Cairo, Eilts happened to hold a meeting with Ashraf Marwan, counselor to President Sadat and one of his senior advisors. Black September and the Khartoum verdicts were not a part of the agenda, for Eilts had received no instructions from Washington on the matter. But Marwan raised the subject. He mentioned, as though in passing, that the Black September men were in Cairo, and he said it was President Sadat's intention to let them go. This, Marwan indicated, was the arrangement that had been made between Nimeiry and Sadat; i.e., the killers would be transferred from Khartoum to Cairo and once there would be released. Marwan did not ask Eilts for an opinion on the proposed release. He was running it by Eilts to see how the American ambassador would react. If Eilts said nothing, the Egyptians would take his silence as tacit American approval for the release of the killers. It was a familiar ploy, and Eilts, a savvy diplomat, immediately recognized it for what it was.

Eilts knew he had to weigh in strongly and act without delay, on his own initiative, for by the time he could get instructions from Washington, the killers would have gone free. So Eilts gave Marwan a blunt warning: he was deeply concerned, he said, that the release of the Black September killers would cause any prospect for the new relationship that Egypt and the United States hoped to establish—and, by extension, the aid that Egypt hoped to receive from the United States—to go by the board. President Sadat, Eilts added, should be made aware of this.

Eilts's response left the Egyptian alarmed. Marwan hurried off to see Sadat. A few days later, he reported back to Eilts that the president of Egypt had decided to hold the Palestinians for the remainder of their sentences.

But there was one puzzling element that no one could resolve. Eight gunmen had left the Saudi embassy on the morning of March 4, 1973, and eight were tried and sentenced by the Sudanese court on June 24, 1974. But according to the Egyptians, only five showed up in Cairo. Where were the other three? Were they released in Khartoum and sent out to some destination other than Egypt? Or were they let loose when they got to Cairo? And who were they? Eilts was never able to get answers to these questions. Several times he asked to know where and in what conditions the five were being detained, and he asked to send someone to look in on them, but the Egyptians never answered any of his requests. The new foreign minister, Ismail Fahmy, assured Eilts that the Black September gunmen were being held in a jail. Sadat did also in one instance. But Eilts suspected they were being held under a kind of house arrest rather than in a regular jail.

Eilts cabled Washington a report of his meeting with Marwan. In due course the State Department sent back its endorsement of the position he had taken. But during all the rest of Eilts's time as ambassador to Egypt—he did not leave Cairo until the summer of 1979—Washington never again raised the matter with him, never sent him any kind of instruction or even inquiry about the Black September killers detained in Cairo.

For in Washington, the process of forgetting had already begun.

21

Dissent in the Ranks

In Washington, the first reaction to Nimeiry's release of the killers was one of shock and outrage. "We are dismayed by the virtual release of these confessed murderers," State Department spokesman Robert Anderson told the press at the noon briefing on June 25 as he announced Brewer's recall. "We cannot accept [it] as adequate punishment." But other than the recall of the U.S. ambassador, Anderson had nothing to say about what measures the administration might take to punish the Sudanese for their action.

From the media and political circles came a chorus of condemnation. "Mocking the dead," the *New York Times* called it in an editorial on June 25. Nimeiry's release of the killers, the paper said, was "a cowardly act," one that put the Sudan on "the dishonor roll of countries which, by surrender to Arab pressures, have made themselves accomplices in the spread of international terrorism." Senator Robert Byrd urged that the United States break off diplomatic relations with the Sudan. "This is a disgraceful situation," Byrd declared in a speech to the Senate, "one that brings us no honor when eight self-admitted murderers of two American diplomats can apparently commit such a dastardly act and pay no penalty for their crimes." Others spoke in like outrage.

Despite the volley of public and congressional condemnation, the administration seemed in no hurry to move against the Sudanese. When Brewer got back to Washington, he was surprised to find that all of the various U.S. aid programs for the Sudan were proceeding as usual. He had told Nimeiry that steps would be taken, so now he had an interest in seeing that they were. The source of the delay, Brewer found, again was Kissinger. The secretary of state wanted to approve everything, but he was too busy, or so his aides said, to deal with the issue immediately. Several weeks were to pass before Kissinger would make himself available to address the matter of sanctions against the government of Sudan. Finally, however, a meeting was held with Kissinger, and it was decided to suspend the U.S. aid program, to cut off Export-Import Bank loans and private investment loan guarantees, and to send home some—but not all—of the Sudanese military officers who were studying at war colleges in the United States. Brewer would remain in Washington for a while. And relations with the Sudan would go into a deep freeze.

Sudanese reaction to these steps was muted, for Nimeiry had not released the Black September killers out of hostility toward the United States, only out of fear of what the Palestinians, Libya, and other radical regimes might do to him if he persisted in holding them. The president of Sudan continued to consider himself a friend of the United States, and his desire for good relations with Washington was strengthened by the growing rapprochement between his Egyptian neighbor and the United States. Nimeiry evidently had expected that the Americans would react rather sharply at first to his letting the killers go, but he also seemed to expect, or at least to hope, that the reaction would not last overly long. On June 26, two days after Moore's and Noel's murderers were released, Sudanese Foreign Minister Mansour Khaled sent Kissinger a saccharine-sweet letter insinuating that this move somehow—he did not say how—served the goal of advancing Middle East peace efforts, an endeavor in which Kissinger was then deeply engaged. Khaled closed his missive with the statement that it was President Nimeiry's "firm belief that our newly born good relations are all important to us, and no passing incident, however painful, should mar them."

The State Department filed Khaled's letter away without answer or even acknowledgment—the description of the murder of the two American diplomats as a "passing incident" was a bit too much to stomach—but this did not discourage the assiduous Sudanese foreign minister. Toward the end of September, at the annual opening of the UN General Assembly, Khaled met with Joseph Sisco, the under secretary of state for political affairs, and suggested that it was time for the United States to send its ambassador back to Khartoum.

Washington was already thinking along those same lines. It was never easy for American diplomacy to resist the blandishments of a government that proclaimed itself friendly. To do so was especially difficult when the country in question was so strategically important as was the Sudan at that particular moment. Kissinger wanted all the Arab backing he could get for his efforts to bring Egypt and Israel along, step by step, toward peace. The support of Egypt's southern neighbor was regarded as all the more needed in light of the hostility shown toward Kissinger's undertaking by Egypt's western neighbor, Libya.

The turmoil in Ethiopia gave added impetus to Washington's wish to thaw the freeze in relations with the Sudan. In September, Emperor Haile Selassie, Washington's staunchest ally in Africa, was deposed by a junta of left-leaning middle-grade military officers. The new government showed an unmistakable interest in moving Ethiopia closer to the Soviet Union.

Late in September, James Akins, a career Foreign Service officer who was ambassador to Saudi Arabia, got wind of the plan to send Brewer back to Khartoum in October. Akins had been a good friend of both Moore and Noel, and he was dismayed over his government's evident reluctance to stand up for them. In June, when Nimeiry had released their killers, he had cabled Washington to propose that Nixon or Kissinger ask the Saudis to issue a public condemnation of the Sudanese action. Washington ignored Akins's proposal. Akins was keenly aware that pressing the issue would not win him popularity with Kissinger or the administration. But he could not restrain himself when he learned that the administration was on the point of sending its ambassador back to Sudan. Akins sent off a long cable saying that the earlier decision, which he knew was Kissinger's, to appoint a U.S. ambassador to Khartoum before the Sudanese had tried and punished Moore's and Noel's killers had been "a mistake." He argued strongly that Brewer's return now would send the wrong signal to the Sudanese and to other governments. "Some counter-weight must be applied by the United States," Akins wrote, against governments that fail to punish terrorists.

Henry Kissinger never liked to be told by anyone that he had made a mistake. Akins soon learned that Kissinger had been mightily irritated by his cable. He also learned, to his disappointment, that he was the only ambassador to speak up on this issue. When Akins was summarily dismissed from his job a few months later, he was sure his criticism of Washington's rush to restore relations with Sudan was one of the reasons.

It was probably less Akins's objections than the Sudanese foreign minister's explicit request to Sisco that kept the secretary of state from ordering Brewer back to Khartoum at the beginning of October. The State Department did not want to be seen to be responding to Sudanese pressure, so Brewer was kept in Washington another few weeks. In mid-November, however, he flew off to the Sudanese capital. But Brewer himself saw to it that he went with instructions to make clear there that his return did not mean that all was forgiven and forgotten, or that American aid programs would soon be resumed.

If no other ambassador dared follow Akins in protesting directly to Kissinger, Brewer's return to Khartoum nonetheless did spark protest within the ranks of the Foreign Service, a group that rarely protested anything. In the manner of such things in that time, it was a muted protest, and it was wholly in-house. Foreign Service officers considered themselves gentlemen dealing with other gentlemen. And gentlemen did not air their disputes in public.

The channel for the protest was the American Foreign Service Association. The association was a kind of labor union whose members did not like to think of it as a union, or themselves as belonging to one. After a contest of several years, the association had won the right to represent the employees of the foreign affairs community (some eleven thousand at the time) in dealings with State Department, USIA, and AID management. It of course did not pretend to engage in collective bargaining—government unions do not negotiate with management over pay—but it did aspire to speak for the interests of Foreign Service personnel. The association drew to its leadership some of the most talented, and the most outspoken, members of the Foreign Service.

A few weeks after Brewer's return, the association sent Secretary of State Henry Kissinger a letter which, although couched in respectfully restrained language, was of a kind that Kissinger was unaccustomed to receiving from subordinates:

> The Association is very concerned about the implications . . . of the return of Ambassador Brewer to the Sudan. Without appropriate addi-

tional action, there is a real danger that Ambassador Brewer's return to the Sudan could be interpreted both by the Sudanese and others as well as our own personnel as indicating that we are not really serious about dealing severely with countries which support, harbour or permit acts of terrorism directed at U.S. personnel.

The letter, signed by F. Allen (Tex) Harris, the association's acting president, closed on a note of mild reproof and with an admonition: "We trust that in the future when decisions are made which affect the safety of our personnel abroad, we will be given a better opportunity to discuss this with you or your responsible officials before a final decision is taken."[56]

Kissinger dismissed the association's protest out of hand. He considered the decision to send Brewer back to Khartoum to be purely a matter of policy, and thus a matter for the sole decision of the chief policy making officer of the State Department, namely himself. The Foreign Service Association had no business meddling in it. Kissinger replied to the association in a brief, pro forma letter. But an aide let the association know that he considered their approach to be out of order, to be an attempt to interfere in a matter over which he had exclusive jurisdiction.

* * *

The unease among America's career diplomats dated back to more than a year and a half earlier. Its proximate cause was President Richard Nixon's press conference remarks on March 2, 1973, a few hours before the killings. Some held Nixon personally responsible for the killings and thought that his swagger and his tough-guy posturing in proclaiming his refusal to "pay blackmail" had in fact triggered the deaths of Moore and Noel. Even those who did not go so far—and they were the majority—considered Nixon's statement a terrible blunder and a shocking display of indifference to the fate of two American diplomats held at gunpoint by fanatical killers.

The unease sparked a quiet debate about the terrorism policy itself—the policy of no negotiations, no deals, and no concessions. Although some gave it their support, or at least paid it lip service, many others felt it unnecessarily rigid and likely to cause more tragedy in the future. King Hussein's release of Abu Daoud in September 1973 raised still more

[56]See Note on Sources for chapter 21.

questions about the policy. For Moore's and Noel's friends and former colleagues, there was a terrible bitterness in what Hussein did. Abu Daoud was the man whose freedom would have reprieved the lives of Curt Moore and Cleo Noel, and now he was being let go just like that, for nothing, it seemed. And then in June 1974 Nimeiry handed Moore's and Noel's killers over to the people who had sent them to kill the two Americans!

As a group, Foreign Service officers prided themselves on taking orders and carrying them out loyally and faithfully, but for many this was simply too much, a kind of last straw. Letters urging that stiff sanctions be applied to the Sudan came in to the Foreign Service Association's headquarters in Washington from chapters at U.S. embassies and consulates around the world. Hume Horan, Akins's deputy at the U.S. embassy in Jidda, Saudi Arabia, and a decade later himself to be U.S. ambassador in Khartoum, sent a long, indignant letter to the association's president, Thomas Boyatt. "We should have broken relations with Sudan when the killers were released," Horan wrote, but at the very least Brewer should not be sent back; his return "would offend the dignity of the United States and contradict the outpourings of U.S. officials on the evils of terrorism." Brewer, Horan proposed, should be given another embassy, and the U.S. embassy in Khartoum should be left in the hands of a chargé d'affaires indefinitely.

Horan was appalled when Brewer was sent back to Khartoum. It was, he wrote in another letter, "an astounding and to me scarcely credible decision."

Horan's outrage had a personal as well as a professional basis, for he had known both Curt Moore and Cleo Noel. In Jidda, however, he was in no position to carry the matter further. But in Washington another Foreign Service officer, a tall, lanky, fast-talking New Yorker named Harry Blaney, had for some time been troubled by the Khartoum murders and by the implications of a policy on terrorism that he felt was only too willing to sacrifice the lives of American personnel but was reluctant to make governments that abetted terrorism pay the price for their actions. Blaney had never served in the Middle East—he was a European specialist—and he had never met Moore or Noel. But he was just as appalled by the administration's faint response to Nimeiry's release of their killers as any who had.

It angered Blaney. He felt that both the policy and the way it was being carried out by the administration were wrong. He proposed that a group be set up within the association to study terrorism and other dangers faced by Foreign Service personnel, and to talk with the State Department's management about better ways to deal with such matters. The officers and members of the association's board agreed, and so Blaney, having proposed the idea, was chosen to head the group.

It came into being in August 1974 and was called the Working Group on Terrorism and Extraordinary Dangers. Two of its eight members had themselves been held hostage in situations that were harrowing, though not tragic in the manner of Khartoum. The words "extraordinary dangers" were intended to cover a variety of other issues. What Blaney and other members of his group had in mind in particular was the State Department management's reluctance at the time to acknowledge the threat to the health of Foreign Service personnel posed by the Soviet government's bombardment of the U.S. embassy in Moscow with microwaves.

Blaney's committee called in a consultant on terrorism and proceeded to do a detailed analysis both of what had happened in Khartoum and of the no-negotiations, no-deals, and no-concessions policy. They quickly came to agreement that the no-negotiations element of the policy was dead wrong. It simply made no sense, they felt, to say to armed kidnappers, "We're not going to negotiate with you, you're not going to get anything, your only option is to give up," as the United States, Jordan, and Israel had done in the Khartoum case. That, Blaney and his associates concluded, was a major mistake; it had gotten Moore, Noel, and Eid killed. Governments should never reject terrorists' demands out of hand, Blaney's group concluded. They should negotiate and negotiate and string things out as long as possible.

But consensus was more difficult to reach when it came to deciding just what to negotiate about. Within the association as within the Foreign Service as a whole, opinion was sharply divided over whether governments should actually pay ransom—in the form either of release of prisoners or of money—to save the lives of hostages. It ran the gamut all the way from those who said yes, bargain terrorists down to their lowest price and then pay whatever may be necessary, to those who insisted that nothing should be paid no matter what the circumstances. Blaney's group came up with a recommendation that it hoped would bridge the gap: the United States would hold to its public position of refusing to pay ransom but in fact would be ready to pay money to kidnappers if that was deemed necessary to save lives; it would not, however, under any circumstances release prisoners or ask others to do so. But the working group was not able to get this recommendation approved by the association's board, and in the end the association's position on the issue hardly differed from that of the administration: terrorists could be given food, water, medical supplies, and safe passage out to a destination of their choice, but not prisoners, weapons, or money.

On another issue, however, the association parted company radically with the administration. If the United States was going to send its people to places where there was a risk of their being taken hostage but tell them that it would not pay to save their lives, then, the association argued, it had to be hard as rock with governments that aided or abetted terrorism, or that failed to punish terrorists. If the no-deals and no-concessions policy was to be politically and morally consistent, it had to be buttressed by a policy of harsh sanctions against governments that helped terrorists or that let them go free.

This was a view that was strongly held even before the establishment of Blaney's group. The association had made the point to Kissinger in its letter some three weeks after Nimeiry let the Black September killer go. Any nation, Tex Harris had written, which refuses to take conscientious action against international murderers and extortionists must face heavy penalties. If this was not to be the case, Harris told Kissinger, then the entire policy on terrorism should be reviewed.

But when Blaney and his associates sat down with the administration to talk about these issues, it was quickly made clear to them that they were regarded as interlopers, and that their views were unwelcome and were going to get, at most, only a perfunctory hearing. "Our positions hit an absolute stone wall with the administration," Blaney was later to say.

The person Kissinger assigned to deal with Blaney and his group was Lawrence Eagleburger. Himself a Foreign Service officer, Eagleburger had been one of Kissinger's top aides at the National Security Council. He came with Kissinger to the State Department and was at first Kissinger's personal assistant and later deputy under secretary for management, the job Macomber held at the time of the Khartoum murders.

Eagleburger had the reputation around the department of being Kissinger's hatchet man; if you did something Kissinger didn't like, it was Eagleburger who would trash you for it. He could occasionally be seen in the halls of the State Department, a short man turning stoutish already in his early forties, with a head that seemed to sit directly on his shoulders. Hunched forward, he charged along with a stern, intense look on his face.

Eagleburger made clear that there would be no compromise on the administration's policy of no negotiations, no deals, and no concessions. But the association's clash with Eagleburger came less over this than over policy toward states that abet terrorism or fail to punish its perpetrators. Blaney argued that the administration was not being consistent with the logic of its own position. It had not taken any steps to punish Libya, which clearly had had a hand in the Khartoum murders, and all it had done against the Sudan in retaliation for the release of the killers was cut off aid programs and keep the U.S. ambassador out of Khartoum for four months. The association wanted Ambassador William Brewer withdrawn permanently and trade as well as aid cut off, and it wanted sanctions against Libya too.

Eagleburger's response was that the United States would strike a tough public stance toward states that abet or fail to punish terrorism, but that the critics had to take into consideration that Washington had policy interests, and these policy interests would on occasion override other considerations. For Blaney and his associates, what Eagleburger seemed to be saying was that if we lose a few people but keep our interests in a given country or region, then well and good. They thought it appalling.

The policy, they suspected, was Kissinger's, but Eagleburger was always careful to protect his boss. He always said, "This is the administration's policy." But the administration, Blaney felt, was not interested in addressing the problem in an intelligent way; it just wanted to strike a macho pose. It was afraid that if it took a more sophisticated position it would look wimpy.

Blaney and his group got nowhere with Eagleburger, and after a few sessions Eagleburger, who by then had been elevated to the post of deputy under secretary for management, tired of them and turned them over to the new coordinator for terrorism, Robert Fearey. Blaney's frustrations mounted. His committee asked for briefings and access to intelligence material. But they found that when they were given briefings, they were told less than what was being told to journalists, even though they all held top-secret clearances. They were being stonewalled, they felt, at every turn. And Fearey, they thought, was interested only in the public-relations aspect of his job; he just wanted to manage how the American people and Congress perceived the administration's policy, and he did not care about going after terrorists or governments that abetted them.

It was Khartoum that sparked the creation of the Committee on Terrorism and Extraordinary Dangers, but as time passed, Khartoum gradually slid from the top of the committee's agenda to be replaced by other issues. This, however, did not cause relations between the committee and the administration to improve. Much to the contrary, antagonism mounted. One day, after a particularly harsh confrontation over what Blaney and the committee members felt was the administration's refusal to deal adequately with the dangers posed to American personnel by Soviet microwave bombardments of the U.S. embassy in Moscow, one of Eagleburger's aides came to see Harry Blaney. He came to convey a terse warning.

"If you don't desist," Eagleburger's man told Blaney, "your name will be shit. You will be finished in the Foreign Service."

22

Proceed to Normalize Relations

In the fall of 1974, even before Brewer returned to Khartoum, President Jaafar al-Nimeiry chose a new ambassador to represent him in the United States. The appointee was Francis Deng. The mission Nimeiry assigned Deng was to bring relations with the United States back to normal from the freeze into which his release of the Black September killers had plunged them.

Nimeiry could not have made a more felicitous choice. In his own person, Deng was the embodiment of the new Sudan, the Sudan of reconciliation between north and south, for he was a black and a southerner and, perhaps not just incidentally, the son of the principal chief of the powerful Dinka tribe. He was also a man who knew the United States and Americans well. He had spent two years at Yale and earned a doctorate in law there, and after that he had worked in New York for the United Nations.

And Deng was as bright as they came. He had been one of the top three students in his class in law school at Khartoum University. His achievements there had won him a Sudanese government scholarship to Oxford, which became his stepping-stone onward to Yale.

Nimeiry had been courting Deng for some time, and had offered him several attractive jobs. But Deng was wary. So long as the government in Khartoum was still at war with the south, he did not intend to lend his name to it. But after the Juba accords of March 1972, Deng's reticence faded; in fact he was eager to give his endorsement and lend his hand to Nimeiry's historic initiative to heal the nation's wounds and bring the south into genuine partnership with the north.

Nimeiry wanted to make Deng a judge in one of the southern districts. Deng pointed out that his experience, and his interest, was in international affairs, so Nimeiry sent him to be the Sudan's ambassador to Sweden and the neighboring Nordic states. Deng was back in Khartoum at the beginning of March 1973, called there by Nimeiry to take part in the celebration of the first anniversary of the Juba accords. So he was a witness to the drama of the Black September's seizure of the Saudi embassy and the killing of the two Americans and the Belgian.

Deng came to Washington in January 1975 and immediately launched his campaign to turn relations between the United States and the Sudan around. The American political system held no secrets for Deng. He knew just how to manipulate it. He did not confine his contacts to the State Department. He went everywhere, to the Hill to meet with senators and congressmen, to the Central Intelligence Agency to meet with its new director, George Bush, to other departments of government, and to the media, everywhere telling of his country's friendship toward the United States and of his government's desire for the resumption of a normal relationship.

At the State Department Deng found he had opponents, not personal ones, for no one held anything against him personally, but members of the career service who continued to feel very strongly that the United States should not forget or forgive Nimeiry's release of the Black September killers. But he also found that he had sympathizers and supporters, and that they, not the opponents, were the ones who held the key positions. Starting from the middle ranks and working up, Deng identified them as Wendell Coote, the new office director for eastern African affairs (responsibility for the Sudan having in the meantime been moved to that office from the office of northern African affairs); William Schaufele, the new assistant secretary for African affairs; Joseph Sisco, the under secretary of state for political affairs; and—Deng was given clearly to understand—Secretary of State Henry Kissinger himself.

So before long Deng was closing in on his objective. In the early fall of 1975 he had a meeting with Sisco, and not long afterwards a State Department official telephoned to tell him that the administration was going to lift its ban on United States Export-Import Bank lending to the

Sudan, as well as on U.S. government guarantees for private American investment there. The official made clear that these were intended to be cautious but deliberate first steps toward the normalization of relations. He also told Deng that the State Department would wait for him to inform his government before it advised the U.S. ambassador in Khartoum. The reason, the official said, was that it was Deng's own efforts that had brought about the move toward normalization, and that he believed in ambassadors' getting due recognition for what they had achieved. The effect of this, of course, was to undercut Brewer's position in Khartoum.

Brewer had gone back to Khartoum in November 1974 faithfully maintaining that his return did not signal any change in the freeze in relations, and he had continued to hew to this line. When the State Department notified Brewer of the lifting of the restrictions on Export-Import Bank lending and investment guarantees, it did not tell him what it had told Deng, namely, that this was a deliberate first step back toward normalization of relations. So when Brewer communicated the measures to the authorities in Khartoum, he did so with the caveat that they meant no change in the overall U.S. policy. This was the exact contrary of what Deng had cabled his government.

The American ambassador in Khartoum was saying one thing and the Sudanese ambassador in Washington the opposite. The confusion was such that Deng was called home at the end of 1975 to explain to Nimeiry just where matters stood.

Nimeiry had a surprise for Deng. He was so pleased with Deng's work that he wanted to move him up a few notches. He told Deng that he was appointing him minister of state for foreign affairs. But Nimeiry also wanted Deng to pursue to its conclusion his work of normalizing relations with the United States. So he sent Deng back to Washington to complete the job and to do another that seemed equally if not more daunting—to arrange for the president of the Sudan to visit the United States and get an invitation to the White House.

Deng returned to Washington early in 1976 and held an intensive round of talks with those in the State Department and elsewhere who were sympathetic to his purpose. Not long afterwards he got a call inviting him to come for a meeting with the secretary of state, his first since he had been accredited as ambassador more than a year earlier.

This looked like the breakthrough Deng had been waiting for. Coote cautioned him that he should not expect too much, but Deng nonetheless went to Kissinger's office hopeful, planning to tell the secretary of state of his government's accomplishments and of its ardent wish for better relations with the United States. He was taken aback when Kissinger addressed him angrily, scolding him for his government's freeing of the Black September killers. Kissinger seemed virtually to say that this action left no basis for collaboration between the United States and the Sudan.

Was this why he had been called to meet the secretary of state? Deng asked himself. The best defense in this circumstance, he decided, was to go on the offensive. So Deng replied spiritedly to Kissinger's words, telling of the threats of reprisal made against the government of Sudan by the PLO had it continued to hold the Black September killers, pointing out that Nimeiry had ended the war in the south, and that he had been the first Arab leader to restore diplomatic relations with the United States. He closed with a warning: if the United States continued to treat his government as a pariah, it risked losing the Sudan's friendship.

Kissinger's tone changed abruptly. "Mr. Ambassador," the secretary of state said, "I agree with you. Beyond a certain point, our policy could be counterproductive."

Kissinger's swift about-face astonished the Sudanese ambassador no less than his initial belligerent sally. Deng waited, expecting the secretary of state to say, "but . . ." But it did not come. Instead Kissinger turned and addressed the State Department aides who had joined him for the meeting.

"So, gentlemen, if you have no objections, I would suggest that you review our policy toward the Sudan and proceed to normalize relations."

Kissinger added a word of caution. "But let's do it judiciously. Let's not do anything that would provoke a counterreaction."

It was, Deng realized, a carefully crafted scenario, a masterful show conducted by a master showman—first the display of anger, done for the record; then sweet reasonableness and the hand extended in friendship.

The secretary of state had still another pleasant surprise for the Sudanese ambassador. "I understand your president wants to visit Washington. He will be welcome, but, again, handle it carefully." It should be a private visit, Kissinger said, but he assured Deng that Nimeiry would be received at the White House by President Ford.

* * *

A few months later, Jaafar al-Nimeiry got his wish. He came to Washington and met at the White House with the president of the United States. To Sally Moore and Lucille Noel he sent flowers, enormous bouquets that seemed to fill half their living rooms.

The unpleasantness at Khartoum in March 1973 had indeed now become only a passing incident. The release of the killers in June 1974 was both forgiven and forgotten, over and done.

Epilogue

The presidential aircraft bearing the remains of George Curtis Moore and Cleo Allen Noel, Jr., landed at Andrews Air Force Base just before 3:00 P.M. on Monday, March 5, 1973. It was a cold, dreary, overcast day, a day in every way fitting for a tragic return home. An honor guard from the United States First Infantry Regiment smartly presented arms as the two coffins were lowered to the tarmac. An air force band played "The Star Spangled Banner." The loud, dull report of a nineteen-gun salute, an honor normally reserved for heads of government, punctuated the notes of the anthem and echoed across the field. A crowd of friends and well-wishers stood silently at attention while the coffins were carried to hearses, to be driven away to the National Presbyterian Church in Washington, where the bodies of the two men would lie in state until the funeral on March 7. Secretary of State William P. Rogers escorted Lucille Noel and Sally Moore and their children from the arrival ramp to the terminal. There were no public remarks.

The Reverend Dr. Edward L. R. Elson, who had married Curt and Sally Moore in June 1950, and who was now chaplain of the United States Senate and pastor emeritus of the National Presbyterian Church, conducted the funeral ceremony. On the long flight back from Khartoum, Sally Moore had remembered the Reverend Elson, and when Bill Macomber asked her whom she would like to have officiate, she chose him, and Lucille Noel agreed.

Curt Moore and Cleo Noel were buried on the afternoon of March 7, 1973, in Arlington National Cemetery, side by side as they had died, and near the gravesite of President John F. Kennedy. Several hundred mourners stood under a leaden gray sky and a chilly drizzle to watch as the caskets were gently lowered into two rectangles sliced neatly in the ground. There was again a nineteen-gun salute, followed this time by three volleys of rifle fire. The U.S. Navy Band did the musical honors. It played tirelessly, on and on; it played "Ruffles and Flourishes," "The

Star Spangled Banner," "America the Beautiful," and, at the end, "Eternal Father Strong to Save." Their refrain rang out across the soggy hillside.

The graveside ceremonies done, Secretary Rogers presented the flags from the respective coffins to Sally Moore and Lucille Noel and accompanied them down the hill to waiting cars.

American flags at installations abroad and at U.S. government premises throughout the United States were lowered to half-mast. This was done, as President Richard Nixon was careful to explain in his appearance at the State Department on March 6, "even though the individuals involved were not Members of the Congress or members of the Cabinet, when normally such action is only taken. . . ."

All honor had been rendered. And now it was over.

* * *

The C-141 that had flown Deputy Under Secretary William B. Macomber to Khartoum stopped in Cairo on its return journey to deposit there the remains of Guy Eid. His casket was met at Cairo airport by members of his family and by the ambassador of Belgium. Eid was interred quietly, without fanfare, in his family's burial plot in Cairo's Greek Orthodox cemetery.

* * *

The Black September itself did not long survive George Curtis Moore, Cleo Allen Noel, Jr., and Guy Eid. Curt Moore and Cleo Noel were known to many Arabs, and they were known as friends. Few Arabs spoke out publicly to condemn their murder, for the Black September inspired terror. But privately there was much criticism. Arabs who had applauded the killing of Israeli athletes in Munich began now to worry that Black September was carrying the Palestinian cause toward senseless, nihilistic violence. If Arabs were now killing their friends, so the comment went, then something had gone badly wrong. Soon they would have no friends. Within the ranks of the Palestinian movement and throughout the Arab world there was deep unease over what Black September had done, and there was much questioning of the organization's basic premises.

Then a little more than a month after Khartoum, Fatah and Black September received a violent jolt. On the night of April 9 to 10, 1973, an Israeli commando team that had trained intensively for several weeks came stealthily ashore in Beirut. In cars rented for them from a local Avis agency by accomplices who had come in as tourists some days earlier, the Israelis drove to the downtown area of West Beirut, to a building just off Hamra Street (the same area in which Curt Moore and Cleo Noel had once lived), where three top Fatah leaders had their homes. They burst into the apartments of Mohammed Yussef al-Najjar, Kamal Adwan, and Kamal Nasser and gunned each down. Mohammed Yussef al-Najjar, known as Abu Yussef, was one of the top figures in Black September; he was said to be the planner of the Bangkok operation, and he probably had had a hand in the Khartoum one as well. Kamal Adwan was a member of Fatah's ruling circle and was, it seems, also involved in Black September. Kamal Nasser was a noted Palestinian poet and the spokesman for the PLO. Unbeknownst to the Israelis, Arafat, Salah Khalaf, and Ali Hassan Salameh were in apartments in a nearby building. Khalaf had intended to spend the night at Kamal Nasser's apartment but at the last minute had changed plans.

Fatah and Black September not only lost three top figures, they lost much of their self-confidence. If the Israelis could strike at them in the heart of their home territory, they would not be safe anywhere. Many Palestinians, and other Arabs as well, imagined the hand of the United States to be behind the Beirut raid and believed it to be retaliation for the Khartoum slayings. Arafat publicly accused the Americans of complicity in the Beirut raid.

The PLO chief threatened reprisal against the United States, and American embassies in the Middle East girded for trouble. But either Arafat did not believe his own accusations or he was too intimidated to act on them. Whichever the case, the Black September Organization was on its way to dissolution. After Khartoum it paused for six months and then, like a volcano sinking into extinction, erupted one last time. On August 5, 1973, two young Palestinians pulled automatic weapons and hand grenades from their luggage in the departure lounge of the Athens airport and opened fire indiscriminately, killing four people and wounding some fifty. At their trial the two declared themselves members of the Black September and said they had been sent to avenge the killing of Abu Yussef in Beirut the previous April; they thought their victims were American Jews on their way to settle in Israel (in fact most of them were Americans who had been on holiday in Greece and were waiting to board a TWA flight to New York).

The attack at the Athens airport in effect marked the end of the Black

September. The organization's more radical elements spun off to the PFLP or mounted wildcat operations under new names. Within Fatah, moderates such as Hani al-Hassan, who opposed international terrorism, were again coming to the fore. Contacts between the PLO and the CIA, broken off following the agency's bungled handling of the December 1970 meeting with Ali Hassan Salameh, resumed in low key during the summer of 1973. After the October war, the prospect of Middle East peace negotiations gave Arafat renewed incentive to turn away from confrontation with the United States. He sent two messages to the Americans asking clarification of their positions on key diplomatic issues.

On October 31, 1973, Secretary of State Henry Kissinger summoned General Vernon Walters, deputy director of the CIA, to his office on the seventh floor of the State Department. Kissinger asked Walters if he could establish contact with the PLO. Walters, a big, jovial man who over the years had carried out dozens of secret missions for administrations both Republican and Democratic, said he had friends who could arrange something. Walters was thinking of King Hassan of Morocco, whom he had known since 1942.

Walters agreed to undertake the mission, but not without some foreboding. He remarked to Kissinger that as deputy director of the CIA he was probably number six or seven on the PLO's hit list. Kissinger replied with a wry smile: "I am probably number one. So you are going." Then he gave Walters specific instructions. He wanted Walters to meet with the PLO but not to negotiate with them. "I want you to tell them certain things, certain pre-conditions that must be met if, as we have been getting indirect word, everything they have been doing is for the purpose of getting our attention to listen to their side of the story. So you go, make contact with them, talk to them and see what it is they are after and in what terms they are thinking." Then Kissinger added: "Try and get them to stop the violence against us— but don't negotiate."

"But," Walters asked, "what do I say if they refuse to stop terrorism against Americans?" Walters knew that U.S. law forbade the CIA to engage in the killing of foreign enemies, even those involved in terrorism against Americans.

Kissinger looked puzzled for a moment and then shrugged the problem off on Walters: "Say something appropriate but nothing illegal."

Walters flew off to Rabat, where on November 3 King Hassan

arranged for him to meet with two senior officials of the PLO, Hani al-Hassan and Bassam Majid Abu Sharif, known by the code name Abu Sharar. King Hassan himself accompanied Walters to the meeting place. Still, Walters was not entirely reassured. He and an aide would be going into the meeting alone and unarmed, Walters told the king of Morocco. He hoped this would be true of the other side as well.

"General, I have the whole place surrounded by my men," Hassan assured him.

Walters's sense of humor never deserted him. "Your Majesty," he declared, "I am not really interested in being revenged."

The king of Morocco smiled. "I am sure that everything will work out all right. There will be no problem."

King Hassan introduced Walters to the two Palestinians. Hani al-Hassan was tall and distinguished-looking. He wore a coat and tie. Majid Abu Sharif was in shirtsleeves and unshaven, in the Arafat mode.

The king of Morocco offered a word by way of introduction. "Blood has flowed between you," Hassan said, "but we all have one thing in common. We all believe in one God, who is the Father of us all. May he give you the wisdom to find some way to put an end to the killing that has come between you." That said, Hassan turned and left the room.

Hani al-Hassan spoke for the two PLO representatives; Abu Sharif listened but did not take part in the conversation. In a clipped British accent, al-Hassan talked at length of the plight of the Palestinians, driven from their ancestral homes by the Jews, he said, and killed.

Then it was Walters's turn.

"I have been charged with transmitting three very important matters to you," he said. "If you are thinking of pushing the Jews into the sea and destroying the State of Israel, there will be no further dialogue between us. If you are thinking of having us do something against King Hussein of Jordan, who is our friend and ally, there will be no further dialogue between us. And if there is any further act of blood between you and us, then this dialogue will cease. I will not return, and I do not know if the U.S. government will find anyone willing to talk to you after such violence."

Neither of the two Palestinians raised objection to what Walters had said, but al-Hassan clearly had a question on his mind. Finally, with a rueful smile, he asked cautiously:

"May I ask you a very awkward and delicate question?"

"Go right ahead," Walters answered. "There are no awkward questions, there are only indiscreet answers, and I am a specialist in them."

"Did you have anything to do with the killing of some of our leaders in Beirut, when the Israelis came ashore in boats and killed them in their apartments?"

"No," Walters replied. "We had nothing whatever to do with it. I give you my word as an American army officer on that."

Al-Hassan seemed surprised but also relieved. "I accept that," he said.

Again it was Walters's turn.

"I will not ask you any questions about the killing of Ambassador Noel and our deputy chief of mission in Khartoum. . . ."

Al-Hassan was visibly embarrassed. "You have got to realize that we belong to an organization made up of people who have lost everything, families, homes, everything. They have suffered so much that there are certain elements we cannot control in their grief and anger." The United States had to understand too, al-Hassan said, that "everything we have done has been aimed at getting your attention and bringing you to listen to us."

Walters had expected something of this sort, and he had his answer ready. "If you think that you will get us to listen by killing our people, you do not understand us. If we do hear, it will be with a deaf ear. The violence against us has got to stop, or much blood will flow, and you may be sure that not all of it will be ours." It was as far as he dared go without overstepping the bounds of U.S. law.

The two Palestinians said nothing but nodded in apparent understanding.

* * *

In November 1974 Yasser Arafat came to New York to address the United Nations. One of the men in Arafat's entourage was Ali Hassan Salameh. Salameh and one or more agents of the CIA met in a room at the Waldorf Astoria Hotel. They sealed a pact in which Fatah forswore terrorism against Americans—a pact that might have been sealed four years earlier had Robert Ames's superiors listened to his advice, and that might have saved the lives of Curt Moore and Cleo Noel.

Salameh was as good as his word. In the civil war that flared in Lebanon in 1975 and 1976, Salameh's men (after the demise of Black September he became the head of Force 17, Arafat's security detail) protected the American embassy in West Beirut and the apartments of American diplomats. He was not able to save Ambassador Francis Meloy and his deputy, Counselor Robert Waring, from assassination in 1976 by elements beyond Fatah's control, but when turmoil reached the point where the Americans had to evacuate their personnel, Salameh managed the security arrangements. To show its appreciation, in December 1976 the CIA invited Salameh to the United States, to Louisiana and Hawaii for vacation and to Washington for talks with Ames and other CIA officials.

But the friendship of the CIA did not shield Ali Hassan Salameh from Israeli vengeance. Salameh was killed by the Israelis in Beirut on January 22, 1979, by a car bomb. If some reports are to be believed, the CIA had an opportunity to save Salameh but let it pass. It is said that before carrying out the operation, the Israelis approached the American intelligence agency to try to learn whether it would object, and when no objection was raised they went ahead.

Four years later it was Robert Ames's turn. On April 18, 1983, Palestinian terrorists drove a pickup truck loaded with two thousand pounds of high explosives into the American embassy in Beirut. It was an operation that Ali Hassan Salameh might have foiled, or might have warned the Americans about, had he lived. Ames was in the U.S. embassy building that day for a working lunch with members of the CIA station. He was among the several dozen Americans and Lebanese employees of the embassy who were killed in the blast.

*   *   *

Abu Daoud was said to have been sent to command a Palestine Liberation Army battalion on the Syrian front in the October 1973 war, following his release from jail in Jordan some two weeks earlier. He did not mend his ways. He was last heard of in France in 1977, arrested for trying to smuggle a bomb aboard an El Al passenger plane, but then quickly released by the French, who did not want a prominent Palestinian terrorist on their hands.

As we have already seen, Abu Jamal and Fawaz Yassin, the two men directly responsible for setting up the Khartoum operation, disappeared from view after leaving Khartoum on the morning of March 1, 1973. Abu Jamal's true identity was never known; he vanished without a trace. Fawaz Yassin was said to have spent a few days in Tripoli before going on to Baghdad, where the PLO jailed him for a time for his part in the operation against the Saudi embassy. That, at least, was what PLO sources told Western journalists, but very likely it was fiction. Other, seemingly more credible reports had it that Qaddafi sent Yassin off into hiding in South Yemen for a while. Whatever the case, he was not seen again.

The five Black September gunmen who were held in jail in Cairo after having been released by Nimeiry in June 1974 stayed jailed there. In the years that followed, Arafat and Salah Khalaf, though they had both publicly called the killings in Khartoum a "rogue operation" and had denied any connection with it, repeatedly pressed the government of Egypt to release them. Sadat, however, refused. He continued to have them held even after their seven-year sentence ran its course, for by then, after his peace treaty with Israel, his relations with the PLO had deteriorated almost to the breaking point. The five gained their freedom only after Sadat's assassination in November 1981. Nothing was heard of them after that, just as nothing further was heard of the three who had been released after the sentences were handed down on June 24, 1974.

* * *

After regaining the friendship of the Americans, President Jaafar al-Nimeiry remained the faithful ally of the United States. Some said he was in the pay of the CIA, and that this was one of the reasons Kissinger went so easy on him. Whatever the truth of this, Nimeiry's government benefited handsomely from his relationship with the United States; the Sudan became for a time the largest recipient of American military and economic aid on the African continent other than Egypt.

Nimeiry's great contribution and proudest achievement was the ending of the civil war in the south and the reconciliation between Arab and black Sudanese. It was a monument to his rule, but ten years after he built it, he methodically set about smashing it. In 1983 Nimeiry revoked the autonomy granted to the south under the Juba accords and imposed Islamic law not just on the Arab and Moslem north but on the animist and Christian south. And so, predictably, the south rose once more in revolt. Perhaps Nimeiry thought that what he had done would allay the growing discontent with his rule among Arab Sudanese. In any event, he acted in the face of much advice to the contrary from his American friends, who nonetheless remained his friends to the very last.

Jaafar al-Nimeiry was overthrown in March 1985, ironically, it might be said, while he was on another visit to the United States. Nimeiry's downfall had been in prospect for some time, ever since he had revoked the Juba accords, but it was triggered by riots in protest of fuel price increases ordained by the International Monetary Fund. As trouble developed in Khartoum, Hume Horan, since 1983 the American ambassador there, tried to warn Nimeiry. But Horan found the president of the Sudan singularly and inexplicably unresponsive.

Nimeiry flew to Cairo, to live in exile there, where eleven years earlier he had sent George Curtis Moore's and Cleo Allen Noel's killers to a different kind of exile.

* * *

The issue of Yasser Arafat's responsibility in the killing of the two Americans and the Belgian lay largely dormant for over a decade after the event. It was not seriously raised until the fall of 1985, when a former U.S. deputy ambassador to the United Nations, Charles M. Lichenstein, launched an effort to get the Department of Justice to seek an indictment against the PLO chief for the murder of Moore and Noel.

Lichenstein's initiative was heavily backed by the American Israel Public Affairs Committee and other elements of the pro-Israeli American Jewish lobby. There was, here again, a touch of irony, for it was the supporters of Israel, a country for which neither Curt Moore nor Cleo Noel had had particular sympathy, who invoked justice for them. In fact, however, the AIPAC initiative had little if anything to do with justice for the dead. That was no longer on anybody's true agenda. It was, quite simply, an attempt to get Arafat. A law passed by Congress in 1984 offered a possible legal framework; it authorized the Department of Justice to pursue and bring to trial abductors of Americans anywhere around the world. And events of the moment offered a motive.

In the fall of 1985 the Department of State launched one of its periodic efforts to bring the Arabs and the Israelis to the negotiating table. This particular one called for an international conference. As before, however, the Arabs would not attend unless the PLO could participate in some guise, and the Israelis would go only if there was no apparent PLO presence. And even if that condition could be obtained, the idea of an international conference did not appeal to many Israelis or to many of their friends in the United States. Indicting Arafat would discredit the PLO and, most probably, kill prospects for U.S. mediation. For a country that had the leader of the Palestine Liberation Organization under indictment on charges of murder would be an unlikely sponsor for a conference that would host members of the organization he headed.

Attorney General Edwin Meese seemed to find much appeal in the idea of prosecuting Arafat. Lichenstein rallied forty-four U.S. senators to sign a petition to Meese calling for the indictment of Arafat on charges of murdering Moore and Noel. The State Department, however, was opposed. Arafat and the PLO, Curt Moore's and Cleo Noel's former colleagues argued, would be key elements in any future Middle East peace settlement. As Eagleburger had told Blaney a decade earlier, the United States had policy interests, and these policy interests would on occasion—in fact, almost always—take precedence over other considerations.

But the main problem faced by those who wanted the PLO chief indicted was that they themselves had no direct evidence against him. There was a lot of circumstantial evidence, and there were press stories, in particular one by *Washington Post* reporter David Ottaway printed in the *Post* on April 5, 1973:

> Yasser Arafat, leader of the main Palestinian guerrilla organization, Fatah, was in the Black September radio command center in Beirut when the message to execute three Western diplomats being held hostage in Khartoum was sent out last month, according to Western intelligence sources. The sources said it was not clear whether Arafat personally or Salah Khalaf, an extremist Fatah theoretician better known as Abu Iyad, gave the order to carry out the executions, using the code word "Cold River." But they have reports that Arafat was present in the operations center when the message was sent and that he personally congratulated the guerrillas after the execution of the three diplomats. . . . According to one source, the U.S. Central Intelligence Agency monitored at least some of the communications between the Beirut command center and the Saudi Arabian embassy in Khartoum where the hostages were being held. Arafat's voice was reportedly monitored and recorded. But it was not clear from this source whether Arafat's voice was identified as the sender of the Cold River message or was only heard later congratulating the guerrillas and later during the negotiations leading to the surrender of the eight Black September terrorists.

But newspaper stories and reports attributed to "intelligence sources" were not the stuff of evidence in an American court. Lichenstein and others pressed the administration to disgorge the CIA tapes, but it would not do so, and no one could be found who would testify in court to personally having heard them or read transcripts of them.

So on April 21, 1986, Assistant Attorney General John Bolton sent the forty-four senators a letter advising that the United States lacked evidence to bring an indictment: "Although much has been alleged about evidence implicating Arafat . . . the evidence currently available from key departments and agencies within our government and from other sources is insufficient for prosecutive purposes." And, Bolton added, even if a case could be brought, "critical national security information would be irreparably compromised if we disclosed during litigation the nature of our searches for evidence."

★ ★ ★

In the early morning hours of April 16, 1988, an Israeli commando team slipped ashore in Hammam al-Shaat, a seaside suburb of Tunis, capital of Tunisia, where the PLO had relocated following its expulsion from Beirut in 1982. The operation it was assigned to carry out was much like the one in Beirut in April 1973. Israeli agents sent in ahead of time rented cars for the commandos and left them at the designated location. This time, however, the target was one man only. The Israelis drove to the home of Khalil al-Wazir, the man known by the code name of Abu Jihad, broke in, shot him to death, and departed without meeting resistance. It was a spectacular operation, but it was done quietly.

Khalil al-Wazir, it will be recalled, was a top figure in the Black September. That, however, was not why the Israelis wanted him, for by the late 1980s the Black September was ancient history. Since Black September's demise, al-Wazir had run numerous terrorist operations against Israel. He had been on Israel's hit list for quite some time, but what moved the Israelis to go after him in April 1988 was the Palestinian uprising in the occupied territories of the West Bank and Gaza, the Intifada, that had broken out at the end of the previous year. The Intifada was the most painful blow ever dealt Israel by the Palestinians. Though it was a spontaneous movement, the Israelis credited al-Wazir with giving it a sense of direction and order.

*   *   *

With the killing of Khalil al-Wazir, the Israelis had eliminated three of the top four men of the Black September. The one who eluded their vengeance was Salah Khalaf, or Abu Iyad, the organization's head.

Jim Hoagland, the *Washington Post* correspondent who had met Curt Moore in Khartoum in May 1971 and who had returned to Khartoum in March 1973 when he was assassinated, interviewed Salah Khalaf in Tunis in November 1989. The man known as Abu Iyad had aged. His mustache and the thinning hair on his temples had gone white, and this, together with a paunch, gave him a grandfatherly air. He had mellowed too. Like Arafat, who a year earlier had forsworn terrorism and declared the PLO ready to recognize Israel's existence, Khalaf now spoke of peace and coexistence with the Jewish state.

But when Hoagland questioned him about the killings in Khartoum in March 1973, Khalaf turned first defensive and then evasive. "It was Nixon's responsibility, and the Sudanese. They could have stopped it." In any event, Khalaf said, he himself had had no knowledge of the Khartoum operation; neither he nor Arafat had been aware of it in advance. He deplored it, called it "a crime against the Palestinian nation."

Khalaf explained that he had talked to "the boys," as he called the gunmen, when they were in jail in Cairo. They had told him they did it because Moore was in Jordan in September 1970 and was responsible for the killing there.

Khalaf then looked at Hoagland and asked: "Is that true?"

No, he didn't think so, Hoagland replied; in fact, Moore couldn't have been in Jordan in September 1970, because he was in Khartoum then.

And what about the CIA? Khalaf asked. Was Moore ever in the CIA?

To this, Hoagland had the same answer. No, he said, he didn't think Moore had ever been in the CIA. When he reflected on it he was sure.

Then what about the possibility that there was another George Moore in Amman in September 1970? Did Hoagland know about that? Khalaf asked.

No, Hoagland replied, about that he did not know.

A Final Note

There was, in fact, a George Moore assigned to the American embassy in Amman. He was George L. Moore, Sr., and he was the comptroller of the United States Agency for International Development mission in Jordan. But to credit Salah Khalaf's suggestion that the Black September could have confounded George L. Moore, Sr., with George Curtis Moore, a man who had never spent more than a few hours in Jordan, and those in the summer of 1957, requires a monumental suspension of disbelief.

According to State Department records, George L. Moore, Sr., was born in Pennsylvania in 1910. He was an accountant in private business until 1955. In that year he joined AID and was sent first to the American embassy in Saigon, then to Djakarta, and then on to other assignments before winding up in Amman in June 1966. At each post he worked as an accountant, tallying figures for the AID mission.

If George L. Moore, Sr., was a CIA master spy, he and his employers did a truly masterful job of disguising him. None of the Americans who knew George L. Moore, Sr., during his assignment in Amman ever thought him anything other than the aid mission's chief accountant, or ever had reason to suspect him of being anything else. Among other things, the job itself was too demanding. It was not a job that one could do while moonlighting from being a spy.

In any event, George L. Moore, Sr., could not have masterminded the slaughter of the Palestinians in Amman in September 1970, for he was not there then. In 1970 he turned sixty, the mandatory retirement age for Foreign Service personnel at the time. He left the U.S. aid mission in Amman, and also the service of the U.S. government, in the early months of that year.

*   *   *

If a terminal date had to be put on the story told in these pages, it would surely be January 14, 1991. At about eleven o'clock that evening,

Salah Khalaf, the one-time head of Black September and the man who bore ultimate responsibility for the seizure of the embassy of Saudi Arabia in Khartoum and the killing on March 2, 1973, of George Curtis Moore, Cleo Allen Noel, Jr., and Guy Eid, met with the PLO's security chief, Hayel Abdul Hamid, at the latter's home. While the two men quietly talked, one of Abdul Hamid's guards burst into the room and shot them to death.

Those who read the press reports closely, and who were familiar with the events of March 1 and 2, 1973, could note a certain irony in the fact that the weapon used to kill Salah Khalaf was a Kalashnikov assault rifle, the same make of weapon used to take the lives of Moore, Noel, and Eid.

In the two years before his death, Salah Khalaf had indeed undergone a conversion. He had become the Palestine Liberation Organization's most ardent advocate of peace and reconciliation. Many credited him with having persuaded Arafat to renounce terrorism and accept Israel's existence. He was said to be supplying Western intelligence agencies with information about Palestinian terrorism and working to disrupt the organization of the most dangerous Palestinian terrorist of the day, Abu Nidal.

Unlike his three Black September colleagues, Abu Yussef, Abu Hassan, and Abu Jihad, Abu Iyad was not killed by the Israelis. According to the PLO's own subsequent investigation, the gunman who ended his life was sent by Abu Nidal, a man who had followed the path that Khalaf had pioneered.

The boomerang had returned to strike down its throwers. The men who had sent other men to kill George Curtis Moore, Cleo Allen Noel, Jr., and Guy Eid had in their turn all been killed.

If it could not truly be called justice, perhaps it could be said to be vengeance, errant, blind, and tardy though it was.

NOTE ON SOURCES

For chapters 1 through 22, the source for remarks in quotes, unless footnoted, is either the speaker him- or herself or another person or persons interviewed by the author who is (are) identified in the text as being present at the time the words were spoken. Material for the chapters and for the epilogue and final note (other than items specifically footnoted) was drawn from the following sources. Full bibliographical details on these sources are given in the bibliography.

Chapter 1: The RAND study, pp. 19–22 ("Preparation for the Operation"); BSO Trial Background Material (Magisterial Inquiry); and an interview with a source who asked to remain unnamed.

Chapter 2: The RAND study; CIA paper "The Khartoum Incident"; the Lansloot memorandum; BSO Trial Background Material (Magisterial Inquiry); interviews with Timothy Wells, Sarah (Sally) Moore, Robert E. Fritts, and Hafeez A. M. Mohammed; and a written note from Hassan, Ambassador Noel's driver. Testimony in the afore-mentioned documents is not wholly consistent. For example, the Lansloot memoran-dum states that invitations to the Saudi ambassador's reception were not issued to the PLO and Fatah chiefs of mission, whereas the CIA paper ("The Khartoum Incident") says: "The Deputy Chief of Fatah in Khartoum . . . entered the Embassy on an invitation which was sent to the Chief of Fatah in Khartoum." The CIA paper's version was confirmed at least in part by the terrorists in their testimony at the magisterial inquiry (BSO Trial Background Material [Magisterial Inquiry]), where they spoke of Rizk al-Qas having entered the Saudi embassy before it was stormed. In another instance, Lansloot identifies Ambassador Noel's car as a Lincoln and says the terrorists' Land Rover rammed it. The vehicle, however, was a Chevrolet, and Fritts found it undamaged when he arrived in Khartoum to assume charge of the U.S. embassy twenty-six hours after the storming of the Saudi embassy. Testimony given in court by both the prosecution and the terrorists makes clear that the car rammed by the terrorists' vehicle belonged to another party.

Chapter 3: Interviews with Lucille Noel, Sally Moore, Katherine Bergeson, Lucy Wyatt, Lucien Kinsolving, and a source who asked to remain unnamed. Data on the Sudan and its relationship with Egypt were drawn from the *Area Handbook for the Democratic Republic of Sudan, 1973;* Holt and Daly, *The History of the Sudan;* and Waller, *Gordon of Khartoum.*

Chapter 4: Interviews with Sally Moore, Robert E. Fritts, Timothy Wells, and a source who asked to remain unnamed; a written communication from Shigeru Nomoto dated November 25, 1990; and the RAND study.

Chapter 5: Written communication from Shigeru Nomoto dated November 25, 1990, and the CIA paper "The Khartoum Incident"; and interviews with Sally Moore, Timothy Wells, and a source who asked to remain unnamed. With regard to Moore's treatment at the hands of the terrorists, the CIA paper states: "The DCM was beaten unmercifully about the head with guns. . . ."

Chapter 6: Interviews with Timothy Wells and David Ignatius. On the PLO and Black September: Cooley, *Green March, Black September;* Dobson, *Black September.* On Hassan Salameh and Ali Hassan Salameh: Bar Zohar and Haber, *The Quest for the Red Prince.* On ties between the CIA and Ali Hassan Salameh: David Ignatius, "The Secret History of U.S.-PLO Terror Talks," *Washington Post,* 12/4/88, and idem, *Agents of Innocence,* which, although a work of fiction, is, its author certifies, a true and accurate account of the CIA-Salameh relationship. State Department confidential telegram DTG 270024Z Mar 73 identifies Salah Khalaf (Abu Iyad) as the planner of the Khartoum operation. A State Department secret/exdis* telegram (DTG [date-time group] not legible) states: "Fatah leader Yasir Arafat has now been described in recent intelligence as having given approval to the Khartoum operation prior to its inception."

Chapters 7 and 8: Interviews with Sally Moore, Theodore Tremblay, and Lucille Noel; and personal papers of George Curtis Moore.

Chapter 9: Interviews with Lucien Kinsolving and Lucille Noel.

Chapter 10: Interviews with Sally Moore, Lucy Wyatt, Katherine Bergeson, and James J. Blake; and personal papers of George Curtis Moore.

Chapter 11: Interviews with John Gatch, Harry Odell, Armin H. Meyer, William B. Macomber, David D. Newsom, Samuel Gammon, George Thompson, Edwin Brawn, and James J. Blake; and author's personal recollections.

Chapter 12: Interviews with Armin H. Meyer, John Gatch, William B. Macomber, and John Burke; paper by Armin H. Meyer, "The Khartoum Tragedy," and Moorehead, *Fortune's Hostages.*

Chapter 13: Interviews with Timothy Wells, Robert E. Fritts, George Thompson, Curtis Jones, William B. Macomber, and two persons who asked to remain unnamed; and State Department documents, the RAND study, and a letter from Samuel R. Peale to Donald F. McHenry dated March 13, 1976.

Chapter 14: Interviews with Armin H. Meyer, William B. Macomber, Robert E. Fritts, Curtis Jones, and Joseph N. Greene; and State Department documents and the RAND study.

Chapter 15: Interviews with Joan Peale, Armin H. Meyer, Curtis Jones, Harry Odell, John Gatch, George Thompson, and David D. Newsom; and State Department documents, the RAND study, and a letter from Samuel R. Peale to Donald F. McHenry dated March 13, 1976.

Chapter 16: Interviews with Robert E. Fritts, Jim Hoagland, Timothy Wells, Sally

---

*Designates a highly restricted distribution.

Moore, and a source who asked to remain unnamed; and State Department and CIA documents, the RAND study, the Lansloot memorandum, a letter from Samuel R. Peale to Donald F. McHenry dated March 13, 1976, and a written communication from Shigeru Nomoto dated November 25, 1990.

Chapter 17: Interviews with Robert E. Fritts, Ilsa Sanderson, Theodore Tremblay, and William B. Macomber; and the RAND study and State Department documents.

Chapter 18: Interviews with Timothy Wells, Robert E. Fritts, Sally Moore, George Thompson, Jim Hoagland, and a source who asked to remain unnamed; and State Department documents and the RAND study.

Chapter 19: Interviews with Robert E. Fritts, Lewis Hoffacker, and William D. Brewer; and State Department documents, the RAND study, BSO Trial Background Material (Magisterial Inquiry), and a letter from Samuel R. Peale to Donald F. McHenry dated March 13, 1976.

Chapter 20: Interviews with William D. Brewer, Lucy Wyatt, and Hermann Frederick Eilts; and BSO Trial Background Material (Magisterial Inquiry) and the RAND study.

Chapter 21: Interviews with William D. Brewer, James Akins, Thomas Boyatt, Harry Blaney, and Hume Horan; and documents made available to the author from the files of the American Foreign Service Association.

Chapter 22: Interviews with Francis Deng and William D. Brewer.

Epilogue: The author's personal recollections; a document made available by a person who asked to remain unnamed; interviews with Hume Horan and Jim Hoagland; *State Department Newsletter,* March 1973; Bar Zohar and Haber, *The Quest for the Red Prince;* Livingstone and Halevy, *Inside the PLO;* and material on the Lichenstein initiative made available to the author from the files of the *Near East Report,* Washington, D.C.

"A Final Note": *Biographic Register,* Department of State, 1969; and Jonathan C. Randal, "Revenge Surfaces as a Motive in Slaying of Top Arafat Aide," *International Herald Tribune,* July 24, 1991.

BIBLIOGRAPHY

Official Documents

Kidnapping of Ambassador Cleo A. Noel and DCM George C. Moore in Sudan, March 1973, A Working Note, prepared for the Department of State/Defense Advanced Research Projects Agency by the RAND Corporation, November 1976 (the RAND study). Formerly classified Confidential, this document was released to the author under letter dated May 30, 1991, from Sheila J. Jackson, Office of Freedom of Information, Department of State. 78 pp. plus chronology.

Department of State, Division of Language Services, translation of memorandum dated March 14, 1973, from Theo L. R. Lansloot, Counselor of the Embassy of Belgium, Cairo, to Ministry of Foreign Affairs, Foreign Trade and Development Cooperation, Brussels. Subject: Attack by the Commandos of the "Black September" Movement on the Residence of the Saudi Arabian Minister at Khartoum (March 1–4, 1973). Captivity and death of the Belgian representative in Khartoum, Mr. Eid, as a result of the attack. 30 pp.

BSO Trial, Background Material (Magisterial Inquiry) Supplement No. 2. An unclassified compilation of transcripts and summaries of the Sudanese court's magisterial inquiry hearings, November 15, 1973, through March 9, 1974. 119 pp.

Forty-one Department of State documents, ranging from unclassified through secret, released to the author in full under letter dated October 19, 1990, from Frank M. Machak, Office of Freedom of Information, Department of State.

Unclassified radio transcripts, released to the author under letter dated October 29, 1990, from John H. Wright, Information and Privacy Coordinator, Central Intelligence Agency.

One hundred seventy-one Department of State documents, ranging from unclassified through secret, released to the author, 132 in full and 39 in part, under letter dated November 7, 1990, from Frank M. Machak, Office of Freedom of Information, Department of State.

Seven Department of State documents, various classifications, six released in full and one with deletions, under letter to the author dated November 20, 1990, from Frank M. Machak, Office of Freedom of Information, Department of State.

Central Intelligence Agency papers, entitled "The Seizure of the Saudi Arabian Embassy in Khartoum" and "The Khartoum Incident," released to the author with deletions under letter dated January 14, 1991, from John H. Wright, Information and Privacy Coordinator, Central Intelligence Agency.

Twenty-three Department of State documents, various classifications, ten released in full and thirteen with deletions, under letter to the author dated January 17, 1991, from Frank M. Machak, Office of Freedom of Information, Department of State.

Note: Copies of telegrams received at the State Department from U.S. embassies that were furnished to the author under his Freedom of Information Act request all bear identifying numbers and date-time groups (DTG), except those from Embassy Khartoum sent in the telecon channel (the secure teletype link), which show only a log-in time stamp. Some copies of State Department telegrams sent to the field bear identifying numbers and date-time groups, but many others are "working copies," i.e., copies of the as yet unprocessed telegram, which show only a date, or date-time group, and a classification.

Books

Published works contributed only a minor part to the writing of this study. The following were perused by the author:

Abbas, Mekki. *The Sudan Question.* London: Faber and Faber, 1952.

Abino, Oliver. *The Sudan: A Southern Viewpoint.* London: Oxford University Press, 1970.

Abu Iyad (Salah Khalaf) with Eric Rouleau. *My Home, My Land.* New York: Times Books, 1981.

Bar Zohar, Michael, and Eitan Haber. *The Quest for the Red Prince.* New York: Morrow, 1983.

Bauman, Carol E. *The Diplomatic Kidnappings.* The Hague: Nijhoff, 1973.

Churchill, Winston S. *The River War.* 3rd ed. London: Eyre and Spottiswoode, 1949.

Cooley, John K. *Green March, Black September.* London: Frank Cass and Co., 1973.

Dobson, Christopher. *Black September: Its Short Violent History.* New York: Macmillan, 1974.

Hart, Alan. *Arafat: Terrorist or Peacemaker?* London: Sedgwick and Jackson, 1984.

Holt, P. M., and M. W. Daly. *The History of the Sudan.* 3rd ed. Boulder, Colo.: Westview Press, 1979.

Ignatius, David. *Agents of Innocence.* New York and London: W. W. Norton, 1987.

Livingstone, Neil C., and David Halevy. *Inside the PLO.* New York: William Morrow and Co., 1990.

Moorehead, Caroline. *Fortune's Hostages.* London: H. Hamilton, 1980.

Seale, Patrick. *Abu Nidal: A Gun for Hire.* New York: Random House, 1992.

Superintendent of Documents, U.S. Government Printing Office. *Area Handbook for the Democratic Republic of Sudan, 1973.* Washington, D.C., 1973.

Wallach, Janet and John. *Arafat in the Eyes of the Beholder.* New York: Lyle Stewart, 1990.

Waller, John. *Gordon of Khartoum.* New York: Atheneum, 1988.

INDEX

Abbas, Mahmud (Fatah), 37
Abboud, Ibrahim (mil. ruler, Sudan), 76
"Abu," as code name for guerrilla chiefs, 43
Abu Ammar. *See* Arafat, Yasser
Abu Daoud (Awda, Mohammed Daoud Mahmud):
demands by BSO for release of, 104, 125, 202;
demands for release of by rival Fatah group, 208;
as Fatah agent, 45; as prisoner in Jordan, 51,
194; release of by Jordan, 208–209, 226–27,
243; role in Munich Olympic raid, 48
Abu Hassan. *See* Salameh, Ali Hassan
Abu Hijle, Abdul Latif (Khartoum PLO head), 191,
200
Abu Iyad. *See* Khalaf, Salah
Abu Jamal, initial role in Khartoum operation, 1–5,
243
Abu Jihad. *See* al-Wazir, Khalil
Abu Kheir (PLO rep., Khartoum), 213
Abu Yussef. *See* al-Najjar, Mohammed Yussef
Adwan, Kamal (Fatah), 37; assassination of, 239
Aid programs, U.S., for Sudan, 20, 223, 230
Aircraft, commercial, hijacking of, 27, 39–41, 47,
49, 115
Aircraft, military, use in U.S. mission to Khartoum,
132–34, 140–41, 143
Airport security, 115
Akhbar al-Yom (newspaper, Cairo), 95
Akins, James (amb., U.S.), protest of U.S. policy
after Khartoum crisis, 224–25
Al Ahram (newspaper, Cairo), 52
al-Assad, Hafez (def. min., Syria), 42
al-Atta, Hashem, coup attempt in Sudan, 87–89, 90
Algiers, role in PFLP's hijacking of El Al plane, 39
al-Hindawi, Rifai (prisoner, Jordan), 129, 202
al-Husseini, Haj Amin (mufti, Jerusalem), 36, 43
al-Jadid, Salah (leader, Syria), 42
al-Malhouk, Abdullah (amb., Saudi Arabia), 7; actions following Khartoum crisis, 172, 179, 182–
83; as hostage, 22, 28, 122, 125, 160–61,
169
al-Malhouk, Mrs., during Khartoum crisis, 23, 159,
160, 169
Al Muharrer (newspaper, Beirut), 51, 174, 215

al-Najjar, Mohammed Yussef (Fatah), 37, 43; assassination of, 239
al-Obeid, Fadl (official, Sudan), 172, 210
al-Qas, Rizk (Ghassan, Abu): BSO Khartoum operation, 3–4, 8, 125, 148, 154, 203; during inquiry
and trial, 212–13, 215; at end of crisis, 175–76;
personality, 164–65
al-Rifai, Zaid (counselor, Jordan), 148
al-Sawrani, Jamal (PLO rep., Arab League), 200
al-Wazir, Khalil (Fatah), 37, 43; assassination of,
247
American Foreign Service Association, protest to
Kissinger, 225–26
American Israel Public Affairs Committee, 245
Ames, Robert (CIA): assassination of, 243; meeting
with Salameh, 45–46, 242
Amman, Jordan, attempted destruction of PLO in,
35
ANM (Arab Nationalist Movement), 40
Anya Nya (guerrilla movement, Sudan), 91
Arabic language: Foreign Service schools, 13, 20,
74; Moore's fluency, 24, 27, 66–67, 81; Noel's
use, 69–70
Arab Nationalist Movement (ANM), 40
Arabs: preoccupation with conflict with Israel, 166;
role in the Sudan, 16; status in Ethiopia, 80
Arafat, Yasser: address to the UN, 242; on Arab
takeover of Saudi embassy in Paris, 208; code
names, 1, 43; proposed indictment for Khartoum
operation, 245–47; public absence during Khartoum crisis, 125, 148; public denial of Fatah
participation, 195, 198; reemergence at end,
178–79; role in Fatah, 36–43, 52–53
Aram, Karam Ahmad, role in BSO Khartoum operation, 3, 203, 211
ARAMCO (Arabian-American Oil Company), 68
Asmara, Eritrea: Moore's assignment to, 80; U.S.
communication station, 18
As Sahafa (newspaper, Khartoum), 196
Athens, Greece, airport raid by BSO gunmen,
239–40
Atherton, Roy (Alfred L., Jr.) (U.S. Foreign Service), role during Khartoum crisis, 107

Avidor, Shimon (amb., Israel), as hostage in Bangkok embassy, 50
Awda, Mohammed Daoud Mahmud. *See* Abu Daoud

Bader-Meinhoff gang, BSO's release demands, 33, 104, 125, 129
Baghir Ahmad, Mohammed al- (int. min., Sudan): during BSO trial, 197, 198, 200, 203; role during crisis, 123–26, 135–37, 139, 145–48, 154–55; role at end of crisis, 175–76
Bangkok, Thailand: Israeli embassy crisis, 27, 49–50; as model for Khartoum operation, 128, 134–35
Bar Lev, Haim (gen., Israel), 38
Barry, John (corr.), 191, 193
Begin, Menachem, 44
Beirut, Lebanon, 2; Arabic language school, 24, 66, 69; assassination of Fatah leaders in, 238–39
Belgium: relations with Israel, 163; role in Khartoum crisis, 157. *See also* Eid, Guy
Benghazi, Libya, Moore's assignment to, 80–81
Ben-Gurion, David (pr. min., Israel), 71
Bergstrom, Alan (U.S. Foreign Service), role during Khartoum crisis, 131–32, 143, 156
Bertens, Jan (dipl., Netherlands), 8–9
Black September Organization (BSO): attacks on Jordanian officials, 46–47; demands during crisis, 32–33, 104, 125, 128–29; at end of the siege, 172–80; Lod airport fiasco, 47; Munich Olympics, 26, 48–49, 113; organization of by PLO, 36; phasing out of, 238–40; planning for Khartoum operation, 1–5; refusal to move hostages to Cairo, 142, 145; takeover of Israeli embassy in Bangkok, 49–50; threats against Sudan, 207; trial of members, 188–89, 195–211, 212–21; use of letter bombs, 49. *See also* al-Qas, Rizk
Blake, James (U.S. Foreign Service), 92, 108–109
Blaney, Harry (U.S. Foreign Service), fight to protect service personnel, 227–31
Blue Nile Insurance Building (Khartoum), 3, 4, 191
Bolton, John (asst. atty. gen., U.S.), 247
Boyatt, Thomas (pres., AFSA), 227
Brawn, Ed (embassy staff), 25, 107, 156
Bray, Charles (White House spokesman), 151–52, 190
Brazil, government role in Elbrick kidnapping, 111–12
Brewer, William D. (amb., U.S.): return to Sudan, 222–26, 234; role in Sudanese BSO trial, 206, 209–10, 211, 214–15, 216–18
Brown, L. Dean (amb., U.S.), role in Amman during Khartoum crisis, 140
BSO. *See* Black September Organization
Bush, George (dir., CIA), 233

Cabinet Committee to Combat Terrorism, U.S., 113–14
Cairo, Egypt: Moore's assignment to, 67; pur-

ported flight of terrorists and hostages to, 141–44, 145
Christensen, Ward (consul, U.S.), kidnapping in Haiti, 117, 119
CIA (Central Intelligence Agency, U.S.): attempted contacts with the PLO, 45–46; disproving forged documents, 91–92; later relations with PLO, 240–43; Moore perceived as agent of, 30, 53, 183, 212, 214; Moore's relations with, 84
Civil war, Sudan, 76, 90–91, 124
Code names, use of by militants, 1
Cold River (*Nahr al-Bard*), as code for execution of hostages, 168, 246
Commodity Credit Corporation Act, 90
Communications: between State Department and Khartoum, 103–104, 108, 142; radio usage in Khartoum, 6, 165, 176
Communist party, Sudan, status of, 87–88, 89
Coote, Wendell (U.S. Foreign Service), 233, 234–35
Coups, Sudanese, 21, 87–89, 244–45

Dawson Field (Jordan), use by PFLP aircraft hijackers, 41–42
Day, Osborne (National Security Council, U.S.), 148–49
Dayan, Moshe, 39, 47
Deng, Francis (amb., Sudan), relations with the U.S., 232–36
Diplomatic community, in Khartoum, 14–15, 28
Duvalier, Jean-Claude (pres., Haiti), role in Knox kidnapping, 118–19

Eagleburger, Lawrence (U.S. Foreign Service), as Kissinger's hatchet man, 229–30
Economy, Sudan: civil war's effect on, 76; ties with the USSR, 86–87
Egypt: actions of after Khartoum crisis, 211, 220–21; as liberator of Palestine, 38, 40; relations with Sudan, 16–17, 77; reluctant assistance of during crisis, 141–42, 188; U.S. relations with, 76
Eid, Guy (dipl., Belg.): burial of, 238; as hostage, 8–9, 108, 125–26; identification of body of, 181; reasons for being a hostage, 162–64, 212
Eilts, Hermann Frederick (amb., U.S.), role in Egypt during transfer of BSO prisoners, 220–21
El Al airlines (Israel), PFLP hijackings, 39, 40–41
Elbrick, Burke (amb., U.S.), kidnapping in Brazil, 27, 110–12
el-Nasri, Mirghani (lawyer, Sudan), 207
Elson, Edward L. R. (chaplain), 237
Embassies, U.S., closure in Arab states, 12–13
Eritrea, 80; insurgency in and U.S. interests, 18; Sudan's aid to guerrilla movement, 91
Ethiopia. *See* Haile Selassie

Fahmy, Ismail (for. min., Egypt), 221
Faisal (king, Saudi Arabia), 146
Fatah, 36, 38–39; Israeli Beirut raid against, 238–

39; organizational role in Khartoum operation, 2–3, 191, 196; return to Khartoum, 200

Fawaz, Yassin. *See* Rahman, Fawaz Yassin Abdul

FBI (Federal Bureau of Investigation), ransom policy in domestic kidnappings, 115

Fearey, Robert, as new coordinator for terrorism, 230–31

Foreign Service, U.S.: interim appointments of diplomats, 11–12; language study schools, 13, 20, 74; reaction to Khartoum crisis, 102–109, 202–204; view of Kissinger's terrorist policies, 222–31. *See also* individual officers

Foreign Service Institute, Arabic language school, 24, 67, 69

Francis, Donald, M.D., 173

Fritts, Robert E. (U.S. Foreign Service), 25, 122; efforts to obtain trial of BSO gunmen, 198–200, 203, 208; role during Khartoum crisis, 129–30, 143, 156, 170–71, 193

Gatch, John (U.S. Foreign Service), 69, 115; role during Khartoum crisis, 103, 106

Gentile, Marvin (U.S. Foreign Service): role during Khartoum crisis, 143; role during Knox's kidnapping, 118

Germany: Moore's assignment in, 65–66; role during 1972 Munich Olympic raid, 48–49; World War II attempt to poison Tel Aviv's wells, 43–44

Ghassan, Abu. *See* al-Qas, Rizk

Gordon, Sir Charles George, death at Khartoum, 17, 210

Greene, Jerry (U.S. Foreign Service), role in Khartoum crisis, 141–44, 145

Guatemala, kidnapping of German ambassador, 112

Guerrilla activities: by Fatah, 38–39; in Uruguay, 112–13

Habash, George (PFLP leader), 39–40

Haboob (sandstorm), 14; during Khartoum crisis, 146–47, 156, 173–74, 176

Haile Selassie: aid to southern Sudan, 91; designs on Eritrea, 80; overthrow of, 224; state visit to Sudan, 7, 22; as U.S. ally, 18

Haiti, 118–19

Hamadallah, Faruk, role in Sudanese coup attempt, 87–88

Hamid, Hayel Abdul (PLO), 250

Harlan, Robert H. (U.S. Foreign Service), 134

Harris, F. Allen (Tex) (pres., AFSA), 226

Hassan (king, Morocco), 240–41

Hassan (driver, U.S. embassy), role during Khartoum crisis, 9–10, 33, 123

Hassan, Hani al- (PLO moderate), 52, 240–42

Hassan, Khaled al- (PLO moderate), 52

Hassan ibn Talal (crown prince, Jordan), actions during Khartoum crisis, 138–39

Heikal, Mohammed (editor, *Al Ahram*), 52

Hijackings, 27, 115; by BSO, 47, 49; by PFLP, 39–41

Hoagland, Jim (corr.), 248; Khartoum crisis reporting, 157, 193–94; on Moore's early days in Khartoum, 85–86

Hoffacker, Lewis, as head of terrorism office, 204–205

Holmes, Julius (amb., U.S.), 82

Horan, Hume (amb., U.S.), 227; in Sudan, 245

Hostages, American: payments for viewed as blackmail, 145–55, 178; U.S. policy on, 25–26, 108, 110–21, 128

Hoyt, Michael P. E. (U.S. Foreign Service), 205

Hussein (king, Jordan): absence during Khartoum crisis, 138, 148; actions following crisis, 194; attempted destruction of PLO, 35–36, 41–42; PLO attempt to overthrow, 52; proposed role in crisis, 109, 152; release of Abu Daoud, 208–209, 226–27

Hussein, Hassan Ahmad, role in BSO Khartoum operation, 2, 211

Ibrahim, Abdul Ghassim Mohammed (min. of health, Sudan), role during Khartoum crisis, 124, 127, 136

Idriss (king, Libya), relationship with Moore, 80–81

Interests section(s): in Dutch embassy in Khartoum, 13, 20, 74–75; replacing U.S. embassies in Arab states, 12–13, 20

Intifada, the, 247

Iran, Moore's impressions of, 70

Ismail, Hafez (emissary, Egypt), 53, 141

Israel: assassination raids by, 238–39, 247; Bangkok embassy seizure by BSO, 27, 49–50; and Fatah guerrilla activities, 38–39, 108; Moore's impressions of, 71–72; and 1972 Munich Olympic raid, 48–49; perceived policy on hostage ransoms, 110; reaction to Arab terrorism, 51–52; role during Khartoum crisis, 152; U.S. as ally, 12

Izvestia (newspaper, USSR), 89

Japanese Red Army, Lod Airport massacre role, 48

Jibril, Ahmad (PFLP member), 40, 41

Jihaz al-Rasd (Fatah intelligence branch), 43, 45, 53

Johnson, Lyndon, 12

Jones, Curtis (U.S. Foreign Service), role during Khartoum crisis, 131, 143

Jones, John Wesley (amb., U.S.), 81

Jordan: attacks by BSO on officials of, 46–47; attempted destruction of PLO, 35; refusal to release prisoners during Khartoum crisis, 138–39

June 1967 War (Six-Day War): Arab defeat and rise of Fatah, 38; effect on Arab-U.S. relations, 12

Kagnew communications station (U.S. base, Libya), 80

Kalashnikov rifles, use of in Khartoum operation, 3, 4, 180

DAVID A. KORN, a former Foreign Service officer, is author of *Ethiopia, the United States and the Soviet Union; Human Rights in Iraq;* and *Stalemate: The War of Attrition and Great Power Diplomacy in the Middle East, 1967–1970.*